GW01457927

Śrī Śrī Guru-Gaurāṅgau Jayataḥ

On Speaking Strongly in Śrīla Prabhupāda's Service

Books Authored by Bhakti Vikāsa Swami

A Beginner's Guide to Kṛṣṇa Consciousness

A Message to the Youth of India

Brahmacarya in Kṛṣṇa Consciousness

Glimpses of Traditional Indian Life

Jaya Śrīla Prabhupāda!

My Memories of Śrīla Prabhupāda

On Pilgrimage in Holy India

On Speaking Strongly in Śrīla Prabhupāda's Service

Patropadeśa

Śrī Bhaktisiddhānta Vaibhava (three volumes)

Śrī Caitanya Mahāprabhu

Śrī Vaṁśīdāsa Bābājī

Vaiṣṇava Śikhā o Sādhana (Bengali)

Books Edited or Compiled by Bhakti Vikāsa Swami

Rāmāyaṇa

The Story of Rasikānanda

Gauḍīya Vaiṣṇava Padyāvalī (Bengali)

On Speaking Strongly in Śrīla Prabhupāda's Service

Bhakti Vikāsa Swami

ISBN 978-93-82109-04-4

www.bvks.com
www.speakingstrongly.com
books@bvks.com

First printing as a separate book (2012): 3,000 copies

The quotation on the back cover ("You young boys ...") is from *My Glorious Master* (by Bhūrijana Dāsa), p. 139.

The words *Conversation, Lecture, Letter,* and *purport* indicate quotations taken from published editions by or involving Śrīla Prabhupāda. *Conversation* subsumes all types of discussions with Śrīla Prabhupāda, variously classified by the Bhaktivedanta Archives as Morning Walks, Press Conferences, Room Conversations, etc. All such quotations are copyrighted by The Bhaktivedanta Book Trust International, Inc.

Unless otherwise stated, quotations from the *Harmonist* (the erstwhile magazine of the Gauḍīya Maṭha) were written by the editorial staff thereof.

Published by Bhakti Vikas Trust, Surat, India
Printed by Lightning Source

With great force, preach Kṛṣṇa consciousness.

(Śrīla Prabhupāda, Conversation, 1 March 1977)

CONTENTS

Legend

BTG—*Back to Godhead* (magazine)

SBV—*Śrī Bhaktisiddhānta Vaibhava* (book by Bhakti Vikāsa Swami)

The following refer to editions published by the Bhaktivedanta Book Trust (BBT)

Bg—*Bhagavad-gītā*

Cc—*Śrī Caitanya-caritāmṛta* (1: *Ādi-līlā*; 2: *Madhya-līlā*; 3: *Antya-līlā*)

SB—*Śrīmad-Bhāgavatam*

SPl—*Śrīla Prabhupāda-līlāmṛta*

PREFACE

I speak too strongly. People don't like it. I burn people out. Or so I'm told. Some devotees warn me to tone down and speak in a way that will make everyone feel satisfied.

I disagree. I have been disagreeing about this for years, and will probably continue disagreeing until my last breath. Pig-headed arrogance? Maybe. However, just as my critics advocate being mild with others, I request them to be mild with me. Kindly consider that my vitriol might not be impelled by ad hominem nastiness but by the desire to satisfy Śrīla Prabhupāda—as will be explained in this book.

The impetus to write this volume came after a preaching skirmish in London in the mid-1990s. Romapāda Dāsa (a disciple of Śrī Gopāla Kṛṣṇa Goswami), who is an old acquaintance of mine, had invited me to address a weekly meeting of Indian Vaiṣṇava youth at a temple in East London.* Knowing my proclivity for straightforward speaking, Romapāda Dāsa cautioned me that the chairman of that temple was temperamental and should be dealt with carefully. After my lecture there, a middle-aged Indian man asked (in a superficially reverent tone that indicated that he

* Romapāda Dāsa has assented to the publishing of this anecdote, and even furnished some details and emended some points that I had incorrectly recalled.

thought he knew a lot), "Swamiji, you have spoken about *bhakti*. However, I have learned that *jñāna*-yoga, karma-yoga, and *bhakti*-yoga are all the same and lead to the same goal. Can you please explain more?"

I posed a counter-question: "Sir, have you read the *Bhagavad-gītā?*" I pointed to the copy of *Bhagavad-gītā As It Is* that I was holding.

The man mumbled something and repeated that he thought *jñāna*, karma, and *bhakti* were all the same.

I raised the *Gītā* in my hand and told him, "Sir, first read this book, and then speak."

The man replied, "But you said that only Kṛṣṇa is God. However, we worship Murugan and Gaṇapati. What is wrong with that?"

I replied, "Worshiping anyone other than Kṛṣṇa is like placing a garland on a dead body."

The man became furious and started jumping up and down as if he was about to hit us. His wife held his shirt to restrain him. Just then the *ārati* ceremony began. The man went to the notice board inside the temple and tore down (and into pieces) the poster that advertised the weekly ISKCON program, and then shouted something in Tamil. (Later Romapāda Dāsa told me that the man had said, "How dare this person come into our temple and tell us that we are worshiping dead bodies?") He again tried to run at us as if to strike us, and again his wife held him back by his shirt.

I gestured to Romapāda Dāsa and said, "I think we should leave now."

We went to a devotee's house nearby, where Romapāda Dāsa, upset over losing the program venue, told me that the angry man was the chairman of the temple. I responded, "He thinks that the temple is his private property. He doesn't think that it belongs to

Kṛṣṇa; he thinks it belongs to him." Later, I also told Romapāda Dāsa that Kṛṣṇa would give them a better location and added, "You should find an independent place, where you can preach Kṛṣṇa consciousness without any compromise."

The next year, when I again met Romapāda Dāsa in London, I asked him if he was still annoyed with me. He cheerfully replied that by Kṛṣṇa's mercy the youth group had indeed found a bigger and better hall for their programs where they were able to freely speak the philosophy of Kṛṣṇa, and resultingly, the group had significantly expanded.

When Romapāda Dāsa had complained of what he perceived as my errancy, I became perturbed—not because I regretted having angered that foolish man, nor due to the fallout of my outburst, but because I was fed up with devotees' objecting to my direct speaking. Having carefully studied Śrīla Prabhupāda's books and listened to hundreds of his recorded talks—with the specific intent of imbibing his preaching mood and learning how he responded to various propositions and challenges—I was confident that forceful, uncompromising presentation of Kṛṣṇa consciousness was a valid way to follow him, and according to my understanding, the best way. I was also confident that the best way to worship Śrīla Prabhupāda is by conveying to others the same message he gave us, and that any supposed worship of Śrīla Prabhupāda is just a sham if not accompanied with living by and faithfully iterating his teachings.

Consequently, being spurred by Romapāda Dāsa's disconcertment, I resolved to publish a justification of my stand, for those who in the future would inevitably protest against my and others preaching Kṛṣṇa consciousness in a manner meant to most closely follow that of Śrīla Prabhupāda's. Hence, I composed this treatise and featured it in my publication *My Memories of Śrīla Prabhupāda.*

Now, some sixteen years later, I consider that there is even greater need to air that message than when it was first produced. Therefore I have expanded and overhauled the original version and published it as this separate volume. In the course of revising it, while reflecting on the preaching tussles and controversies I have been involved in over the last thirty-seven years since being admitted into ISKCON, I regretted that I had not been stronger, bolder, and more outspoken. I now find myself more convinced than ever of the "crying necessity of the moment for silencing the aggressive propaganda of specific untruths that is being carried on all over the world."[1]

It is fitting that *Speaking Strongly* be my first publication after *Śrī Bhaktisiddhānta Vaibhava*. By perusing *Speaking Strongly*, devotees who appreciated the robust preaching of Śrīla Bhaktisiddhānta Sarasvatī (as depicted in *Śrī Bhaktisiddhānta Vaibhava*) may further appreciate that such robustness was not meant to be limited to him but imparted to all his followers, as it clearly was to his foremost disciple, His Divine Grace A.C. Bhaktivedanta Swami Prabhupāda.

Almost certainly, *Speaking Strongly* will be controversial, and many devotees will find its import difficult to accept. While expecting criticism, I request would-be critics to first read the book in its entirety. I must apologize to whoever may become offended by any of my statements; but some things need to be said even at the risk of upsetting others (why so is discussed herein). Admittedly, a seemingly contradictory case could be made for a more restrained approach in preaching (although it is doubtful that nearly as much evidence could be supplied to support that position as has been provided in *Speaking Strongly*).

---

1 *Harmonist* 29.173 (Dec 1931); SBV, vol. 3, p. 146.

On Speaking Strongly in Śrīla Prabhupāda's Service is solidly based on more than five hundred quotes from Śrīla Prabhupāda's teachings and other authoritative sources, and further substantiated by the inclusion of several of the hundreds of recorded anecdotes that demonstrate his straightforwardness and provocativeness. These combinedly establish that my strong speaking, for which I am somewhat known within ISKCON, is not merely my own idiosyncrasy, but a sacred order from Śrīla Prabhupāda that is meant to largely define his movement, notwithstanding his sometimes cautionary words.

Hence, this tract is intended not only as a personal manifesto, for addressing misgivings that devotees may have about my often abrasive style, but also to educate followers of Śrīla Prabhupāda about his seemingly largely forgotten precept and practice of outright speaking, and to convince all present and future followers of Śrīla Prabhupāda of the necessity for bold, strongly worded preaching. It is particularly aimed at devotees who possess, or aspire to possess, full faith in the teachings of *śāstra* and the Gauḍīya *paramparā*. (Although such faith is the basic qualification of a Gauḍīya Vaiṣṇava, it is often alarmingly absent in members of ISKCON today). Moreover, it offers guidelines for speaking pointedly and effectively in a manner consonant with Śrīla Prabhupāda's desires.

In the initial portion of this monograph, I attempt to show why devotees should speak strongly, clearly, and boldly, and how they can best serve Śrīla Prabhupāda by doing so. Later, I add balance by examining, and to some extent accommodating, other approaches to preaching besides all-out attack, yet also warning of the dangers of being too reticent. I discuss the pros and cons of speaking out, with consideration of time, place, and circumstance, and respond to the oft-mooted query, "Who is qualified to speak strongly?" If my analysis of various angles and nuances of these subjects seems repetitive, it is because I have tried to treat all common perspectives on them, many of which overlap. Furthermore, "Repetition of something is necessary in order that we understand the matter thoroughly, without error."[1]

A measure of the effectiveness of this book will be the extent to which it engenders further discussion. Herein, several important topics have been broached but not developed comprehensively. Not least among them is the very purpose and mission of ISKCON. Also, in focusing primarily on strong speaking targeted at nondevotees, this work offers only limited guidelines for contentious exchanges within Vaiṣṇava circles. Not everything can be included in one volume. I pray that Kṛṣṇa grant me the time, resolve, health, intelligence, and purity to complete the several other important theses that I plan for addressing these and other issues vital to the Kṛṣṇa consciousness movement.

My thanks are extended to those devotees who continue to selflessly help me in the production of my books (see Acknowledgments, p. 251), and to the many more who have encouraged me by expressing appreciation of my writings. Special mention is also due to those devotees who, by their abhorrence of strong speaking, have afforded me sustained inspiration for the compilation of this treatise.

I request all devotees to please pray that throughout this life, and perhaps also in many more lifetimes, I may continue to speak strongly and to persevere in this vocation of writing, and that in so doing I may always aspire to be a humble instrument in the service of Śrīla Prabhupāda and his followers. Furthermore, I pray to Śrīla Prabhupāda and the previous *ācāryas* that they continue to mercifully engage me in their mission, and that they may eternally inspire within me the intelligence to serve them in the manner they see fit.

Bhakti Vikāsa Swami, 3 January 2012

---

1 Bg 2.25, purport.

PROLOGUE
I WORSHIP ŚRĪLA PRABHUPĀDA

I worship Śrīla Prabhupāda, who to a young man who declared "I am God" roared back, "You are not God! You are a dog!"[1]

I worship Śrīla Prabhupāda, who at a meeting of influential Hindus in Japan suddenly shouted "Stop him!" in the middle of their Māyāvādī guru's speech.[2]

I worship Śrīla Prabhupāda, who matter-of-factly told a press reporter that the supposed astronauts could not travel to the moon because the moon is farther from earth than is the sun.[3]

I worship Śrīla Prabhupāda, who told us to make great propaganda on two points: the scientists have not gone to the moon and they cannot even manufacture a chicken egg.[4]

I worship Śrīla Prabhupāda, who ordered that *Life Comes from Life* be printed and widely distributed as an unabashed assault on the cheating of the pseudo-scientists.[5]

I worship Śrīla Prabhupāda, who said "I cannot make any compromise. So long I shall live I shall make no compromise. Why shall I mislead people?"[6]

---

1 See p. 11.

2 See p. 3.

3 Conversations, 26 Dec 1968 & 4 Jun 1976.

4 Conversation, 25 Oct 1975.

5 Letter, 21 Apr 1974.

6 Conversation, 24 Aug 1976.

I worship Śrīla Prabhupāda, who never tired of teaching "You are not the body. You are an eternal servant of Kṛṣṇa, the Supreme Personality of Godhead. Unconditional surrender to His lotus feet is the purpose of human life."

I worship Śrīla Prabhupāda, who knew our disease and repeatedly taught "Give up sex. Sex is the binding force within this material world."

I worship Śrīla Prabhupāda, who declared: "I am not anxious to go to Goloka Vṛndāvana. I just want to expose all these rascals who pretend to be yogis and swamis."[1]

I worship Śrīla Prabhupāda, who spoke of urinating on and kicking the face of a bogus avatar, openly called him a cheater during a press conference, and recommended to his disciples the somewhat milder tactic of throwing a pie into that rascal's face.[2]

I worship Śrīla Prabhupāda, whose books are the perfect antidote for all forms of rascaldom, and the best form of preaching.

I worship Śrīla Prabhupāda, the lord of my life, the ambassador of the spiritual world, and a personal friend of Kṛṣṇa. He never compromised in preaching, and I pray to him for the courage and conviction to eternally follow in his divine lotus footsteps.

1 *Life with the Perfect Master* (by Satsvarūpa Dāsa Goswami), ch. 5.

2 Conversation, 13 Aug 1973; *My Glorious Master* (by Bhūrijana Dāsa), p. 198.

ONE
PREACHING MEANS FIGHTING

Śrīla Prabhupāda fought for Kṛṣṇa. He made no secret that his manifesto was "meant to bring about a revolution in the impious life of a misdirected civilization."[1] To effect this, he tirelessly promoted Kṛṣṇa consciousness, also emphasizing the need to do so energetically, effectively, and even aggressively. He challenged everyone in the world and every theory that even subtly opposed the acceptance of Kṛṣṇa as the Supreme Personality of Godhead and the maxim that the sole duty of every *jīva* is total, unmitigated surrender at Kṛṣṇa's lotus feet:

> Our fighting is against atheism. They say, "There is no God," "God is dead," "I am God," "You are God." We are fighting against these principles. So our fighting is very strong. Don't think that we are sitting idly. I have come here to fight with these atheists. We go everywhere. We are fighting with atheists all over the world.[2]

> Atheists may be very expert in mental speculation and may be so-called great philosophers, but they can be defeated by a Vaiṣṇava firmly situated in his conviction and God consciousness. Following in the footsteps of Śrī Caitanya Mahāprabhu, all the preachers engaged in the service of ISKCON should be very expert in putting forward strong arguments and defeating all types of atheists.[3]

1 SB 1.5.11 (as quoted in the preface of SB).

2 Conversation, 13 Dec 1970.

3 Cc 2.9.51, purport.

> We have to fight, otherwise what is the meaning of preaching? If you think that everything will be accepted very easily, then what is the necessity of preaching?[1]

> These rascals will not understand Kṛṣṇa. Just like the owl. The owl will never open his eyes to see that there is sunlight. However you may say "Mr. Owl, please open your eyes and see the sun"—"No, there is no sun. I don't see." This owl civilization. So you have to fight with these owls. You must be very strong, especially the sannyasis. We have to fight with the owls. We have to open their eyes by force. This Kṛṣṇa consciousness movement is a fight against all the owls.[2]

> Fight must go on. Fight cannot be stopped. So fight like brave soldiers. Kṛṣṇa will help you. Don't make any compromise. No truce with these demons. Fight must be.[3]

In *Śrī Caitanya-caritāmṛta* (3.3.149) it is stated:

প্রেম-প্রচারণ আর পাষণ্ড-দলন ।
দুই-কার্যে অবধূত করেন ভ্রমণ ॥

prema-pracāraṇa āra pāṣaṇḍa-dalana
dui-kārye avadhūta karena bhramaṇa

> For two purposes—to spread the cult of *bhakti* and to defeat and subdue the atheists—Lord Nityānanda, the most dedicated devotee of the Lord, moved throughout the country.

Prema-pracāraṇa means preaching the cult of *bhakti*. *Pāṣaṇḍa-dalana* means subduing atheists. In his purport to this verse, Śrīla Prabhupāda commented:

> Lord Kṛṣṇa appears in every millennium for two purposes, namely to deliver the devotees and kill the nondevotees. His devotees also have two similar purposes—to preach the *bhakti* cult of Kṛṣṇa consciousness and defeat all kinds of agnostics and atheistic demons.

---

1 Conversation, 11 Dec 1973.

2 Lecture, 19 Jul 1975.

3 Conversation, 3 Feb 1977.

> Nityānanda Prabhu carried out the order of Lord Śrī Caitanya Mahāprabhu in this way, and those who strictly follow Nityānanda Prabhu perform the same activities.

As a strict follower of Nityānanda Prabhu, Śrīla Prabhupāda was uncompromising, and to many must have seemed extreme in insisting that surrender to Kṛṣṇa is the only goal of life and that all else is nonsense. He was not always belligerent, but his "occasional aggressive tactics showed us that holy men sometimes have to be hell-fire men."[1] As Śrīla Prabhupāda said, "Sometimes when we preach we have to act like *kṣatriyas*."[2] But it was not only "sometimes" that Śrīla Prabhupāda would provoke and antagonize people. For instance, once in Japan, where few people were interested to assist the devotees, he blasted the Māyāvāda concepts of an Indian man who until then had been helping his disciples—thus alienating him. Later, Śrīla Prabhupāda commented, "Never mind. One day he will appreciate how we have chastised him for his rascaldom."[3] Another time, speaking to a man in Kolkata:

> Prabhupāda said, "Kṛṣṇa is the Supreme Lord, and all others are demigods." The man became a little nervous and quoted a popular Bengali impersonalist who taught that all gods and all methods of worship are the same.
>
> "He's an upstart," Prabhupāda said. "That is not the teaching of the *Gītā*. What is this other teaching? It is all utter confusion."
>
> "If you go on speaking like this," the man said angrily, "I'll have to leave this place. Please don't criticize this *paramahaṁsa*."
>
> "Why not?" Prabhupāda said. "He is a concocter." The man got up and left, calling out, "You don't know Kṛṣṇa!" as he left the room.[4]

---

1 Mukunda Goswami, *Vyāsa-pūjā* (2010).

2 Told by Hṛdayānanda Dāsa Goswami.

3 *See My Glorious Master*, pp. 137–56.

4 SPl ch. 28, "India Revisited: Part 2."

Similar to this, on several occasions Śrīla Prabhupāda got into shouting matches, mostly with Indians.[1] He described his preaching technique:

> I am a little temperamental. I used to use words like *rascal* and so on. I never compromised. They used to call it "preaching with a pickax in one hand and a *Bhāgavatam* in the other." That is how I preached.[2]

The Vedic tradition, although not one of crusades, inquisitions, pogroms, or jihads, has nevertheless always been (until relatively recently) philosophically highly polemic. Why so was established by Ādi-Śaṅkara:

> An opponent might say that indeed we are entitled to establish our own position but there is no apparent point in a refutation of other opinions, a proceeding that produces nothing but hate and anger. We reply that there is a point: There is some danger that men of inferior intelligence will look upon Sāṅkhya and similar systems as requisite for perfect knowledge because those systems have a weighty appearance, have been adopted by authoritative persons, and profess to lead to perfect knowledge. They may therefore think that those systems with their abstruse arguments were propounded by omniscient sages and, on that account, might have faith in them. For this reason we must endeavor to demonstrate the intrinsic worthlessness of such systems.[3]

All great Vaiṣṇava *ācāryas,* particularly Madhva and his discipular adherents, were unabashed in dismantling the faulty philosophical constructs of their adversaries (primary among whom were Ādi-Śaṅkara and his followers). Madhva established, practically as the modus operandi of his *sampradāya,* what Śrīla Bhaktisiddhānta Sarasvatī would later term "the chopping technique"—that a devotee who is firmly grounded in service to the truth speaks

---

1 Examples are in conversations on 18 Jan 1971, Allahabad; 22 Dec 1976, Pune; and several times with Dr. Chaturbhai P. Patel in Mumbai.

2 *TKG's Diary,* 13 Oct.

3 *Brahma-sūtra Bhāṣya,* Śrī Ādi Śaṅkara, 2.1.1.

clearly and forcefully in a manner that offers no scope for wrong conclusions; he thoroughly criticizes all mistaken ideas, even those that have had longstanding wide acceptance among respected persons. All of his refutations are backed by evidence, to benefit others so that they can unmistakenly distinguish reality from illusion and, without any lingering reservations, also apply themselves to the service of the truth.

Similarly, Śrī Rāmānujācārya and his followers achieved eternal glory by risking their lives in speaking frankly.* Such genuine *ācāryas* not only accept honor and facilities or only talk "nicely" about Kṛṣṇa but also are committed to uphold, against all opposition, the principles of their *sampradāya*—which entails speaking vigorously not merely within one's own group, but also venturing out to deliver the message of Godhead to the misguided and often inimical populace.

Śrīla Prabhupāda's own spiritual master was the legendarily staunch Śrīla Bhaktisiddhānta Sarasvatī, who preached so unreservedly that his enemies tried to kill him. He shocked the intellectuals of the day by his fierce, totally uncompromising condemnation of anything less than unmotivated devotional service to Kṛṣṇa, who alone is to be recognized as the Supreme Personality of Godhead, the proper object of worship. Many responded by openly questioning his credentials as a sadhu. Śrīla Bhaktisiddhānta Sarasvatī replied through numerous speeches and articles, explaining why a true sadhu *must* speak strongly. He went on speaking contentiously throughout his life, not caring for outside opposition nor even his own disciples' dissatisfaction.†

* For a summary of such pastimes of Rāmānujācārya and his followers, see "The Ācārya's Unequalled and Unsurpassed Greatness," in *Śrī Bhaktisiddhānta Vaibhava* (vol. 3, p. 53).

† Descriptions of Śrīla Bhaktisiddhānta Sarasvatī's legendary staunchness appear throughout *Śrī Bhaktisiddhānta Vaibhava*. For his stance on strong speaking, see "The Revolutionary Preacher of Truth" therein (vol. 1, p. 135).

> When my guru-mahārāja was present, even big, big scholars were afraid to talk with his beginning students. My guru-mahārāja was called "living encyclopedia"—he could talk with anyone on any subject. He was so learned—so we should be like that as far as possible. No compromise—Ramakrishna, avatars, yogis, everyone was enemy to Guru-mahārāja. He never compromised. Some godbrothers complained that this preaching was chopping technique and it would not be successful. But we have seen that those who criticized fell down. For my part, I have taken up the policy of my guru-mahārāja—no compromise. All these so-called scholars, scientists, philosophers who do not accept Kṛṣṇa are nothing more than rascals, fools, lowest of mankind, etc.[1]

Once a senior disciple of Śrīla Bhaktisiddhānta Sarasvatī complained that a young *brahmacārī* had spoiled a preaching engagement by openly vilifying a popular charlatan. The meeting had dissolved into chaos. It was terrible publicity. But instead of rebuking that *brahmacārī*, Śrīla Bhaktisiddhānta Sarasvatī commented, "He has done well." Śrīla Bhaktisiddhānta Sarasvatī appreciated the combative spirit.[2]

Some *prākṛta-sahajiyās* fault Śrīla Bhaktisiddhānta Sarasvatī, claiming that Śrī Caitanya Mahāprabhu was not so confrontational. Śrīla Bhaktisiddhānta Sarasvatī explained that although Mahāprabhu by no means entered into barren dogmatic debates, He established His position by meaningful scriptural grapples with the most erudite philosophers of the day.[3] During the time of Mahāprabhu, within learned circles arguments were conducted according to exacting Vedic rules of logic and hermeneutics, and participants both understood and accepted when they had been defeated. But nowadays such principled debate is largely unknown. Almost everyone thinks himself qualified to express opinions on various issues, even without having thoroughly studied them, and

1 Letter, 27 Jul 1973.

2 SPl ch. 4, "How Shall I Serve You?"

3 SBV, vol. 2, p. 15.

does not even understand when he has been defeated. Therefore in the present era, in serving the mission of Mahāprabhu by awaking people to His message, our recent *ācāryas* have prescribed a more forceful and shocking approach than that personally adopted by Mahāprabhu. As Śrīla Bhaktisiddhānta Sarasvatī stated, "The aggressive pronouncement of the concrete truth is the crying necessity of the moment for silencing the aggressive propaganda of specific untruths that is being carried on all over the world."[1]

Some devotees may claim that although chopping techniques were suitable in the time of Śrīla Bhaktisiddhānta Sarasvatī and Śrīla Prabhupāda, they are no longer suitable today. But actually those words of Śrīla Bhaktisiddhānta Sarasvatī's in 1931 are eternal beacons to preachers in this world, which is populated by an overwhelming majority of *jīvas* intent on forgetting Kṛṣṇa, plus a tiny minority trying to "arrest the perverted current tide and redirect it toward the eternal source."[2] What was a crying necessity in 1931 is now even more pronounced. And thus Śrīla Prabhupāda, as the best servant of Śrīla Bhaktisiddhānta Sarasvatī, having fully imbibed the mood of his spiritual master, fought against the demonic civilization to establish Kṛṣṇa as the Supreme Absolute Truth. Śrīla Prabhupāda avowed himself to be "the greatest enemy of modern civilization," and added, "It is a regular war declared."[3] Once, when disciples pleaded that he rest and recuperate his health, he gravely responded, "I want the benediction to go on fighting for Kṛṣṇa, like Arjuna."[4]

And fight Śrīla Prabhupāda did, even from the outset of his ministration in the West—for instance, when he became livid at the impersonalism of his earliest followers:

---

1 *Harmonist* 29.169 (Dec 1931); SBV, vol. 3, p. 146.

2 *Harmonist* 25.9 (Jun 1927); SBV, vol. 3, p. 41.

3 *TKG's Diary*, 21 May.

4 SPl ch. 50, "The Lame Man and the Blind Man."

Swamiji [Śrīla Prabhupāda] particularly criticizes the Radhakrishnan commentary to the *Bhagavad-gītā* verse (9.34) in which Kṛṣṇa tells Arjuna, "Engage your mind always in thinking of Me, offer obeisances, and worship Me. Being completely absorbed in Me, surely you will come to Me."

Upon this verse, Radhakrishnan comments that it is not to the personal Kṛṣṇa that we have to surrender but to "the unborn, beginningless, eternal who speaks through Kṛṣṇa."

"Just see!" Swamiji says when this verse and commentary are read at the evening class. "I told you Dr. Radhakrishnan was an impersonalist. This Māyāvādī philosophy is worse than atheism."

We are not really certain what "Māyāvādī" means. When asked, Swamiji says that impersonalists are called Māyāvādīs because they consider Kṛṣṇa's transcendental, eternal body to be *māyā*, or illusion. "For them," he says, "the impersonal Brahman is the Absolute Truth, and Kṛṣṇa is subordinate to Brahman. But in *Bhagavad-gītā* Kṛṣṇa says that He is the Supreme Absolute Truth and that the impersonal Brahman is subordinate to Him."

Surprising us all, Keith [later initiated as Kīrtanānanda] rallies to the defense of Dr. Radhakrishnan. "I think he's right," he says. "After all, Kṛṣṇa is in all of us. So if we surrender to the unborn within us, then we attain the Absolute Truth."

To support his view, Keith quotes Śaṅkara and Huang Po, Buddha and Christ, Spinoza and St. Paul. Swamiji just sits on the dais, and for the first time I notice him turn red. This is surprising, considering his golden complexion. When Keith pauses, Swamiji asks, "Are you finished?"

Keith isn't finished. He talks on about the Self and the One Mind, quoting liberally from various scriptures before winding down.

"Are you finished?" Swamiji asks again.

"Yes," Keith says.

"So, you have understood what we have been saying—that Kṛṣṇa is God?"

"Yes," Keith says.

"And that worship is due God?"

"Yes," Keith says.

Suddenly Swamiji, red and furious, stands up. "Then why do you want to take it away from Kṛṣṇa?" he roars, shaking the small storefront. "It's Kṛṣṇa! It's Kṛṣṇa!" He slams his hand down on the lectern. "It's no unborn within Kṛṣṇa! It's Kṛṣṇa!" We all sit stunned, as if a lion had pounced on the dais. "Kṛṣṇa, the Supreme Personality of Godhead, is directly telling Arjuna, 'To Me. Worship Me.' And Dr. Radhakrishnan says that it is not to the person Kṛṣṇa but to some void. Just see what a nonsense rascal! Do you want to worship some unborn void instead of Kṛṣṇa? Kṛṣṇa is the Absolute Truth. His body, mind, and self are absolute. And He says, 'Think of Me, be devoted to Me, worship Me.' And even Śaṅkara says, *bhaja govindaṁ, bhaja govindaṁ, bhaja govindam:* 'Worship Govinda, worship Govinda, worship Govinda. Your nonsense will not save you at death!' And yet this rascal wants to take it away from Kṛṣṇa. Do you want to follow such a rascal? Kṛṣṇa says, 'Worship Me.' Do you not understand? Then why are you saying it is not to Kṛṣṇa? Why? Why not to Kṛṣṇa?"

We all look at Keith as if he'd suddenly turned into an untouchable. This surprises us all, since usually he is so expert. Yet he simply articulated the Māyāvādī mentality of us all. We sit in stunned silence, not daring to venture further.

"Did you see how red Swamiji got?" I ask Wally [later initiated as Umāpati] afterwards. "Boy, was he angry!"

"But he's right," Wally says. "All the commentators try to avoid Kṛṣṇa. You've read *Bhagavad-gītā* before. Until meeting Swamiji, did you ever think of worshiping Kṛṣṇa?"

I have to admit that it never crossed my mind.

> Thus we discover that we are also Māyāvādī impersonalists. Addicted to inactivity and hedonism, we know nothing of spiritual personality and action. Swamiji has to shout loud indeed to make us understand that God is a person and that action for His sake is on the spiritual platform.
>
> "This is *Bhagavad-gītā's* most essential message," Swamiji says the next morning. "Lord Kṛṣṇa tells Arjuna to fight, but He says, 'Do it for Me.' When we work for Kṛṣṇa and chant His name, we are already liberated and living on the spiritual plane. Just as a person feels heat when he touches something hot, you are liberated as soon as you enter into the service of Kṛṣṇa."
>
> We all feel as though we've just touched something very hot. There is no doubt that our long slumber is being disturbed.
>
> "We are declaring war," Swamiji says. "War on *māyā*."[1]

By declaring war in his storefront, Śrīla Prabhupāda risked losing his fledgling flock—the only followers (if at that stage they could be considered thus) that he had after months in America—but he instead won them in a manner that would not have been possible had he not unreservedly exorcised their deep-rooted misconceptions.

Shortly after being initiated, Umāpati Dāsa told Śrīla Prabhupāda that he could not accept his assertion that a family should live together as if strangers in a hotel. Śrīla Prabhupāda then showed him the relevant statement from the *Bhagavad-gītā*, but Umāpati remained dissatisfied, and soon thereafter left the association of the devotees.* When after nine months Umāpati returned, Śrīla Prabhupāda told him that because another devotee had left shortly before he had, he (Śrīla Prabhupāda) was worried that Umāpati's departure would catalyze a spate of further defections.

---

* The relevant statement was almost certainly the first half of Bg 13.10.

---

1 *The Hare Krishna Explosion* (by Hayagrīva Dāsa), ch. 3.

At that time, Śrīla Prabhupāda's entire movement consisted of approximately twenty disciples, yet even though faced with the prospect of losing all or most of them, Śrīla Prabhupāda never budged from the truth.[1]

Mukunda Goswami, who also was among the earliest disciples of Śrīla Prabhupāda, similarly stated that from nearly the very beginning he realized that Swamiji was not just a teacher but a fighter who really did not like impersonalism and who would never compromise.[2]

Śrīla Prabhupāda never modified his stance. In 1972, at a public lecture in Glasgow, a young man stood up and loudly declared, "I am God!" to which Śrīla Prabhupāda roared back: "You are not God! You are dog!"[3] *

At a pandal program in Delhi, in the middle of his lecture, Śrīla Prabhupāda called a belligerent American hippie onto the stage:

> "Have you realized yourself?" the young man demanded. "Have you realized the soul in the innermost depths of your being?"
>
> "Yes!" Śrīla Prabhupāda replied.
>
> At first the man was taken aback, but then he again challenged, "Now you tell me another thing. When was the *Bhagavad-gītā* written?"
>
> "Now you answer my question," Śrīla Prabhupāda said. "What is the process of receiving knowledge from the *Bhagavad-gītā*?"
>
> "No," the young man retorted. "You tell me—when was the *Bhagavad-gītā* written? In your lecture you said five thousand years ago, but

* This was a regular response of Śrīla Prabhupāda's to people who told him that they were God. (See Conversation, 23 Dec 1969, and the discussion after Lecture, 16 Jul 1972)

1 Told by Umāpati Swami to Bhakti Vikāsa Swami.

2 *Miracle on Second Avenue* (by Mukunda Goswami), pp. 54 & 71.

3 SPl ch. 40, "Around the World but Absorbed in Bombay."

according to other swamis, it was written only fifteen hundred years ago. Answer my question. I asked you first!"

Śrīla Prabhupāda raised his voice angrily. "I am not your servant. I am Kṛṣṇa's servant. You must answer my question!"

A heated argument began, with the hippie yelling at Śrīla Prabhupāda and Śrīla Prabhupāda arguing back. Finally the devotees removed the boy from the stage.

The incident confused the audience. Many people began to leave. "Why did your Guru Mahārāja become angry?" some of them demanded from the devotees. "He should have answered the man's question." Some of the civic leaders supporting the pandal program also became upset, fearing Śrīla Prabhupāda had made an unfavorable impression on the public. Those who were devotional, however, remained in their seats to hear further what Prabhupāda had to say.

To the devotees it was inconceivable. Why had Prabhupāda, in the middle of his talk, invited a crazy hippie onto the stage, given him a microphone and a seat, and then argued with him to the point of yelling and shouting? And all before an audience of twenty thousand!

[Bhavānanda:] One man who had helped organize the pandal protested, "Oh, Swamiji has gotten angry. This is not good." But Śrīla Prabhupāda seemed to have done it purposefully. He had spoken for a long time that evening on how to understand the *Bhagavad-gītā,* and then he had this hippie brought on the stage. It was bewildering to us. We couldn't figure it out.

[Girirāja:] Śrīla Prabhupāda was actually using the entire incident to illustrate the process of understanding *Bhagavad-gītā.* After the man left, Prabhupāda completed his lecture by stating that one must approach Kṛṣṇa or Kṛṣṇa's representative with a submissive attitude, by serving and inquiring, not simply asking challenging questions. The whole incident had illustrated this point.

[Yadubara:] Many in the audience misunderstood the incident. It caused a split. But those who understood what Śrīla Prabhupāda had done could see that this hippie was a rascal, and this had been a time for transcendental anger against his nonsensical opinions.

[Tejīyas:] After everything was over, Prabhupāda told us, "Just as the *gopīs* were lusty for Kṛṣṇa, Arjuna would also get angry for Kṛṣṇa. So it is not bad that a devotee becomes angry for Kṛṣṇa." But many people in the crowd could not understand this point—how a devotee is not impersonal.[1]

Śrīla Prabhupāda could have dismissed the hippie with a terse comment. But he did not. He called the hippie onto the stage and publicly engaged in a shouting match with him. In this instance, Śrīla Prabhupāda, the empowered representative of Kṛṣṇa, chose to fight onstage with a hippie even though it was likely that many attendees would disapprove.

While touring America in 1975, Śrīla Prabhupāda caused another uproar by stating on television that women are less intelligent than men. Several female reporters came to interview Śrīla Prabhupāda, who remained unfazed even after one of the journalists angrily stormed out of the room. The press coverage went from bad to worse, but Śrīla Prabhupāda stood by his principles.[2]

A critic might contend that Śrīla Prabhupāda could have handled those situations in a more sensitive and careful manner. Although on many occasions Śrīla Prabhupāda *did* deal tactfully, he often chose to fight, sometimes by all-out attack.

[Journalist:] I think an awful lot of our readers, and an awful lot of people in the United States, are terribly confused with the many people who claim to be gurus and gods and who pop up in this country, one after the other, and they say that ...

[Prabhupāda:] I can declare that they are all nonsense.

1 SPl ch. 37, "The Land Is Yours."

2 Conversation, 9 Jul 1975.

> [Journalist:] I wonder if you could elaborate on that a little bit?
>
> [Prabhupāda:] I can say, furthermore, they're all rascals.[1]

In the beginning days of Kṛṣṇa consciousness in the West, a group of budding devotees complained to Śrīla Prabhupāda that he was too hostile against impersonalism, false yogis, and so on. Śrīla Prabhupāda responded, "A preacher must attack."[2]

Śrīla Prabhupāda not only fought, but he also commanded his disciples to fight:

> You young boys should also preach strongly. You must learn the truth—*mamaivāṁśo jīva-loke**—and preach strongly, as I am doing all over the world. Preach the truth just as Kṛṣṇa is speaking in *Bhagavad-gītā* and *Śrīmad-Bhāgavatam*, and do not compromise Kṛṣṇa's words.[3]

> These are all nonsense—simply nonsense, *mūḍha*. Of course, we use this word *mūḍha*, and people become very angry, but what can we do? *[Laughter]* The *mūḍhas* must be explained as *mūḍhas*. And because the *mūḍhas* are going as intelligent, therefore there is chaotic condition. So our Kṛṣṇa consciousness movement is to become intelligent—not to remain *mūḍhas*—and to expose these rascal *mūḍhas*. That is our Kṛṣṇa consciousness movement. So you must be prepared. While making propaganda, expose these *mūḍhas*. That is one of the services of Kṛṣṇa. Don't remain foolish. Wherever there is required, fight with these *mūḍhas* and tell them rightly, straightforwardly, that "You are *mūḍhas*." Thank you very much.[4] †

---

* "The *jīvas* are parts of Kṛṣṇa" (Bg 15.7).

† Although the word *propaganda* is often used in a negative sense, indicating widespread dissemination of untruth, Śrīla Prabhupāda generally used this word in a positive sense, to indicate the widespread disseminating of truth.

---

1 *Journey of Self-Discovery*, 4.1.

2 Umāpati Swami, personal recollection.

3 *My Glorious Master*, p. 139.

4 Lecture, 2 Apr 1975.

The Kṛṣṇa consciousness movement declares war against bogus incarnations. The bogus propaganda put out by people claiming to be God has killed God consciousness all over the world. Members of the Kṛṣṇa consciousness movement must be very alert to defy these rascals who are presently misleading the whole world. One such rascal, known as Pauṇḍraka, appeared before Lord Kṛṣṇa, and the Lord immediately killed him. Of course, those who are Kṛṣṇa's servants cannot kill such imitation gods, but they should try their best to defeat them through the evidence of *śāstra,* authentic knowledge received through the disciplic succession.[1]

Our aim is to destroy the position of the mundane scholars. We have to prove to the world that anyone who is not Kṛṣṇa conscious is a *duṣkṛtina* and *mūḍha.*[2]

You can eulogize your guru-mahārāja, but you have to learn how to face the public and be strong to defend yourself. That is success. Not simply by praising your guru-mahārāja. You'll praise your guru-mahārāja—that is not very difficult. But be victorious over the opposing elements. Then you will praise your guru-mahārāja nicely. At home, you can praise your guru-mahārāja, and guru-mahārāja will be satisfied: "Oh, my disciples are praising me." That is good, respectful. That is the qualification. But you have to fight. Then your guru-mahārāja will be glorified.[3]

I am very glad that you are challenging all of these so-called swamis and gurus. My guru-mahārāja appreciated devotees who boldly present our Vaiṣṇava philosophy. We must take advantage of every opportunity to defeat these rascals and drive them away, so please continue this strong attitude.[4]

Very strongly preach this philosophy to the student class of men. That is the greatest service.[5]

---

1 Cc 2.22.9, purport.

2 Letter, 17 Apr 1977.

3 Conversation, 26 Dec 1975.

4 Letter, 30 Nov 1971.

5 Letter, 20 May 1972.

> No other movement or cult has such vast background of authority, so we are not afraid to challenge anyone and everyone to defeat their philosophy on the basis of that authority.[1]
>
> These rascals are passing as scientists and philosophers and thus misleading persons. This is our greatest grief. Therefore I am requesting you all: just make a plan to face these rascals and defeat them. They are misleading the whole human society. Now the Kṛṣṇa consciousness movement should take this turn.... Kṛṣṇa has two engagements: *paritrāṇāya sādhūnāṁ vināśāya ca duṣkṛtām*—giving protection to the sadhus, the devotees, and killing the demons. Of the two engagements, His killing of the demons was His major occupation. If we examine how much time He devoted to killing and how much time He devoted to protecting, we shall find that He devoted more time to killing. Similarly, those who are Kṛṣṇa conscious should also kill—not by weapons, but by logic, by reasoning, and by education. If one is a demon, we can use logic and arguments to kill his demoniac propensities and turn him into a devotee, a saintly person. Especially in this present age, Kali-yuga, people are already poverty-stricken, and physical killing is too much for them. They should be killed by argument, reasoning, and scientific spiritual understanding.[2]

Like his own guru-mahārāja, Śrīla Prabhupāda also was inclined toward his bolder preachers.[3] He wanted them to be lionlike—to challenge, fight, and win:

> You have understood our philosophy rightly, that we boldly challenge anyone—philosopher, scientist, educationist—to understand our philosophy, and for that, we enter without hesitation into the heart of the biggest cities and preach to anyone and everyone the message of Lord Caitanya, who Himself was like the lion in strength.[4]
>
> I wish that every one of you should be lion's descendant. Our Lord Kṛṣṇa assumed the form of a lion and killed the atheist, Hiraṇyakaśipu,

1 Letter, 8 Dec 1971.

2 Lecture, 3 May 1973.

3 Letter, 21 Dec 1972.

4 Letter, 19 Feb 1972.

and by disciplic succession we shall also kill all impersonalist atheist. Absolutely there is no Kṛṣṇa Consciousness for the impersonalist.[1]

Best preachers ... will not stand by idly and listen to any nonsense ideas or Māyāvādīs.[2]

The whole world is running on a false theory that life is born out of matter. But that is not a fact. So how to defeat this theory? That is our business. We have to defeat this rascal theory. We have to challenge all these rascals and defeat them. We have to make a program. Because this is most misleading, the whole human society is affected by this misleading theory, we have to make program: go from place to place and invite all big men, all scientists. That program we have to make. We cannot allow this nonsense theory to go on. We must do something. So we have to challenge, protest, defeat. This will be our work. Our worshiping of Kṛṣṇa is our internal affair. The external affair: we need to establish this theory. Make plan how to meet them, how to defeat them. Catch them on their throat. We are not ordinary so-called swamis and sadhus. We are going to give to the world something which they forgot.[3]

The people of the world should be taught to hear the transcendental topics of the Lord, and the devotee of the Lord must speak loudly so that they can hear.[4]

We shall speak very loudly and expose these bogus men. Let our philosophy be challenged by anyone and we shall defeat them.[5]

Regarding the rascal Bharati, yes, capture this rascal and defeat him in debating, and prove him as a rascal number one.[6]

Somebody [claims that he] is Kṛṣṇa Himself, somebody is greater than Kṛṣṇa, somebody says Kṛṣṇa has no form, somebody says that Kṛṣṇa is dead and so on. Our program is to offer vehement protest against all these nonsensical declarations.[7]

---

1 Letter, 2 Nov 1967.

2 Letter, 21 Dec 1972.

3 Conversation, 3 May 1973.

4 SB 2.3.20, purport.

5 Letter, 22 Nov 1971.

6 Letter, 2 Nov 1973.

7 Letter, 16 Feb 1971.

> Make a plan. Go from town to town, all over the world. This has to be done. If you are mischievous, you are criminal. But if you tolerate mischievous activities, that is also criminal. Challenge these rascals. Stop their rascal theories.[1]

> So many wrong things are going on in the name of nationalism, in the name of scientific advancement, and people are suffering. Everybody has bluffed so long. Now we have to stop them. This is our movement. The rascals are flourishing by cheating and bluffing. This should be stopped. How much important is your movement—just try to understand. Their whole program is to defy God. And our program is to declare war against these rascals.[2]

In war, there is a time for fighting and a time for making peace. But war is mostly fighting. The battlefield is no place for pacifists or cowards. Those who do not fight are already defeated. Without attacking, no one can win.

Śrīla Prabhupāda exulted over his disciple Haṁsadūta Swami's public defeat of one Dr. Kovoor, who at that time was Sri Lanka's most prominent proponent of atheism.* Upon having Haṁsadūta Swami's points read to him, Śrīla Prabhupāda noted, "He is putting very strong arguments. This is preaching!"[3]

There is virtually no limit to how aggressive a devotee may be in attacking the agents of *māyā*. In 1977, devotees were taken to court in New York on charges of brainwashing. Śrīla Prabhupāda ordered a disciple who was defending the nationally publicized case to be shockingly provocative in response:

---

* Śrīla Prabhupāda enthusiastically endorsed that the altercation between Haṁsadūta Swami and Dr. Kovoor be included within a publication featuring certain of Śrīla Prabhupāda's own conversations that debunk pseudo-scientific theories. Thus, the Kovoor exchange appears as an appendix to *Life Comes from Life*, a BBT book that has been printed in the millions.

---

1 Conversation, 3 May 1973.

2 Conversation, 9 Dec 1973.

3 SPl ch. 52, "I Have Done My Part."

> "Yes, brainwashing. Because you have got so much stool in your brain, we require to wash it. It is my thankless duty to wash it. You should have thanked me, but you are so fool, you are condemning." Tell them like that. "You are proud of your civilization. Licking of the vagina, different, obnoxious smell. You are less than the dog. The dog likes to smell the vagina. You are like that. Why you are searching after dog vagina, this vagina, that vagina, that vagina? Is that civilization?" Expose them like that. "Your brain is filled with so much stool, so we are washing it." This is a good opportunity in the court, so that it will be published. People will know what is our philosophy. Licking the vagina civilization. Publish.[1]

Undoubtedly, devotees "cannot expect a very smooth life in preaching."[2] Fighting is not easy:

> Preaching is always difficult—that I am repeatedly saying. You cannot take preaching as very easygoing. Preaching must be a fight. Do you mean to say fighting is easy? Fighting is not easy. Whenever there is a fight, there is danger, there is responsibility. What is preaching? Because people are ignorant, we have to enlighten them. That is preaching.[3]

Kṛṣṇa consciousness will not immediately be accepted, but nevertheless, we should fight to win, and Kṛṣṇa will help us:

> It is not that everyone will immediately accept your Kṛṣṇa consciousness. We have to meet opposing elements. The more we successfully meet them, that is the success of preaching. We have to always win. Yes, we always win if we have complete faith in Kṛṣṇa. Then as we preach and answer, we will always win. Kṛṣṇa is God. If we are on His side, we will win always.[4]

1 Conversation, 19 Feb 1977.

2 Conversation, 26 Jan 1977.

3 Conversation, 12 Dec 1973.

4 *ISKCON in the 1970s*, vol. 1, p. 29.

TWO
NO COMPROMISE

Strong speaking may be considered in two divisions: clear delineation of the message of Kṛṣṇa consciousness, and forcefulness and provocativeness in delivering that message. The essence of strong speaking lies in the former. Since the message of Kṛṣṇa consciousness is inherently strong and clear, real preaching of that message must also be strong and clear, without any compromise. Compromise means to understate, obfuscate, or deliberately misstate the message given by Kṛṣṇa and the *ācāryas*. As is apparent from the entire message of *Bhagavad-gītā*—Kṛṣṇa's exhorting Arjuna to annihilate ungodly elements—it is even a compromise to fail to oppose all misconceptions and falsehoods, to avoid the fight that genuine preaching entails:

> The word *jīva-hiṁsā* (envy of other living entities) actually means stopping the preaching of Kṛṣṇa consciousness. Preaching work is described as *paropakāra*, welfare activity for others. Those who are ignorant of the benefits of devotional service must be educated by preaching. If one stops preaching and simply sits down in a solitary place, he is engaging in material activity. If one desires to make a compromise with the Māyāvādīs, he is also engaged in material activity. A devotee should never make compromises with nondevotees.[1]

1 Cc 2.12.135, purport.

Śrīla Bhaktisiddhānta Sarasvatī termed those who compromised "good for nothing,"[1] and also averred:

> If I were to desist from speaking the impartial truth for fear that some listeners might be riled, I would be deviating from the path of Vedic truth to accept that of untruth. I would become inimical to the Vedas, an atheist, and would no longer possess faith in Bhagavān, the very embodiment of truth.[2]

As the perfect servant of his lionlike guru, Śrīla Prabhupāda never compromised—nor did he want his disciples to compromise:

> The fact is that I am the only one in India who is openly criticizing, not only demigod worship and impersonalism but everything that falls short of complete surrender to Kṛṣṇa. My guru-mahārāja never compromised in His preaching, nor will I, nor should any of my students. We are firmly convinced that Kṛṣṇa is the Supreme Personality of Godhead and all others are His part-and-parcel servants. This we must declare boldly to the whole world.[3]

> We are facing so many difficulties. We don't care for it. We never compromise. All my students will never compromise. Why shall I compromise? If I am confident that I am speaking the truth, why shall I compromise? Those who are not confident of his position will compromise. One who does not know where he stands will compromise. And if I know where I am standing, why shall I compromise? Let others do whatever they like. This is our position.[4]

> When you become actually preacher of God consciousness, you cannot make any compromise. You must call a spade a spade.[5]

> When we deliberately discuss on *śāstras*, there is no question of compromising. We must face the bare facts.[6]

> We don't make any flattery to satisfy the whims of the audience. We speak from *Śrīmad-Bhāgavatam*, we speak from *Bhagavad-gītā*, and

1 BTG 27 (1969).
2 SBV, vol. 1, p. 144.
3 Letter, 3 Jan 1972.
4 Conversation, 31 Dec 1976.
5 Lecture, 16 Oct 1972.
6 Lecture, 5 Apr 1971.

> present them as it is, without any adulteration. This is our position. If you like, then you make progress. If you don't like, that is your option. But we cannot make any compromise. We must present the *śāstra* as it is.[1]
>
> Kṛṣṇa says, *sarva-dharmān parityajya mām ekaṁ śaraṇaṁ vraja:* "Let aside everything. Just become My devotee, a surrendered soul." So we are preaching that. We don't make compromise. Therefore all people are against me, because "This man simply says 'Kṛṣṇa.'" But I cannot say anything more.[2]
>
> We cannot compromise to satisfy others.[3]
>
> We don't make any compromise. What we believe, we are preaching that. People are accepting. So you believe or not believe—it doesn't matter for us.[4]
>
> We have got a very nice diamond. Try to sell it. If there is a purchaser, he will purchase; otherwise not. It is our duty to canvass. But we cannot sell iron instead of diamonds.[5]

At a festival in Hawaii in 1969, on encountering a bogus group that was glorifying a supposed incarnation of Rāma and Kṛṣṇa, Govinda Dāsī began to speak loudly so that all could hear:

> You have no scripture, you have no disciplic succession. You are blindly following the teachings of this rascal! What proof do you have that this man is God? Has he shown you any evidence? Kṛṣṇa lifted Govardhana Hill as a child when He appeared on this planet, but this man has not done any wonderful thing. Rather, I see by his picture that he is old and wrinkled and ugly, ready for death to take him. And yet you so foolishly believe that he is God! In the Vedas, the avatars' appearances are fully described along with the birthplace and philosophy of each avatar. There is no mention of this rascal. You say that he is the last avatar of this age, but the Vedic

1 Lecture, 27 Sep 1974.

2 Lecture, 28 Dec 1973.

3 Letter, 30 Sep 1973.

4 Conversation, 13 Nov 1975.

5 Conversation, 10 Apr 1977.

authorities say that Kalki will come in 427,000 years. You fail to mention Lord Caitanya, who appeared 486 years ago and propagated the *saṅkīrtana* movement all over India, who drenched the universe in love of Godhead. His mission, His golden color—everything—was described by Vyāsadeva, the compiler of all the Vedas five thousand years ago. But instead of accepting the authorized incarnation of Lord Caitanya, you believe the word of an ordinary man who tells you, "I am God, and you can become God too," without even asking for scriptural evidence or proof of his lordship. This is very unfortunate.

In the last half-century, so many of these cheaters have come to this country from India to mislead the people, proclaiming, "I am God," and holding in their hand a cigarette or a wine bottle. What kind of foolishness is this? We are all suffering in this material world, kicked this way and that like dogs, and yet you say you are God? You can never become God! You are conditioned, controlled by God. God is supreme; you are minute. Qualitatively you are one with God—in your pure spiritual state you have godly qualities—but you can never become quantitatively as great as God. We are simultaneously one and different—qualitatively one but quantitatively different, like the gold ring and the gold mine. The quality is the same, but one is far more vast. Kṛṣṇa states it plainly in the *Bhagavad-gītā:* "My dear Arjuna, all these living entities are My parts and parcels." But instead of accepting Kṛṣṇa's words as they are, you are listening to some fool who will only mislead you. He can never give you any proof of his lordship. Kṛṣṇa showed His universal form. He said to Arjuna, "You just surrender unto Me!" But rather than do that simple thing, you choose to follow the imperfect speculations of some so-called swami, and consequently you are being completely misled.[1]

One man who was unable to defeat the further arguments presented by Gaurasundara Dāsa (Govinda Dāsī's husband) became so irate that he severely struck Gaurasundara on the chin. On receiving the report of this preaching adventure, Śrīla Prabhupāda penned a reply:

---

1 From "Heroine Govinda Dāsī," BTG 29 (1969) [edited].

> I am so much pleased by reading your letter of June 26, 1969, describing your preaching activities in Hawaii, both husband and wife together. It is very much pleasing to me. I was shocked when I heard that Gaurasundara was hurt on the chin, but at the same time, I was so much enlivened by hearing of your spirited preaching activities. I am proud that a little young girl like you is so much spirited in preaching Kṛṣṇa consciousness. Undoubtedly I was very much sorry to learn about Gaurasundara being attacked by a fanatic, but don't be disheartened. Even Nityānanda also faced such difficult problems, but try to avoid them as far as possible. The whole world is full of fanatics and atheist classes of men, so sometimes we have to face such difficulties. But this is all *tapasya.* Without *tapasya,* nobody can approach Kṛṣṇa. So preachers who boldly face all kinds of difficulties are considered to be under *tapasya,* and Kṛṣṇa takes note of such *tapasya* of the devotee, and the devotee is recognized by Him. I have asked the BTG men to publish your heroic preaching activities under the heading of "Heroine Govinda Dāsī." So I am sure Kṛṣṇa is very much pleased of this incident, and He will surely bestow His blessings both on you and Gaurasundara.[1]

To preach straightforwardly without compromise or timidity was Śrīla Prabhupāda's policy and also his instruction to his followers. Indeed, it is the right and duty of a *brāhmaṇa* to openly enunciate what is correct and what is not. "*Brāhmaṇa* means as it is, they will describe. That is *brāhmaṇa.*"[2]

It is particularly the duty of sannyasis, who are meant to be strong-minded, fearless preaching leaders, to present the message of *śāstra* persuasively, forcefully, and without compromise. It is therefore particularly disappointing and inapt when sannyasis habitually fail to do so.

Some disciples of Śrīla Prabhupāda once informed him that at an interfaith meeting in Toronto in 1975, one of Śrīla Prabhupāda's sannyasi godbrothers had presented Vaiṣṇavism as if it were just

---

1 Letter, 7 Jul 1969.

2 Lecture, 21 May 1976.

another way, without giving any strong argument—not "as it is" or in a manner similar to how Śrīla Prabhupāda would have spoken—and that an ISKCON devotee present there had proposed switching the discussion from relative considerations of different religions to an analysis of what is the Absolute Truth, whereupon the godbrother had scolded that devotee as being unknowledgeable and contentious.[1] In a later conversation about this incident, Śrīla Prabhupāda dismissed that sannyasi godbrother as a rascal who was simply after some following.[2]

Of course, it is not that only sannyasis must speak strongly. Many of Śrīla Prabhupāda's most caustic writings are from his pre-*sannyāsa* days. Even during his *gṛhastha* life, Śrīla Prabhupāda always unpretentiously delineated the truth, which he knew can—and should—be known by everyone, the same truth that the Absolute Truth Himself declares: "I am easily available (*sulabha*) to those who are sincere enough to accept Me."[3] Anyone who sincerely seeks to know and serve the truth is a real sadhu. Those who have any other agenda constitute cheaters and the cheated. Śrīla Prabhupāda's unambiguous revelation of the Absolute Truth—Kṛṣṇa, as He is—left no excuse to anyone for not surrendering unto Kṛṣṇa. With courage founded on absolute conviction, Śrīla Prabhupāda refused to meekly evade conflict, and he directly addressed challenges.

Sometimes one Dr. Patel, accompanying Śrīla Prabhupāda on walks on Juhu Beach, Mumbai, would criticize Śrīla Prabhupāda for his unceasing denunciation of everything and everyone bogus:

> [Dr. Patel:] You are so very hard and harsh.
>
> [Prabhupāda:] I must be hard! The whole world is spoiled by these Māyāvādīs. Therefore I am very hard. We must be harder and harder. I don't make any compromise with these rascals.[4]

1 Conversation, 30 Jun 1975.

2 Conversation, 21 Apr 1976.

3 See Bg 8.14.

4 Conversation, 23 Mar 1974.

[Dr. Patel:] With all due respect, sir, we must have some sort of forbearance for others' views.

[Prabhupāda:] No, no. Because if we have got to preach, we cannot make any compromise.

[Dr. Patel:] You feel that way—we have no objection. But we should also respect somebody else's views.

[Prabhupāda:] No, we have got all respect, but not unnecessary respect.

[Dr. Patel:] But even unnecessary respect—sometimes you unnecessarily go beyond, according to the …

[Prabhupāda:] No, no. We have respect. But a thief should be called a thief. That is truth.

[Dr. Patel:] You are the magistrate, and you are the judge, and you are the …

[Prabhupāda:] No, no. I am not the judge. I am talking on the basis of *Bhagavad-gītā. Na māṁ duṣkṛtino mūḍhāḥ prapadyante narādhamāḥ:* "One who is a *narādhama*—he does not surrender to Kṛṣṇa." This is the judgment. As soon as we see that one is not surrendered to Kṛṣṇa, we accept him as a *narādhama.* That's all. Whatever he may be.[1]

[Dr. Patel:] You have been bracketing so many good people with the bad, and I feel strongly about this philosophy of yours.

[Prabhupāda:] Where are good people? All rascals! Let them come. Yes, I shall kick on their face, I am so strong. Where is good man? I have already kicked that Bala Yogi—"He's a dog!"—in a public meeting. If anybody is a Māyāvādī, he's a dog. Kick him on his face![2]

When introduced to a Ph.D. candidate in biology in Atlanta, Śrīla Prabhupāda remarked, "Poor frogs," and pointed out the fault of killing them (a standard practice in biology).[3] Similarly,

1 Conversation, 5 Apr 1974.

2 Conversation, 23 Feb 1974.

3 SPl ch. 35, "This Remote Corner of the World."

in Philadelphia in 1975, a professor from Temple University came to meet Śrīla Prabhupāda, who promptly inquired, "What do you teach?"

"Hinduism," the man answered.

"What do you mean by 'Hinduism'?"

The professor, thinking to give a clever reply, said, "I don't know."

Śrīla Prabhupāda retorted, "Then you are a cheater! For you are purporting to teach that which you do not know."

The professor became livid. It got heavier and heavier. A shouting match began, but eventually the professor admitted, "Yes, I am a cheater, but I am an honest cheater." Refusing this olive branch, Śrīla Prabhupāda shot back, "You say you are honest, but the judgment of a cheater cannot be accepted." The professor demanded that Śrīla Prabhupāda should tell him what Hinduism is, and Śrīla Prabhupāda said, "First you become shaven-headed like these. Then I will teach you. *Tad viddhi praṇipātena paripraśnena sevayā.*"[1] The professor responded, "I did. When I came in, I offered my *praṇāmas.*" He folded his hands together. Then Prabhupāda said, "Then my first instruction to you is stop this cheating business." Some graduate students who were present could hardly believe what Śrīla Prabhupāda was doing to him.[2] *

* Ravīndra Svarūpa Dāsa was studying at the religion department of Temple University, and the professor, an Indian born in a Vaiṣṇava family, was also in that department. Ravīndra Svarūpa Dāsa had invited the professor to meet Śrīla Prabhupāda, but after this incident the professor became openly inimical to Śrīla Prabhupāda and ISKCON—which made life at the university difficult for Ravīndra Svarūpa Dāsa. However, after many years the professor realized that Śrīla Prabhupāda had been correct, and he again embraced his Vaiṣṇava roots.

1 Bg 4.34.

2 SPl ch. 46, "Preaching to America: Part 1"; *Following Srila Prabhupada,* DVD 11; Ravīndra Svarūpa Dāsa, personal recollection.

Also in 1975, when some theologians from the University of Southern California visited Śrīla Prabhupāda at the Los Angeles ISKCON temple, he spoofed their term "modern theology," told them that they were "illogical," and declared, "You do not know God. You are trying to find out God. This is not theology. Theologist means one who knows God and abides by His order." Śrīla Prabhupāda insisted, "We are presenting God: 'Here is God.' And big, big *ācāryas* have accepted—Rāmānujācārya, Madhvācārya, Viṣṇu Svāmī, Lord Caitanya, and, in our disciplic succession, my guru-mahārāja. And I am preaching, 'This is God.' I am not presenting a God whimsically. I am presenting a God who is recognized. So why don't you accept? What is the difficulty?" When Dr. Judah, who was openly appreciative of Śrīla Prabhupāda and his followers, suggested that because the theologians were older it was difficult for them to change, Śrīla Prabhupāda responded, "Then you are not serious about God."[1] Nartakī Devī Dāsī, who had been present, later commented:

> He had to be strict because actually they are cheating. They are presenting themselves as authorities and teaching at big universities, and they get all kinds of degrees, and naturally a young student will take them as an authority. But that is cheating because they don't even know about God and are presenting themselves as someone who does know. And therefore people are wasting their time hearing these kinds of speculations.[2]

Bahulāśva Dāsa further observed:

> When most of these professors came, Prabhupāda was always ready to take them on. He didn't get friendly with many of these professors, but he would always encourage me to bring more. Then we would work hard to cultivate a relationship to get them to come to see Prabhupāda, and then Prabhupāda would just smash whatever their philosophy was or whatever their point of view was. But there were a

1 Conversation, 24 Jun 1975.

2 *Following Srila Prabhupada*, DVD 11.

> few that Prabhupāda liked, like Dr. Judah. And I think that was more because they came with a devotional attitude. They didn't come as if they were the great erudite scholars. When they came, they had a sense of who Prabhupāda was. They knew they were in the presence of a holy person, and then Prabhupāda would treat them differently. But if they came all arrogant and puffed up, then Śrīla Prabhupāda would immediately say, "And so, what is your philosophy? What are you thinking about this?" And he would immediately challenge them and just tear them to shreds. Prabhupāda would go right at them and usually be very challenging. I think Prabhupāda wanted to use these interactions as ways to give the devotees the confidence not to be afraid to speak up. Prabhupāda was showing how to do it—regardless of what their positions were, to present Kṛṣṇa consciousness fearlessly, not to hold back and be overly polite.[1]

Although some devotees object that to adopt such aggressiveness will spoil ISKCON's preaching, actually the opposite is true: without clear delineation of *siddhānta* (proper philosophical conclusions regarding Kṛṣṇa consciousness) all other processes for bringing people to Kṛṣṇa consciousness remain unfulfilled. As Hari Śauri Dāsa observed, "The revolutionary instinct is one of the things that has made Prabhupāda so successful in his preaching. He tells things 'as it is.'"[2]

Thus, real preaching necessitates presenting the message of Kṛṣṇa transparently and without compromise. Devotees should neither re-cast nor obfuscate Śrīla Prabhupāda's teachings, for instance, by merely acquiescing with standard, socially accepted viewpoints—"Yes, we also feed the poor, run schools and hospitals, recycle our trash, support government initiatives against terrorism, ..." Such banalities suggest that devotees have nothing original to contribute, that they parrot the same trite formulae as everyone else, and thus are hardly worth listening to. But:

---

1 *Following Srila Prabhupada*, DVD 11.

2 *A Transcendental Diary*, vol. 2, p. 15.

या निशा सर्वभूतानां तस्यां जागर्ति संयमी ।
यस्यां जाग्रति भूतानि सा निशा पश्यतो मुनेः ॥

yā niśā sarva-bhūtānāṁ tasyāṁ jāgarti saṁyamī
yasyāṁ jāgrati bhūtāni sā niśā paśyato muneḥ

What is night for all beings is the time of awakening for the self-controlled; and the time of awakening for all beings is night for the introspective sage.[1]

Kṛṣṇa consciousness means to see the world as the Supreme Personality of Godhead sees it.[2] Therefore a devotee's understanding is categorically different from that of a nondevotee. If a devotee for whatever reason habitually speaks like a nondevotee, he thereby virtually becomes a nondevotee.

1 Bg 2.69.

2 See SB 4.29.69.

THREE
LOYALTY TO KṚṢṆA

Throughout the ages, Kṛṣṇa consciousness has been preached in varying circumstances, yet the essential philosophical presentation has always been the same. That is because the foundational truths of *sambandha-jñāna*—of Kṛṣṇa's supremacy and of the subordination to Him of the *jīvas* and of all else that be—are eternal and immutable. Furthermore, whatever the external circumstances, the allurements that *māyā* presents to the conditioned souls always fall into the same general categories of karma (worldly sense gratification) and *jñāna* (intellectual or quasi-intellectual predilections that generally tend toward impersonalism). Śrīla Prabhupāda made some behavioral adjustments necessary for pioneering Kṛṣṇa consciousness outside its traditional cultural milieu, yet he presented the teachings of Kṛṣṇa consciousness in basically the same way as had all previous *ācāryas*, for the simple reason that regardless of prevailing conditions, the philosophy never changes: Kṛṣṇa is always supreme, and all else is eternally subordinate to Him. Therefore the formula for successful preaching is simple:

> "Who God is" can be summed up in only five words. Kṛṣṇa is the supreme controller. If you become convinced of this, and preach it enthusiastically, success is assured, and you will be doing the greatest service for all living entities. So you continue more and more to serve Kṛṣṇa, and He will help you.[1]

---

1 Letter, 5 May 1972.

This is the message of Kṛṣṇa and the *paramparā*, and sincere servants of Kṛṣṇa and the *paramparā* never consider transmitting anything different:

> We sincerely serve Kṛṣṇa, we are sincere servants of His Lordship, and we present things as presented by Kṛṣṇa, and that is the test of our bona fide position and our bona fide presentation.[1]

As the origin, sustainer, and ultimate goal of Vedic culture, Kṛṣṇa reinforces its core quality of intolerance toward various deviations from the correct understanding of Vedic knowledge. Throughout the *Bhagavad-gītā*, He repeatedly condemns various fallacies, stating that their adherents are fools and rascals. He summarizes the whole panoply of ignorance and ignoramuses thus:

न मां दुष्कृतिनो मूढाः प्रपद्यन्ते नराधमाः ।
माययापहृतज्ञाना आसुरं भावमाश्रिताः ॥

na māṁ duṣkṛtino mūḍhāḥ prapadyante narādhamāḥ
māyayāpahṛta-jñānā āsuraṁ bhāvam āśritāḥ

> Those miscreants who are grossly foolish, who are lowest among mankind, whose knowledge is stolen by illusion, and who partake of the atheistic nature of demons do not surrender unto Me.[2]

Śrīla Prabhupāda said that this verse is "very important."[3] And he explained that his use of explicit words was not according to his personal opinion, but that he was simply restating what Kṛṣṇa had said:

> *Na māṁ duṣkṛtino mūḍhāḥ prapadyante narādhamāḥ*. These are the words used in the *Bhagavad-gītā*. It is not our manufactured word. People may be very unhappy or angry, but we have to quote from these scriptures.[4]

1 Letter, 15 Nov 1968.
2 Bg 7.15.
3 Conversation, 11 Jul 1976.
4 Lecture, 22 Apr 1974.

> We must condemn anyone who is not Kṛṣṇa conscious. I don't condemn, Kṛṣṇa condemns: *na māṁ duṣkṛtino mūḍhāḥ*.[1]

> Everyone is rascal. How we so boldly say that everyone is? Because Kṛṣṇa says. We are Kṛṣṇa-ite. We have to follow. Just like a small child follows the talkings of his father and mother, so similarly, we learn from Kṛṣṇa. Kṛṣṇa says, *na māṁ duṣkṛtino mūḍhāḥ*. Kṛṣṇa says. So we have learned from Kṛṣṇa.[2]

> As soon as we see that he is not a devotee of Kṛṣṇa, then he's a rascal. How do we say? He is not my enemy, but we have to say because it is stated by Kṛṣṇa.[3]

> A man who is worshiped by so many people we call rascal? On what strength? The strength is this Kṛṣṇa consciousness. We can prove that he is rascal. I am not speaking—Kṛṣṇa is speaking. Kṛṣṇa says in the *Bhagavad-gītā, na māṁ duṣkṛtino mūḍhāḥ*. *Mūḍha* means rascal. So I am repeating Kṛṣṇa's word. Anyone who does not surrender unto Kṛṣṇa, he is rascal. So we can quote from *Bhagavad-gītā*. If somebody brings case against us, so we can freely say that "I am not speaking—it is said in the *Bhagavad-gītā*. Bring a libel case against *Bhagavad-gītā*. Why you are troubling me?"[4]

If devotees feel discomfort instead of pleasure in hearing these words of Kṛṣṇa's, and avoid repeating such statements, it suggests that they do not have full faith in them. To not speak the truth is itself a contamination. One thus speaks half-truths or nontruths. Despite having made some progress toward Kṛṣṇa, such devotees are still inclined toward the outlook of the *duṣkṛtīs* (rascals).

> Those who have no practical experience of the beauty and purity of Kṛṣṇa or of Kṛṣṇa consciousness may be confused by such uncompromising denunciations of material, bodily gratification. But those who are enlightened in Kṛṣṇa consciousness will be enlivened and enthused by such absolutely truthful statements.[5]

1 Conversation, 2 Oct 1975.

2 Lecture, 31 Dec 1973.

3 Lecture, 17 Jul 1973.

4 Lecture, 24 May 1969.

5 SB 10.60.45, purport.

One who has real faith in Kṛṣṇa follows in the footsteps of Arjuna and accepts all that Kṛṣṇa says. Arjuna did not accept only some of Kṛṣṇa's statements and whimsically ignore others. Rather, Arjuna declared:

सर्वमेतदृतं मन्ये यन्मां वदसि केशव ।

sarvam etad ṛtaṁ manye yan māṁ vadasi keśava

O Kṛṣṇa, I totally accept as truth all that You have told me.[1]

Genuine followers of Kṛṣṇa do not edit what He says, but accept it in toto:

> We accept Kṛṣṇa's words. We don't tolerate this Māyāvādī nonsense. We are right. Everyone who disagrees with Kṛṣṇa is wrong.[2]

The devotee has been ordered to preach Kṛṣṇa-*upadeśa,* the instructions of Kṛṣṇa.[3]

> Kṛṣṇa consciousness movement means to follow the instruction of Caitanya Mahāprabhu. And Caitanya Mahāprabhu's instruction is this, to preach Kṛṣṇa-*upadeśa.* And this is Kṛṣṇa-*upadeśa: na māṁ duṣkṛtino mūḍhāḥ prapadyante narādhamāḥ.*[4]

A devotee cannot avoid such instructions. Kṛṣṇa calls nondevotees "fools," "rascals," and "the lowest of mankind." Śrīla Prabhupāda demonstrated his loyalty to Kṛṣṇa by unabashedly reiterating such terms, and devotees who are loyal to the principle of *guru-mukha-padma-vākya cittete kariyā aikya, āra nā kariho mane āśā*—to accept the words of the self-realized spiritual master as all-in-all, rejecting all else—follow Śrīla Prabhupāda's example by speaking forthrightly. In so doing, by repeating what Kṛṣṇa says, as He says it, strong speakers are likely to be disparaged by others. But Kṛṣṇa likes them. He empowers such sincere emissaries, and they advance in Kṛṣṇa consciousness:

1 Bg 10.14.

2 *My Glorious Master,* p. 156.

3 Cc 2.7.128.

4 Lecture, 3 Sep 1976.

> One who preaches this confidential knowledge without any compromise—he is the confidential servant of Kṛṣṇa. There is no compromise. This is real religion. Kṛṣṇa says, *na ca tasmān manuṣyeṣu kaścin me priya-kṛttamaḥ*. This is the person who has received the authority to draw mercy water from the ocean of mercy of Kṛṣṇa.[1]
>
> This Kṛṣṇa consciousness movement is a challenge to all the rascals and fools. So those who have taken this movement very seriously should be very sober, and understand at least you must expose all these rascals. That will be very much appreciated by Kṛṣṇa.[2]
>
> Kṛṣṇa immediately recognizes a preacher of Kṛṣṇa consciousness who takes all risks to deliver his message.[3]
>
> Kṛṣṇa appreciates such strong preachers as His dearmost servants, so let us work very enthusiastically to drive away rascal philosophy and establish the real religion of *Bhagavad-gītā* as it is.[4]
>
> The more you fight with these rascals, the more you advance in Kṛṣṇa consciousness. You are a fighting soldier. Kṛṣṇa very much appreciates.[5]

Or, as Śrīla Prabhupāda paraphrased Kṛṣṇa as saying, "Nobody is dearer to Me than he who takes all risks for preaching God consciousness."[6]

1 Lecture, 30 Nov 1976.

2 Lecture, 9 Dec 1973.

3 Letter, 11 Dec 1975.

4 Letter, 8 Dec 1971.

5 Conversation, 12 May 1975.

6 Lecture, 30 Dec 1968. (This statement is based on Bg 18.69)

FOUR
USE OF STRONG TERMS

Śrīla Prabhupāda's everyday vocabulary was full of words like *fool, rascal, demon, mūḍha, nonsense,* and *stool.* He would routinely, matter-of-factly, brand as rascals not only the horrendously wicked but also many persons who would commonly be considered decent folk. As he clarified, their not being Kṛṣṇa conscious qualified them for such denunciation:

> *Śva-viḍ-varāhoṣṭra kharaiḥ saṁstutaḥ puruṣaḥ paśuḥ.** There are many so-called great men and they are very much praised by the general people. So *Bhāgavata* says that anyone who is not a devotee, who never chants the Hare Kṛṣṇa mantra—he may be very great man in the estimation of rascals but he is nothing but an animal. "How you can say that such a great man is an animal?" Our business is a very thankless task. We say any man who is not a devotee of Kṛṣṇa—he is a rascal. We say generally. It is a very harsh word, but we have to use it.[1]
>
> In Montreal a Bengali gentleman inquired, "Swamiji, you are using very strong words—*fools* and *rascals*. Can it be explained otherwise?" And I replied, "No. These are the only words, that you are all rascals and fools."[2]

Considering that Śrīla Prabhupāda used the word *rascal* so often, it behooves his followers to understand how he used it and what

* SB 2.3.19. For the full verse, see p. 48.

1 Lecture, 17 Jul 1973.

2 Conversation, 18 Oct 1975.

he meant by it. *Rascal* can have a forcefully pejorative sense, to mean "a low, mean, unprincipled or dishonest fellow; a rogue," but nowadays it is more commonly used "without serious implication of bad qualities, or as a mild term of reproof."[1] Śrīla Prabhupāda's usage followed that still current in India—clearly insulting, not jocular, and meant to inflict a sting. Śrīla Prabhupāda gave some examples of the kind of people fit to be called rascals:

> Anyone who does not know what is *Bhagavad-gītā* and Kṛṣṇa, he is a rascal.[2]

> Rascal means the nondevotees. They have no good qualification.[3]

> There cannot be any good qualification of a person who is not Kṛṣṇa conscious, who is not a devotee. This is our conclusion. We have got some test tubes. We can study man. He may become a very good scholar, very good politician, very big minister, but we test whether he has got any sense of Kṛṣṇa consciousness. If he's not, immediately I understand that "Here is a rascal number one."[4]

> Without Kṛṣṇa consciousness everyone is a rascal, is a thief, is a rogue, is a robber, these qualifications. Therefore our conclusion is anyone who does not understand Kṛṣṇa, he has no good qualification. Neither he's honest, neither he has knowledge. Therefore he's a third-class man. This is not dogmatism, this is fact.[5]

> Although people declare themselves great scientists, economists, philosophers, politicians, and sociologists, they are actually nothing but rascals.[6]

> Anyone who denies the existence of God, he's a rascal. Rascal means poor fund of knowledge.[7]

---

1 Both of these definitions are from Oxford English Dictionary, 2nd ed. (CD-ROM, v. 4.0), Oxford University Press, 2009.

2 Lecture, 31 Oct 1975.

3 Conversation, 30 Nov 1975.

4 Lecture, 21 Jun 1973.

5 Conversation, 27–29 Feb 1972.

6 SB 5.14.27, purport.

7 Conversation, 25 Feb 1973.

> Rascaldom means to accept a man as God and to accept God as man. We can understand who is an intelligent man and who is a rascal by this criterion.[1]
>
> Rascal means the Māyāvādī, *karmī, jñānī*, yogi, all they are rascals. It is our open declaration.[2]
>
> Rascal means that however [one may] kick him on his face, still, he'll insist. They'll never take good lesson. And sensible means he takes good lesson. *Na māṁ duṣkṛtino mūḍhāḥ*. And why they remain rascal? Because they are *duṣkṛtinaḥ*, very, very sinful. Very, very sinful. Don't you see? They are maintaining slaughterhouse. They are maintaining brothel. They are ruining everyone's life by sense gratification. These are all sinful activities. Therefore they remain rascal forever. They cannot improve. Because they are so sinful, they have to suffer, go to the darkest region. They'll have to become worms of the stool. That is awaiting them. But they do not know how things are going on. They are thinking, "We are safe." That is foolishness. That is rascaldom.[3]
>
> Rascal means one who has no common sense even.[4]

Śrīla Prabhupāda's definitions for terms like *fool* and *nonsense* were along similar lines. His usage of *demon* paralleled the Sanskrit term *asura*, and corresponds to the dictionary definition: "a person of malignant, cruel, terrible, or destructive nature."[5]

The unfortunate fact is that nowadays the modern civilization is rascaldom,[6] and the world population is just a royal edition of the animals.[7] For the sake of reforming them, Śrīla Prabhupāda directly informed such rascals and animals that they were rascals and animals. It is the duty of Śrīla Prabhupāda's followers to not shy away from also stating such facts.

1 Lecture, 30 Jun 1973.

2 Lecture, 26 Jun 1973.

3 Conversation, 7 Dec 1973.

4 Conversation, 23 May 1975.

5 Oxford English Dictionary.

6 Lecture, 16 Mar 1974.

7 SB 1.3.43.

FIVE
THE DUTY OF PREACHERS TO PRESENT THE TRUTH

The prime duty of preachers is not to make or avoid making enemies, nor even to make friends, but to present the truth. And in this wretched world, truth is hardly welcome, while untruth dressed as truth reigns everywhere. Truth has many enemies, and falsity many friends. Accordingly, much of what is considered factual or axiomatic in fields as diverse as science, education, history, politics, and current affairs is whatever powerful vested interests want the masses to believe. Even in the society of devotees, persons dedicated to deceiving themselves and others become lauded as pure devotees and great preachers by presenting Kṛṣṇa consciousness as they would like it to be or imagine it should be, or according to public expectations of what religion should be.

However, to preach the actual truth as received through guru-*paramparā* is a very different matter. Devotees should be like copper wire, which unimpededly transmits electricity from its source. Devotees who profess to represent Śrīla Prabhupāda yet fail to directly speak the message of *Bhagavad-gītā* as it is—in its pristine, potent magnificence—at least implicitly acquiesce with those demonic impersonalists who mangle truth, reality, and the teachings of *śāstra* with demonic propositions such as "all paths are the same." Clearly, if even the most apparently successful of preachers delivers anything but straightforward Kṛṣṇa consciousness, he fails to deliver the genuine truth of Kṛṣṇa consciousness as given by *śāstra* and the previous *ācāryas*. He insults the previous *ācāryas* by claiming to represent them while actually presenting a diluted imitation of their message, thus implying that the *ācāryas* are as insipid as himself. In the name of preaching he actually increases the cesspool of ignorance.

Devotees do not partake in the concept of being "well balanced," which is part of the catechism of the materialistic status quo meant to ensure that semi-intellectual dupes remain acquiescent and mediocre. "Balance" is generally understood to mean a middle position between two viewpoints—but devotees reject from the outset such pabulum epistemology. Devotees are devotees of the truth, which is axiomatically independent of and categorically superior to the opinions of imperfect and misinformed persons. It is this truth, the truth of the *jīvas'* utter dependence on the Supreme Person, that devotees should preach, not being waylaid by reasonable-sounding but ultimately atheistic theorems. Indeed, Śrīla Bhaktisiddhānta Sarasvatī particularly specified that the duty of a Vaiṣṇava preacher is to point out the futility of any process besides surrendering to the Supreme Lord.[1] Similarly, Śrīla Prabhupāda stated:

> Unfortunately people do not know who God is and how to make Him happy. Our Kṛṣṇa consciousness movement is therefore meant to present the Supreme Personality of Godhead directly to the people.[2]

It is simply cheating if despite having knowledge of the highest truth—of Kṛṣṇa and of the nectar of surrender to Him, which can come only by accepting Kṛṣṇa's words in toto—devotees do not act as message-bearers of the truth but instead deliver some

1 SB 11.2.46, commentary.

2 *The Science of Self-realization*, ch. 6 (c).

drivel. Unless devotees clearly speak the truth, how will others ever become aware of it? "If not us, who? If not now, when?"[1]

Undiluted speaking on relevant issues and the decrying of all that is not Kṛṣṇa conscious are necessary duties of a genuine preacher. The message of the absolute truth must be presented explicitly to definitively distinguish it from the ubiquitous nontruth:

> The loyal servant of the absolute truth is required to be the active opponent of all violent enemies of the truth. It is his imperative duty to protest against the violence of nontheists in uncompromising terms and take all consequence of such protest.[2]

> A *sādhu* is to speak to the householders about the naked truth of life so that they may come to their senses about the precarious life in material existence.[3]

The preacher must aim at transforming his hearers and slashing their worldly attachments. *Santa evāsya chindanti mano-vyāsaṅgam uktibhiḥ:* "The words of a saintly person emphatically cut the mental attachments of materially attached people."[4] Śrīla Bhaktisiddhānta Sarasvatī explicated this theme:

> The only duty of merciful persons is to transform the contrary inclination of conditioned souls.[5]

> The only duty of sadhus is to cut away all the accumulated wicked propensities of every individual. This alone is the causeless natural desire of all sadhus.[6]

Everyone in this world has accumulated wicked propensities, having been barraged from birth with untruths propagated by so-

1 Slogan by revolutionary students in Prague in Nov 1989, quoted in the *Observer* (London, 26 Nov 1989).

2 *Harmonist* 29.113 (Oct 1931); SBV, vol. 1, p. 144.

3 SB 1.13.23, purport.

4 SB 11.26.26.

5 SBV, vol. 1, p. 217.

6 *Harmonist* 28.243 (Jan 1931); SBV, vol. 1, p. 143.

called friends and relatives, the media, and the educational system. Yet the combined power of all that is material can be overcome by the power of the truth, even when spoken by an apparently insignificant person. The message of the truth directly addresses the inner being of the hearer and assaults the false ego, the persona by which each individual seeks to shield himself from the reality of being subordinate to and controlled by the Supreme Truth. The message of the truth will pain and shock egoistic persons, but genuine seekers of the truth will rejoice upon receiving it.

It is particularly to benefit such sincere persons that devotees should not fail to speak the truth. Such precious souls can sense what is genuine and what is bogus and are quick to embrace the truth and reject hedging and duplicity. The light-and-airy approach, deliberately avoiding weighty issues, may superficially appeal to many superficial people, whose interest in Kṛṣṇa consciousness is unlikely to go beyond the superficial. As Śrīla Prabhupāda observed, "Those who want to be cheated do not take the solution even when it is at hand but prefer to be cheated."[1] Therefore Śrīla Prabhupāda warned to "not compromise our principles," because "those who are actually sincere about spiritual life will gradually see the purity of our movement as you are conducting it and they will become attracted to the real thing."[2] Śrīla Prabhupāda also noted that "if we speak the truth, those will hear who are intended to hear by being qualified or prepared."[3]

Persons who are ready to receive the truth are the best candidates for becoming dedicated devotees and spiritual leaders capable of bringing many people to genuine Kṛṣṇa consciousness. Just as appeals to the emotions will tend to attract sentimentalists, only intelligible presentations of śāstric truths are likely to induce thoughtful persons to make a conscious, reasoned commitment to

1 Letter, 1 Jan 1974.

2 Letter, 1 Jan 1974.

3 Letter, 15 Nov 1971.

devotional life. An example of this was Ravīndra Svarūpa Dāsa, who recounted his first visit to an ISKCON center:

> I never heard anything as welcome as the lecture after the chanting. The devotee spoke very strongly about the need to become free from material desires. He laid down four regulative principles, the pillars of spiritual life: no meat-eating, no intoxication, no illicit sex, no gambling. I know that many people who hear this in a Kṛṣṇa temple are put off. I was attracted at once. At last, I thought, someone is willing to tell the truth.[1]

Such truth-seekers are relatively rare, yet they are precious: "We do not expect that cent percent of people will become Kṛṣṇa conscious. That is not possible. But if there is one ideal Kṛṣṇa conscious person, he can do benefit to many thousands."[2] But actually, more people than we might imagine are sick of impersonal mumbo jumbo and are thirsting to hear some straightforward, honest words that make sense and appeal to the soul. We can never discover such people unless we speak the straightforward, honest message of Kṛṣṇa conciousness that they crave to hear.

Certainly it is a great loss if anyone, upon hearing an immature presentation of Kṛṣṇa consciousness, becomes disinclined toward this perfect process, but it is a still greater loss if a sincere seeker misses the opportunity to hear the truth due to a devotee's unwillingness (for whatever reason) to unambiguously and unreservedly disseminate the truth. I learned this in the early 1980s when a respectable young British man visited our ISKCON ashram in Dhaka, Bangladesh, and told us that he was seeking direction in life. I was as excited to preach to him as he was eager to hear, but the two godbrothers of mine who were present suggested that we just be low-key and friendly and not impose on him. I acquiesced, but later learned that the man had become a

1 BTG 15-06 (1980).

2 Lecture, 20 Jul 1976.

Christian. We failed him and we failed Śrīla Prabhupāda by not giving the clear guidance that he craved.

Therefore all followers of Śrīla Prabhupāda should make one with their heart (*cittete kariyā aikya*) his order to "deliver this pure science of God to everyone and give them the chance to make their lives successful."[1] Even though it is not expected that numerous people will immediately accept the message "as it is," still, as more and more gradually do so, the effect will become cumulative and increasingly powerful. Conversely, if we neglect to offer unadulterated Kṛṣṇa consciousness, then no one will know of it and have an opportunity to accept it—although some might take a diluted version. Hence, Śrīla Prabhupāda urged his disciples "to give all men this Kṛṣṇa philosophy" and assured them that by doing so "many real devotees will come with us back to home, back to Godhead."[2]

1 Letter, 5 May 1972.

2 Letter, 27 Nov 1971.

SIX
FIGHT WITH ŚĀSTRA

Devotees must learn how to fight, not like ruffians but by wielding the sword of knowledge received from the *ācāryas*. In the battle against *māyā, śāstra* (Vedic scripture, the words of Kṛṣṇa) is the *astra* (weapon). Speaking according to *śāstra* not only gives strength to the preacher but is his very hallmark of authenticity. If he does not speak according to *śāstra*, he is simply bogus:

> Śrīla Narottama Dāsa Ṭhākura says, *sādhu-śāstra-guru-vākya, cittete kariyā aikya*. One should accept a thing as genuine by studying the words of saintly people, the spiritual master and the *śāstra*. The actual center is the *śāstra*, the revealed scripture. If a spiritual master does not speak according to the revealed scripture, he is not to be accepted. Similarly, if a saintly person does not speak according to the *śāstra*, he is not a saintly person. The *śāstra* is the center for all.[1]

Therefore: "Neither a *sādhu* (saintly person or Vaiṣṇava) nor a bona fide spiritual master says anything that is beyond the scope of the sanction of the revealed scriptures."[2] The attempt to practice or preach Kṛṣṇa consciousness without adherence to *śāstra* cannot at all be beneficial:

श्रुतिस्मृतिपुराणादिपञ्चरात्रविधिं विना ।
ऐकान्तिकी हरेर्भक्तिरुत्पातायैव कल्पते ॥

1 Cc 2.20.352, purport.

2 Cc 1.7.48, purport.

śruti-smṛti-purāṇādi- pañcarātra-vidhiṁ vinā
aikāntikī harer bhaktir utpātāyaiva kalpate

> Devotional service of the Lord that ignores the authorized Vedic literatures like the *Upaniṣads, Purāṇas* and *Nārada Pañcarātra* is simply an unnecessary disturbance in society.[1]

The words of *śāstra,* especially of *Bhagavad-gītā* and *Śrīmad-Bhāgavatam,* carry immense potency for slashing ignorance. Devotees slash ignorance (*santa evāsya chindanti mano-vyāsaṅgam uktibhiḥ*)[2] by repeating the words of *śāstra,* which are meant to pierce the heart and sever all misgivings (*bhidyate hṛdaya-granthiś chidyante sarva-saṁśayāḥ*).[3] In this vein, Lord Kṛṣṇa told Arjuna:

तस्मादज्ञानसम्भूतं हृत्स्थं ज्ञानासिनात्मनः ।
छित्त्वैनं संशयं योगमातिष्ठोत्तिष्ठ भारत ॥

tasmād ajñāna-sambhūtaṁ
hṛt-sthaṁ jñānāsinātmanaḥ
chittvainaṁ saṁśayaṁ yogam
ātiṣṭhottiṣṭha bhārata

> Therefore the doubts which have arisen in your heart out of ignorance should be slashed by the weapon of knowledge. Armed with yoga, O Bhārata, stand and fight.[4]

Devotees in the modern age perform *bhakti-yoga* by fighting for Kṛṣṇa, armed with the weapon of śāstric knowledge:

> In each and every meeting you should go and challenge these persons, but you must be equipped very strongly with the conclusions of *Bhagavad-gītā.*[5]

Śrīla Prabhupāda attributed his success to his imparting the knowledge of *Bhagavad-gītā* as it is, without adulteration, for

1 *Bhakti-rasāmṛta-sindhu,* 1.2.101.
2 SB 11.26.26.
3 SB 1.2.21.
4 Bg 4.42.
5 Letter, 18 Nov 1968.

"a little bit of a pure thing is much better than huge volumes of impure, adulterated things."[1]

> Perhaps, throughout the whole world, it is the first time: we are preaching *Bhagavad-gītā* as it is. We are the only institution in the world that is preaching *Bhagavad-gītā* as it is, and people are liking it. Before that, for the last two hundred years, so many swamis and yogis tried to preach Hindu philosophy, Vaiṣṇavism. Not a single person became a devotee of Kṛṣṇa, not a single person. Now you see so many young men. Why? Why this difference? Because we did not present *Bhagavad-gītā* adulterated—presented as it is, that's all. What is the use of preaching adulterated things?[2]

For the modern age, *śāstra* primarily means Śrīla Prabhupāda's books, and preaching means to preach from those books:

> The three books which I have already prepared, namely, the *Bhagavad-gītā As It Is, Teachings of Lord Caitanya,* and *Śrīmad-Bhāgavatam,* all these books are the ultimate source of knowledge. If you simply reproduce what I have tried to explain in those books, surely you will come out victorious, even in the midst of so many great mundane scholars. The descriptions given in these books are not mundane speculations, but they are authorized versions of liberated souls, presented by our humble self. So the strength is not in us, but the strength is in the Supreme Lord. And we have simply to present them without any adulteration, in humble service spirit. That is the secret of success.[3]

Śāstric teachings should be conveyed without change, yet also with consideration of the eligibility of the target audience. Śāstric lore covers the whole spectrum of spiritual knowledge, up to the highest level of Rādhā-Kṛṣṇa *prema.* But people in general, who are inculturated to think of this world as nice, first need to hear that it is not at all nice, that they do not belong here, and that

1 Letter, 27 Aug 1969.

2 Conversation, 12 Apr 1975.

3 Letter, 27 Sep 1968.

they should endeavor to get out. Śrīla Prabhupāda never tired of making these points, and he repeatedly quoted some of the most devastating śāstric verses that demonstrate them. As Tamāla Kṛṣṇa Goswami recalled, "No matter how important the person was, Prabhupāda spoke about dogs, hogs, camels, and asses."[1]

श्वविड्वराहोष्ट्रखरैः संस्तुतः पुरुषः पशुः ।
न यत्कर्णपथोपेतो जातु नाम गदाग्रजः ॥

śva-viḍ-varāhoṣṭra-kharaiḥ
saṁstutaḥ puruṣaḥ paśuḥ
na yat-karṇa-pathopeto
jātu nāma gadāgrajaḥ

Men who are like dogs, hogs, camels and asses praise those men who never listen to the transcendental pastimes of Lord Śrī Kṛṣṇa, the deliverer from evils.[2]

Some more "Prabhupāda favorites," from Ṛṣabha-deva's teachings:

नायं देहो देहभाजां नृलोके
कष्टान् कामानर्हते विड्भुजां ये ।
तपो दिव्यं पुत्रका येन सत्त्वं
शुद्ध्येद्यस्माद् ब्रह्मसौख्यं त्वनन्तम् ॥

nāyaṁ deho deha-bhājāṁ nṛloke
kaṣṭān kāmān arhate viḍ-bhujāṁ ye
tapo divyaṁ putrakā yena sattvaṁ
śuddhyed yasmād brahma-saukhyaṁ tv anantam

Of all the living entities who have accepted material bodies in this world, one who has been awarded this human form should not work hard day and night simply for sense gratification, which is available even for dogs and hogs that eat stool. One should engage in penance and austerity to attain the divine position of devotional service.

1 *TKG's Diary*, 30 Apr.

2 SB 2.3.19.

By such activity, one's heart is purified, and when one attains this position, he attains eternal, blissful life, which is transcendental to material happiness and which continues forever.[1]

नूनं प्रमत्तः कुरुते विकर्म
यदिन्द्रियप्रीतय आपृणोति ।
न साधु मन्ये यत आत्मनोऽय-
मसन्नपि क्लेशद आस देहः ॥

nūnaṁ pramattaḥ kurute vikarma
yad indriya-prītaya āpṛṇoti
na sādhu manye yata ātmano 'yam
asann api kleśada āsa dehaḥ

When a person considers sense gratification the aim of life, he certainly becomes mad after materialistic living and engages in all kinds of sinful activity. He does not know that due to his past misdeeds he has already received a body which, although temporary, is the cause of his misery. Actually the living entity should not have taken on a material body, but he has been awarded the material body for sense gratification. Therefore I think it not befitting an intelligent man to involve himself again in the activities of sense gratification by which he perpetually gets material bodies one after another.[2]

पुंसः स्त्रिया मिथुनीभावमेतं
तयोर्मिथो हृदयग्रन्थिमाहुः ।
अतो गृहक्षेत्रसुताप्तवित्तै-
र्जनस्य मोहोऽयमहं ममेति ॥

puṁsaḥ striyā mithunī-bhāvam etaṁ
tayor mitho hṛdaya-granthim āhuḥ
ato gṛha-kṣetra-sutāpta-vittair
janasya moho 'yam ahaṁ mameti

---

1 SB 5.5.1.

2 SB 5.5.4.

> The attraction between male and female is the basic principle of material existence. On the basis of this misconception, which ties together the hearts of the male and female, one becomes attracted to his body, home, property, children, relatives and wealth. In this way one increases life's illusions and thinks in terms of "I" and "mine."[1]

There are many similar verses in *Śrīmad-Bhāgavatam*, which is the essential subject of the Vedas (*vedyaṁ vāstavam atra vastu*)—the highest truth, reality (*vāstavam*) distinguished from illusion for the welfare (*śiva-dam*) of all, which uproots the threefold miseries (*tāpa-trayonmūlanam*) and at the outset rejects cheating religiosity (*dharmaḥ projjhita-kaitavaḥ*).[2] Although such pronouncements are not what most people generally expect or like to hear, they are the truth that Śrīla Prabhupāda preached and told his disciples to preach:

> To preach *Bhāgavata* religion, sometimes we have to quote from the *śāstras* what is not palatable to unscrupulous, so-called religious persons. But in preaching we cannot do without quoting the proper verses. Sometimes they take it adversely and we become subject to unwanted criticism. We are presenting Kṛṣṇa's philosophy and teaching as it is, and what can we do more? But this process of presentation has become fortunate and we have become successful. I do not wish to change the process. I hope you will appreciate this process of preaching the facts as they are confirmed by all Vaiṣṇava *ācāryas*.[3]

Representatives of the *paramparā* are duty-bound to present the words of Kṛṣṇa:

> If we are really Kṛṣṇa conscious, then our business is to repeat the words of Kṛṣṇa—that's all. What is the difference between Kṛṣṇa's representative and non-representative? The representative of Kṛṣṇa will simply repeat what Kṛṣṇa says—that's all. He becomes

1 SB 5.5.8.

2 SB 1.1.2.

3 Letter, 16 May 1974.

> representative. It doesn't require much qualification. You simply repeat with firm conviction.[1]

One who assumes the position of a devotee of Kṛṣṇa, the speaker of the *Bhagavad-gītā,* but nonetheless fails to properly represent Kṛṣṇa by unmitigatedly speaking the truth of the *Gītā,* indulges in deceit and hypocrisy, and steps outside the *paramparā.**

---

* Preaching to the many people who do not accept *śāstra* is discussed in ch. 13, "Scientific, Not Dogmatic."

1 Lecture, 17 Jul 1973.

SEVEN

CONVINCED, BOLD, CLEAR, PROVOCATIVE, FRESH

Strong and clear preaching is required to convince people to embrace Kṛṣṇa consciousness with full commitment—which is the only way to become fully Kṛṣṇa conscious. And it is conviction in the veracity and necessity of Kṛṣṇa consciousness—"There is no question of accepting or not accepting Kṛṣṇa consciousness. It is not optional; it is compulsory. If we do not take to Kṛṣṇa consciousness, our life is very risky"[1]—that impels devotees to continue battling throughout their lives against opposing elements within themselves, within Vaiṣṇava society, and within the entire world.

The exemplar for upfront preachers in the modern age is, of course, Śrīla Prabhupāda, who expertly presented the truths of Vaiṣṇava philosophy in a cogent and forceful manner, explaining why he was right and others wrong, so that listeners would be compelled to either accept his position or be exposed for their foolishness.

One of the innumerable examples of Śrīla Prabhupāda's boldness occurred during 1973 when he was officially honored by the City of Paris, represented by the vice president of the Paris City Council (a post equivalent to the mayor of an American city). Before the devotees' arrival, they were informed of the protocol: after entering

1 SB 10.8.49, purport.

the reception, everyone should stand, and then the vice president would present an address, to which Śrīla Prabhupāda could reply. But upon entering, Śrīla Prabhupāda sat. The vice president seemed nervous, and everyone was looking at Śrīla Prabhupāda. Yogeśvara Dāsa leaned over and said, "Śrīla Prabhupāda, they're waiting for you to stand." Śrīla Prabhupāda replied, "I am supposed to stand for who?" So the vice president delivered his greeting to a seated Śrīla Prabhupāda. That was probably the first time in the history of the country that anyone had been received in Paris City Hall without their standing up. Yogeśvara Dāsa narrated:

> The vice president stated that Paris had always been conscious of spiritual values and was very happy to receive an ambassador of Indian spirituality. He spoke many words of appreciation of Śrīla Prabhupāda. When the vice president ended his address, Śrīla Prabhupāda stood and explained that within the body is a soul, that "in the human form of body we can understand our real constitutional position," and then rhetorically asked, "If the leaders of human society do not give education to the human society, how can the spirit soul get out of the clutches of birth, death, old age, and disease?"[1] Śrīla Prabhupāda continued, interspersing praise of France with observations such as that even big heroes like Napoleon eventually had to leave their country. Warning that if due to love of one's country one is reborn therein as a cow and is sent to the slaughterhouse, Śrīla Prabhupāda quoted, *parābhavas tāvad abodha-jāto/ yāvan na jijñāsata ātma-tattvam:* whatever he is doing, unless a person is interested in his spiritual identity, he is simply being defeated.[2]

After Śrīla Prabhupāda's broadside, his hosts (particularly the vice president) looked very nervous. Then the devotees distributed *prasāda*, and everyone became relaxed. Regarding this incident, Yogeśvara Dāsa commented:

> He was strong, and that was Prabhupāda's style. He didn't mince words. He could be very understanding and was always sensitive,

1 Lecture, 9 Aug 1973.

2 SB 5.5.5.

> but never compromising. An opportunity like this in the City Hall of Paris before the mayor, before the press, before dignitaries—Śrīla Prabhupāda was the *ācārya*, the representative of Kṛṣṇa and Kṛṣṇa's world, and there was no compromising the message at all, ever. [1]

A devotee who has faith in Kṛṣṇa's teachings is not embarrassed to present them as confidently as Śrīla Prabhupāda did. Devotees should know that they are on very solid ground, that they are not presenting nebulous, unverifiable dogmas but undeniable facts of spiritual understanding, which, if systematically imparted, should be easily understandable by any clear-thinking person—that the self is distinct from the body, that everyone in this world is inexorably subject to the miseries of birth, death, old age, and disease, that all is not "one," and that human life without the quest for self-realization is in essence little different from that of the animals.

Devotees should be convinced that "our philosophy has the full potency to deliver anyone from the darkest realms of ignorance to the enlightened realm of complete cognizance."[2] Those who are convinced can convince others: "First you must yourself become fully convinced of this philosophy—your preaching will meet with all success."[3] Devotees who are seized of the need to surrender to Kṛṣṇa are also seized of the need to convey this necessity to others. With this conviction, they can go anywhere, challenge anyone, and be victorious everywhere, as was Śrīla Prabhupāda:

> You scientists—you are all rascals. You do not know anything. Chewing the chewed, making research. What research you can do? You do not know anything. The Vedic injunction is: *yasmin vijñāte sarvam evaṁ vijñātaṁ bhavati.*[4] If you know the Absolute Truth, then all other things become known. But you do not know the Absolute

1 This quotation, and the whole Paris anecdote as told by Yogeśvara Dāsa, is from *Following Srila Prabhupada*, DVD 5.

2 Letter, 15 Nov 1971.

3 Letter, 15 Nov 1971.

4 Redacted from *Muṇḍaka Upaniṣad* 1.3.

> Truth. Therefore you are in ignorance. We are not official scientists or philosopher or anything. "But why you are challenging, you are talking so boldly?" "Because we know one thing: Kṛṣṇa. Therefore we can say so boldly and challenge anyone." How I can challenge you? Because I know Kṛṣṇa. If you know Kṛṣṇa, the Absolute Truth, then all other things will be known automatically. We are preaching Kṛṣṇa consciousness, challenging all kinds of men in society. So many scientists are coming, so many psychologists coming. So how we are confident to talk with him? Because we have learned little about Kṛṣṇa. You are a qualified scientist. Why I challenge you? Not that because you are my disciple you are accepting all my challenges. You have got your reasons. You are not a fool. So how it is possible? Practically, how it is possible? Because we are trying to know little about Kṛṣṇa. If you know Kṛṣṇa, you know everything.[1]

> We can talk with anyone. Marx, Darwin, all professors and politicians, we can challenge and defeat them. Our philosophy is so perfect. So go on exposing them, that is the purpose of *Back to Godhead* paper, to expose their materialistic ideas as all nonsense and present the real philosophy that the Lord gives. This is the real knowledge.[2]

Indeed, the ability to counter and overcome opposition is a sign of becoming elevated in devotional service:

> The more one can meet the opposite elements successfully the more one is supposed to be advanced in Kṛṣṇa consciousness.[3]

Advanced devotees have the faith and conviction to speak the message of the *ācāryas* as they spoke it. Such devotees thereby receive the blessings of Śrīla Prabhupāda and the *ācāryas* for bringing people to *ahaituky apratihatā* (unmotivated and uninterrupted) pure devotional service.[4] Those who lack the faith and conviction to straightforwardly repeat the message of

---

1 Conversation, 28 Apr 1973, with Svarūpa Dāmodara Dāsa (a scientist by vocation) and other devotees.

2 Letter, 26 Sep 1975.

3 Letter, 16 Mar 1967.

4 *Ahaituky apratihatā*—from SB 1.2.6.

the *ācāryas* might get the *ācāryas'* mercy in another form—that of *dhana-jana-sundarī*, the seeming success of collecting funds and properties, many followers, and hordes of adoring female disciples.[1]

But advanced devotees care nothing for the illusory benefits that may accrue from mixed devotional service. Because they are resolute in their principles, character, and determination, their every word resounds with clarity, intelligence, and the mettle to declare that which needs to be stated even at the risk of upsetting others and making themselves unpopular. Kṛṣṇa invests potency into the utterances of such devotees: "The potent words of realized souls penetrate the heart, thereby eradicating all misgivings accumulated through years of undesirable association."[2] Such empowered devotees (referred to by Śrīla Bhaktisiddhānta Sarasvatī as "living sources") present Kṛṣṇa consciousness unabashedly, with clear understanding of its principles and its necessity.

On the other hand, weak or vague presentations intrinsically lack power and cannot help anyone become fixed in Kṛṣṇa consciousness. To sincere and discerning people, vagueness conveys ignorance, indifference, confusion, compromise, dissembling, and cowardice. One who is vague and evades the real issues probably will not upset others, but neither will he be able to impress upon them the seriousness and urgency of Kṛṣṇa consciousness.

Vagueness and indirectness appeal especially to impersonalists, who want to enjoy feeling spiritual without making any spiritual commitment, who have no actual spiritual knowledge but simply mouth what they think sounds spiritual. Māyāvādīs must be vague, because they have no clear understanding and do not know what they are talking about. Furthermore, they are envious of Kṛṣṇa. Even those Māyāvādīs who speak of God do so without stipulating

1 *Dhana jana sundarī*—derived from *Śikṣāṣṭaka* 4.

2 Cc 1.1.59, purport.

who He is, as if *God* were just an abstract word to be defined according to each individual's liking. However much Māyāvādīs may talk of God, they are actually atheists, for implicit in their terminology is denial of the supreme person to whom all other living beings must submit, who alone is correctly denoted by the word *God*.

Similarly, devotees whose "preaching" intentionally avoids delineation of the uncompromised, scientific truth of Kṛṣṇa consciousness cannot induce in others the disposition toward full surrender to Kṛṣṇa. Such "preaching" often resembles and is likely to reinforce the envious misconceptions of impersonalists. By not presenting Kṛṣṇa consciousness in the natural way, as it is, a devotee who speaks vaguely necessarily presents something else: his own (incorrect) perspective on reality. Because he is not convinced that Kṛṣṇa consciousness makes sense, or for whatever reason fails to present it sensibly, he willingly speaks nonsense. By obfuscating the clarity of the Kṛṣṇa conscious message, he acts as an enemy of the truth.

Anyone who deviates from the principle of repeating the message of the *ācāryas* thereby subtly or brazenly promotes himself. Another type of self-promoter uses the powerful message and analogies of *śāstra* and the *ācāryas* yet fails to acknowledge the source of this knowledge, thus posing as a self-enlightened repository of wisdom. And those who speak the message of *śāstra* but never bring it to the conclusion of surrender to Kṛṣṇa, the Supreme Personality of Godhead, simply propound the kind of "wisdom" confined to mundane moralizing and personal improvement that is marketed by yet another genre of self-promoting pseudo spiritualists.

On the other hand, a devotee who is truly convinced of the truth of Kṛṣṇa consciousness cannot pliantly acquiesce with the hypocritical, incomplete, imperfect, and latently envious pronouncements of persons ignorant of or opposed to the principle of pure devotional service to Kṛṣṇa. A properly situated devotee correctly perceives that the only real defect in the world is a shortage of Kṛṣṇa consciousness. Only devotees who are thus convinced can offer a realistic, philosophically sound alternative to the stereotyped worldviews that both materialistic and supposedly spiritual people rarely question or, even if they do, are seemingly unable to progress beyond. Statements that seem ordinary to devotees are extraordinary for the uninformed, and can revolutionize people's lives. For instance, many people simply do not know that the self is not the body but an eternal spirit soul, and that human life is not meant for sense gratification but for spiritual realization. Even persons who have heard these truths are mostly numb to the implications of such vital existential facts. They tend to think of spiritual knowledge as otherwordly, impractical, and irrelevant to what they perceive as the "real world." Yet devotees proffer not simply arcane theories but original, refreshing, and viable solutions for all world problems—for instance, that poverty, ecological imbalance, terrorism, and all other anomalies, factual or imagined, can be overcome only by Kṛṣṇa consciousness. Obviously, it is required that such bold claims be well explained and not simply stated dogmatically:

> They must know what is God, how to trust Him, why we shall trust God, what is the benefit. These things should be known, properly educated. We have got the science. We are not speaking blindly or sentimentally.[1]

Śrīla Prabhupāda suggested how to present such topics:

> Human life begins when there is systematic education in the science of God consciousness. Just some days ago, I was discussing with Professor Alister Hardy, head of Religious Experimental Research Unit, Oxford. It was his opinion that the problems of human life are overpopulation, environmental pollution, etc. But from *Bhagavad-gītā* we understand that God is the father of all living beings. So

1 Conversation, 11 Dec 1973.

> the father must be competent to provide for all the children, and in the case of the Supreme Father this is actually so. We get it from Vedic literature, *nityo nityānāṁ cetanaś cetanānām* (*Kaṭha Upaniṣad* 2.2.13): "Amongst all the eternals there is one chief eternal being, and He is engaged in supplying and fulfilling the desires of all the others." Therefore our conclusion was that the real problem is not overpopulation or pollution, malnutrition, etc., but the actual problem is Godlessness. So you are all intelligent boys and girls. Therefore my request to you is that you study this science of Kṛṣṇa consciousness, and solve all the problems of the world by systematic propaganda as far as you are able to do it.[1]

> Actually, this world is like a hospital. We are all like sons of rich men running mad in the streets. Our father—Kṛṣṇa, or God—is the wealthiest father, and we are all His sons gone mad. Someone is thinking, "Oh, give him food—that will help," or "Give him house or clothes, this or that"—but the madness is still there. Actually, they have got sufficient of everything from their father, but they have run off mad. So this kind of bodily welfare work will not help. The world is supposed to be a place for curing men of their varieties of diseases of madness and sending them back home, like a hospital. But men have now got the mistaken idea to make a permanent settlement in this madhouse! Just like the hog is eating stool and is thinking, "Oh, I am enjoying like anything. And when I am finished, then sex with any she-hog—wife, daughter, sister, it doesn't matter—and for so many children I shall have to have big house; and on and on like this, all because of his madness, that he thinks, 'I am enjoying.'" So preach like this, and I think many people will appreciate our philosophy and gain respect for this Kṛṣṇa consciousness movement. Do everything very cleanly and nicely.[2]

One facet of Śrīla Prabhupāda's brilliance was his ability to convey this most profound science of spirituality in a manner accessible even to laymen. He did not speculate, juggle words, or play at being a sadhu or an armchair theorist. He delivered śāstric

1 Letter, 27 Jul 1973.

2 Letter, 18 Feb 1972.

arguments in an authoritative and strikingly intelligent manner that compelled honest persons to take them seriously. Śrīla Prabhupāda's presentation was hearteningly clear, a hallmark of actual knowledge—in contrast to the opaque convolutions of Māyāvādīs, which are designed to keep others guessing and which suggest that only the Māyāvādīs know the truth and others cannot.

Māyāvādīs typically utter stock phrases like "inner landscape," "inner life," and "spiritual journey," cheating their willingly gullible followers by deliberately leaving such terms undefined and thus conveying abstractions that sound intriguingly spiritual (although no one knows what they mean). Their insights keep everyone on the outside; their revelations reveal nothing but their own speciousness and ignorance. Śrīla Prabhupāda exposed these so-called knowers as bluffers, for they are merely guessing, and their guesses are badly wrong.

Unfortunately, the world is inundated by countless permutations of bogus ideas. Massive demonic indoctrination urges people to act in ways highly detrimental to their own and others' self-interest. Considering that even mundane propaganda requires insistent repetition to make an impact (this understanding being the basis of the advertising industry's relentless touting of sense gratification), surely only the most dynamic counterpromotion of genuine spiritual values has any hope of being noticed.

Hence pushy preachers, impelled by the pressing necessity to arouse dupes to their real welfare, regularly exhort others to immediately take to Kṛṣṇa consciousness as the only real necessity, and inform them of the ominous consequences of not doing so, for they "cannot tolerate that people who have achieved the rare human birth, a birth suitable for worshiping the Lord, simply tread the path of misfortune, of nondevotion."[1]

---

1 Śrīla Bhaktisiddhānta Sarasvatī, SBV, vol. 1, p. 150.

Considering that generally they will meet any specific individual from the general populace only once, and that it may be billions of lifetimes before that person will get another opportunity to receive transcendental knowledge, bold preachers are inspired to induce people to at least once hear the message of the absolute truth. Knowing that an exchange of pleasantries is hardly likely to be life-changing or even remembered, real preachers do not emit ineffectual, instantly forgettable mush. Rather, they can be purposely inflammatory, speaking in a manner intended to upset—in accordance with Śrīla Bhaktisiddhānta Sarasvatī's utterance that people need to be jerked into awakening their original consciousness.[1] Some people are too proud or self-absorbed to even begin to contemplate any position other than their own, no matter how politely or empathetically the Vedic truths are presented to them. Shock tactics—such as shouting or telling people that their civilization is centered on vagina-licking—may be required to jolt such dullards out of their complacent stupor.*

Although some devotees complain that such techniques are too provocative, provocation is exactly the aim of the direct preacher—following the example of Śrī Kṛṣṇa, who began *Bhagavad-gītā* by telling Arjuna that he was talking big but did not know what he was talking about. Similarly, because a direct preacher is genuinely concerned about the well-being of others, he does not try to put superficial hearers at ease, but might deliberately make them feel uncomfortable, or even take the trouble and risk of purposely speaking words so bitingly true as to startle them into at least a rudimentary awareness of their precarious position and the actual purpose of life.

* An example of this is the case of Arnoldas (see p. 91). No amount of reasoned arguments could have even scratched his ego, but one blunt sentence changed his life.

1 SBV, vol. 1, p. 30.

One of the many examples of Śrīla Prabhupāda's being blunt and provocative was his reply to an American hippie who had questioned him skeptically: "You cannot understand because you are crazy."[1]

Śrīla Bhaktisiddhānta Sarasvatī explained the necessity for such provocation in a parable about a boy flying a kite on a roof terrace. Totally absorbed, his eyes fixed in the sky, the boy does not see that he is close to the edge and in danger of falling off. Any commonsensical observer would call out to warn him. Only a madman would think, "He is enjoying himself, so why should I disturb him?" A sane person must shout, "Be careful!" If the boy is a fool and a rascal, he will either ignore his well-wisher or rebuke him: "Why are you distracting me? Do you think I don't know what I'm doing?" Just to jerk the rascal to his senses and save him from certain doom, the observer may earnestly berate him: "You fool! You rascal!"[2]

Almost invariably, a straightforward preacher will be misunderstood by the very persons he attempts to benefit. Although materialists might tolerate or even venerate a sadhu who unobtrusively endeavors for self-elevation, they consider disturbing behavior to be uncouth, and cannot associate it with saintliness. Mistaking the scolding of a genuine sadhu to be like the unpleasant speech of ordinary people, which is meant to belittle others, materialists reject the sadhu as a non-sadhu and the worst of cheaters. However, if a materialist has been sufficiently bothered, and if he is at least somewhat thoughtful and sincere, then the inherent truth spoken by the sadhu will continue to nag him. Such disquietude will naturally lead him to ruminate as to why anyone would undergo trouble and risk to perturb others, and he may thus begin to comprehend how sadhus have wholly dissimilar motivations from

1 SPl ch. 52, "I Have Done My Part."

2 Adapted from Śrīla Prabhupāda's rendition of this parable (Conversation, 26 Jan 1977).

everyone else in the world. Becoming intrigued, he may start the process of further inquiry.

In other words, even if people are at first shocked by a sadhu's apparently pungent comments, if they have any sincerity they will gradually come to appreciate the veracity of his message.* They then will be grateful that devotees have taken pains to attack their illusion. Thus, by vigorous preaching, devotees can penetrate skepticism, overcome opposition, and convince persons who otherwise would have remained indifferent and inimical. Indeed, many people who have become devotees would not have done so if they had not been the recipient of forceful preaching.

In 1977 at Kumbha-melā, a young Māyāvādī sadhu confronted Śrīla Prabhupāda. When Śrīla Prabhupāda responded heavily, Bhakti Cāru Swami thought, "Why is Śrīla Prabhupāda being so hard on him? Maybe if he were treated softly, the sadhu could become a devotee." But actually, that man joined ISKCON a few months later, and to this day has remained a full-time devotee.†

It could be expostulated that it is counterproductive to speak in a manner likely to upset others, for nothing is gained and unnecessary tension is caused. In response, it is true that sharp words are likely to provoke fierce reactions. But if a devotee is competent to rebut

---

* As a disciple once related to Śrīla Prabhupāda, "I went to that New York storefront first of all, and I was a rascal, so they called me a rascal. So I became very offended. Later on, I saw that they were right." (Conversation, 4 Feb 1975)

Hayagrīva Dāsa similarly narrated: "George Henderson, now teaching mathematics at Rutgers [University], visits [New Vrindaban] for a couple of days. Laughing, he recalls the time Prabhupāda challenged him to display the universal form. When he leaves, he gives us a check for two hundred dollars." (*The Hare Krishna Explosion*, ch. 16)

See also the footnote on p. 27.

† His initiation name is Mādhāi Dāsa.

objections, then his aggressiveness will have created a platform for demonstrating both the fallacies of various popular misconceptions and the foolishness of persons who adhere to such fallacies. If a devotee's presentation is sound and clear (as it should be) then even if the persons with whom he directly engages refuse to accept the point, others who are less bigoted are likely to appreciate it.

But can't such belligerence be avoided? Can't devotees preach without being blunt? Why needlessly antagonize others? The answer is that the need for Kṛṣṇa consciousness is so urgent, and the antipathy of the conditioned souls is so formidable, that stinging words are often required. A preacher's mercy is his unpleasant reproaches, which are meant to cause people to understand their precarious position and thus save them from the much greater unpleasantness of prolonged suffering in material existence. Endless litanies of "no treading on toes" smoothness are unlikely to ever pierce the false ego, whereas a few incisive shots from an expert preacher can immediately lacerate misconceptions that might otherwise fester for lifetimes.

> Without doubt, a sadhu's words possess power to destroy the evil propensities of one's mind. In this way, sadhus benefit everyone who associates with them. There are many things which we do not disclose to the sadhu. The real sadhu makes us speak out what we keep concealed in our hearts. He then applies the knife. The very word *sadhu* has no other meaning than this. He stands in front of the block with the uplifted sacrificial knife in his hand. The sensuous desires of men are like goats. The sadhu stands there to kill those desires by the merciful stroke of the keen edge of the sacrificial knife in the form of unpleasant language. If the sadhu turns into my flatterer, then he does me harm; he becomes my enemy. If he flatters us, we will be led to the road which brings worldly enjoyment but no factual well-being.[1]

---

1 Śrīla Bhaktisiddhānta Sarasvatī (*Harmonist* 28.264, Feb 1931); SBV, vol. 1, p. 143.

> Those sadhus who speak sharp words to drive away the witch of the illusory energy are actually the only real devotees of Kṛṣṇa and friends of the living entities. The conditioned living being experiences the distressful quarreling of his wife and close relatives and is rudely treated by them until death, yet he never desires to leave their association; rather, he absorbs himself in trying to appease and serve them. But when a devotee of the Lord, who is always desirous of the living entity's ultimate welfare, chides him just once with instructions meant to drive away *māyā*, then that conditioned entity immediately makes plans to leave the saintly person for his entire life. If you actually want to perform devotional service properly, then you must accept the harsh language of the sadhu as the medicine by which *māyā* can be given up.[1]

This harshness of a sadhu should not be confused with that mentioned in *Bhagavad-gītā* (16.4)—*pāruṣyam*—as being typical of demons. Indeed, the overall message of *Bhagavad-gītā* teaches that harshness is sometimes required to uphold dharma. As Śrīla Viśvanātha Cakravartī Ṭhākura instructs, "Speaking harshly is a bad quality, but if used for someone's benefit it becomes a good quality, analogous to neem juice, which, although bitter, cures sickness."[2]

The harshly-speaking sadhu perceives everyone in this world as bewildered by myriad delusions, of which they need to be disabused before they can even begin to comprehend the truth of Kṛṣṇa consciousness. He sees that although many people like to appear open-minded, reasonable, and concerned with higher values, very few are sincerely seeking the quintessential truth. Having entered a pact to remain forever within *māyā*, almost all are actually inimical to the truth.

Even supposed religion and the supposed search for truth are ultimately cheating if they do not come to the point of

---

1 Gaura Kiśora Dāsa Bābājī (quoted in *Bābājī Mahārāja*, p. 36).

2 Commentary on SB 4.4.12.

Kṛṣṇa consciousness. This is experienced by preachers of Kṛṣṇa consciousness who, when presenting the plain, easily understandable, illuminating truths of *Bhagavad-gītā*—such as the difference between the temporary body and the eternal soul, or that material existence is miserable, or that everyone is constitutionally tiny and obliged to directly or indirectly submit to the supreme authority—are often met with evasiveness, ridicule, dogmatic sectarian replies, or the most inane or convoluted counterarguments. This simply demonstrates that although many people want to appear as if good, sincere, religious, thoughtful, open-minded, or searching for the truth, all of them—save those who accept the straightforward teachings of *Bhagavad-gītā* when presented to them—are simply deluding themselves and others by avoiding Kṛṣṇa.

> As soon as there is talk of this goodness and sinful activity, immediately they go away. Immediately. Yesterday that gentleman came, and just when I began to talk about pious activities and impious activities, he immediately left, "I have got another meeting."[1]

Even when the actual truth is conveyed most tactfully to persons who are apparently interested in discussing the theoretical nature of truth, in many cases their underlying disposition of aversion to Kṛṣṇa is revealed:

> Worldly persons possess a double nature; they express one kind of sentiment but internally cherish a different purpose. Moreover, they want to advertise this duplicity as a mark of liberalism, or love of harmony.[2]

Just because a person may be superficially nice does not mean that we should overlook his faults or act as his enemy by not attempting to correct him. We should understand that most pseudo-seekers

1 Lecture, 1 Jun 1974.

2 Śrīla Bhaktisiddhānta Sarasvatī (*Harmonist* 28.264, Feb 1931); SBV, vol. 1, p. 143.

and ostensibly pious persons are actually attached to their minuscule perverted worldviews, which in their minds justify and facilitate sense gratification in various gross and subtle forms, and keep them forever distant from Kṛṣṇa.

मतिर्न कृष्णे परतः स्वतो वा
मिथोऽभिपद्येत गृहव्रतानाम् ।
अदान्तगोभिर्विशतां तमिस्रं
पुनः पुनश्चर्वितचर्वणानाम् ॥

matir na kṛṣṇe parataḥ svato vā
mitho 'bhipadyeta gṛha-vratānām
adānta-gobhir viśatāṁ tamisraṁ
punaḥ punaś carvita-carvaṇānām

Because of their uncontrolled senses, persons too addicted to materialistic life make progress toward hellish conditions and repeatedly chew that which has already been chewed. Their inclinations toward Kṛṣṇa are never aroused, neither by the instructions of others, by their own efforts, or by a combination of both.

न ते विदुः स्वार्थगतिं हि विष्णुं
दुराशया ये बहिरर्थमानिनः ।
अन्धा यथान्धैरुपनीयमाना-
स्तेऽपीशतन्त्र्यामुरुदाम्नि बद्धाः ॥

na te viduḥ svārtha-gatiṁ hi viṣṇuṁ
durāśayā ye bahir-artha-māninaḥ
andhā yathāndhair upanīyamānās
te 'pīśa-tantryām uru-dāmni baddhāḥ

Persons who are strongly entrapped by the consciousness of enjoying material life, and therefore have accepted as their leader or guru a similar blind man attached to external sense objects, cannot understand that the goal of life is to return home, back to Godhead,

> and engage in the service of Lord Viṣṇu. As blind men guided by another blind man miss the right path and fall into a ditch, materially attached men led by another materially attached man are bound by the ropes of fruitive labor, which are made of very strong cords, and they continue again and again in materialistic life, suffering the threefold miseries.[1]

Many people are so completely deluded that they cannot even begin to recognize their affliction, and are disinclined to take seriously even obvious truths—for instance, that no one in the material world can escape the miseries of birth, death, old age, and disease. An intense approach is required for cutting the arrogance of such fools, to pierce through the misconceptions and attachments that cover their hearts and to revive their original consciousness, beyond false egoism and exploitive desires.

অজ্ঞ জীব নিজ-'হিতে' 'অহিত' করি' মানে।
গর্ব চূর্ণ হৈলে, পাছে উঘাড়ে নয়নে ॥

ajña jīva nija-'hite' 'ahita' kari' māne
garva cūrṇa haile, pāche ughāḍe nayane

> An ignorant person considers detrimental that which is for his benefit. Only after his pride is pulverized do his eyes open.[2]

Most people have never thought deeply about, let alone consciously registered, the assumptions upon which they base their life. They have been imperceptibly yet thoroughly trained to accept falsity as truth, to the extent of considering that which is harmful to themselves and others as being beneficial. As well-programmed workers and consumers, they resent any worldview that impinges on their imagination of being independent and having freedom of choice and thought. They presume that whatever they are doing is fine (even if, as is normal today, their existence is hellish) and that they have no need to change anything in their life. Thus they

1 SB 7.5.30–31.

2 Cc 3.7.119.

become much disturbed if confronted with the Kṛṣṇa conscious understanding, perceiving that it threatens to undermine their whole existence. The bold preacher aims to cut through the stupidity of such vacuous fools by declaring that "the population is just a royal edition of the animals,"[1] that man did not descend from monkeys, that there is no happiness in the material world, that the whole endeavor of modern civilization is idiocy, exploitation, and cheating, that free sex, feminism, and democracy are bogus, or that even much that masquerades as altruism, religion, or spirituality are also just other forms of cheating. Having shaken them to attention, the bold preacher must then vindicate to them the rationale of such seemingly radical concepts.

Even in addressing persons who from the outset are sufficiently pious and interested to respectfully hear the message of Kṛṣṇa consciousness, firmness and clarity are required. Although the general approach may be to encourage such persons in their pious tendencies, corrective instructions should also be given. For instance, as Satsvarūpa Dāsa Goswami recalls:

> I was with His Divine Grace Śrīla Prabhupāda in Australia in 1974 when he spoke on several occasions to church leaders and audiences of seminarians. While telling about Lord Caitanya's universal *saṅkīrtana* movement of chanting God's holy names, Śrīla Prabhupāda would explain that Christians could also take part by chanting the name of Jesus Christ. He pointed out that the word *christ,* coming from the Greek word *christos,* is philologically related to the name Kṛṣṇa. He also said that if, along with chanting "Christos," Christians would give up slaughtering animals and eating meat, they would advance in spiritual realization.[2]

In discussions with Christians, Śrīla Prabhupāda almost always hammered on the point "Thou shalt not kill."

1 SB 1.3.45, purport.

2 BTG 15-10 (1980).

> I asked the Christians so many times, that "Your Bible says, 'Thou shalt not kill.' Why you are killing?" They cannot give any satisfactory answer.[1]

For instance, when speaking with Cardinal Danielou, the head of the Catholic Church in France, Śrīla Prabhupāda belabored the point "How can you support that animal killing is not sin?"[2]

1 Conversation, 5 Sep 1973.

2 Conversation, 9 Aug 1973.

EIGHT

WHO IS QUALIFIED TO SPEAK STRONGLY?

To fight for Kṛṣṇa is a privilege accorded to topmost devotees—transcendental titans of the order of Hanumān, Arjuna, Madhvācārya, Rāmānujācārya, Śrīla Bhaktisiddhānta Sarasvatī, and our own most worshipable Śrīla Prabhupāda. It is the great mercy of these eternal associates of Kṛṣṇa that they have accorded to even much less qualified persons like ourselves the opportunity to enroll as footsoldiers in the battle against all in the world that is not Kṛṣṇa conscious. Particularly, Śrī Caitanya Mahāprabhu ordered all devotees to preach:

যারে দেখ, তারে কহ 'কৃষ্ণ'-উপদেশ।

yāre dekha, tāre kaha 'kṛṣṇa'-upadeśa

Speak the instructions of Kṛṣṇa to whomever you meet.[1]

Śrīla Prabhupāda often quoted this edict, and he himself obeyed it by speaking the instructions of Kṛṣṇa in their pristine forceful brilliance. Nevertheless, there is a common misconception that Śrīla Prabhupāda's manner of delivery is not to be attempted by persons of lesser stature and realization, that devotees must become as pure as he before they can speak as plainly as he did. To support this theory, an anecdote is often cited, how after Śrīla Prabhupāda had spoken pointedly to an Indian consul regarding some official work, he told an attendant disciple:

> I can do this, but you cannot. I am an old man. They don't take me seriously. But if you were to speak to someone who was older than

1 Cc 2.7.128.

you or your age, and if you speak very strongly, they will become offended. But I am an old man, so I can do this. But you cannot.[1]

Similarly, one time in London, Śrīla Prabhupāda called two visitors "cats and dogs"—which they admitted to. After they had departed, Śrīla Prabhupāda told his disciples, "I can say things like that, but you may not be able to do so."[2]

These anecdotes certainly indicate that not all devotees are qualified to speak as straightforwardly as did Śrīla Prabhupāda. Yet they do not nullify his multiple instructions to disseminate the unadulterated truth. After his strong words to the consul, Śrīla Prabhupāda mentioned the prerogative of being old (not pure) for rebuking others. From this may be derived the important lesson that few people are ready to accept sermonizing from persons who are considerably younger than themself. Still, notwithstanding Śrīla Prabhupāda's having once counseled a young-bodied devotee to not be forceful with seniors, there are many occurrences of his ordering his followers to speak out—loud and clear—and of his pleasure when his disciples did so.[*] Therefore it is not true that Śrīla Prabhupāda debarred non-geriatrics from assertive preaching—although the elderly may possess a special allowance for doing so, particularly in cultures wherein seniority is respected (as among Indians, many of whom were recipients of Śrīla Prabhupāda's stern mercy).[†]

* Such instances are copiously presented in this book. See particularly the quotations that follow the statements "He also commanded his disciples to fight" (p. 14) and "He wanted them to be lionlike" (p. 16).

† While writing this at age fifty-five, I invoke a somewhat premature special "old-age" dispensation to exonerate myself from accusations of extremism. Furthermore, I exhort all elderly devotees desirous of following Śrīla Prabhupāda's example to sally forth in the last stage of life and, availing of their age advantage, uninhibitedly speak the truth as Śrīla Prabhupāda spoke it.

1 *Prabhupāda-līlā*, ch. 7-9: "Zurich and New York.

2 Told by Bhakti Caitanya Swami to Bhakti Vikāsa Swami.

Nor is there any record of Śrīla Prabhupāda's having stated that one must become as pure as he as a prerequisite for preaching as strongly as he did. On the contrary, Śrīla Prabhupāda rejected such a proposal:

> [Guest:] You can't preach until you are purified.
>
> [Prabhupāda:] No, purification will go on.[1]

> If you make a condition that "First of all you become qualified, then you preach," that will never come.[2]

But, it may be questioned, is it not inappropriate that devotees who are still influenced by the illusory energy (as are most devotees in this world) condemn all that is nondevotional? According to some, because Śrīla Prabhupāda was especially empowered he was entitled to speak strongly, but others are not, and anyone who attempts to do similarly is simply imitating. In Vaiṣṇava parlance, imitation means to copy form and style as if to pose as on a level with the person imitated. So although devotees should not imitate Śrīla Prabhupāda—for instance, by making a habit of grabbing opponents' shirts*—they should attempt to follow his example of preaching dynamically yet without pride or false ego, knowing that the indispensable qualification for speaking the truth of *śāstra* is not ultimate purity or full realization but the faith and sincerity to distribute that truth unchanged.

> If I am a child, and I ask my father, "What is this, my father?" The father says, "My dear child, it is called coconut." Then if I distribute this knowledge—"This is coconut"—my knowledge is perfect. I may not be perfect, but because I have heard it from my father, who is perfect about the knowledge of this fruit, so I have taken that word from my father and I am preaching "This is coconut," and this is

* Śrīla Prabhupāda did this in an incident described in *Prabhupāda-līlā*, 7-3: "A Visit to Boston, 1983."

1 Conversation, 14 Aug 1971.

2 Conversation, 30 Sep 1975.

> perfect. So our Kṛṣṇa consciousness movement is like that. We are simply repeating the perfect statement of our predecessor.[1]

> If I receive the knowledge from Bhagavān, and if I distribute the same knowledge as Bhagavān has said, without any interpretation of my cheating policy, then the knowledge which I distribute is also perfect. I may not be perfect, but if I present the knowledge which I have taken from Kṛṣṇa as it is, without any interpretation, then what I give you is perfect.[2]

Although a devotee may not be fully realized, that he firmly believes in the message of *śāstra* as delivered by Śrīla Prabhupāda is itself an important realization and is the qualification to preach as he did and as he ordered us to. Śrīla Prabhupāda directly authorized devotees of lesser realization to speak the message of *śāstra*, with the proviso that they simply repeat the teachings of Kṛṣṇa as given in *śāstra*:

> [Hari-śauri:] When we go out and preach and we just repeat or try to repeat whatever we've heard from the spiritual master, but we may not have fully realized what we're speaking about, does that somehow or another reduce the potency of the *Gītā* or the *Bhāgavatam* or ...

> [Śrīla Prabhupāda:] Yes, realization takes time. Therefore there is no question of realization. Caitanya Mahāprabhu says you simply repeat as Kṛṣṇa says. That will save you.[3]

The idea that only the completely pure are entitled to preach strongly is as absurd as the proposition that only parents who are perfect in all respects are fit to impart moral instructions to their children, or that the police and judiciary should be comprised only of wholly irreproachable persons. Certainly, parents, police, and judges need be of good character to properly discharge their responsibilities, but to demand that no one but an utter saint should accept such roles would be so unpragmatic as to be socially

1 Conversation, 14 Mar 1975.

2 Lecture, 3 Aug 1973.

3 Conversation, 31 Dec 1976.

irresponsible. Similarly, to insist that forthright presentation of Kṛṣṇa consciousness be limited to *paramahaṁsas* not only attempts to dissolve the duty of devotees to broadcast the truth (which alone can bestow genuine welfare to all living beings), but also attempts to abrogate the śāstric injunction that it is not *paramahaṁsas* but *madhyama-adhikārīs* (advanced yet possibly not fully purified devotees) who are primarily meant for preaching.[1]

The *madhyama-adhikārī*, by definition and right, is qualified and duty-bound to repeat the weighty message of guru-sadhu-*śāstra*.* Unfortunately, devotees who are committed to faithfully iterating the message of guru-sadhu-*śāstra* are denounced as imitators by persons who have no intention to follow Śrīla Prabhupāda's example of combatting everything bogus. But should we simply tolerate bogus avatars, bogus philosophies, bogus everything? Should we just smile at people and think, "Later, if I become pure, I might say something"—or maybe offer a polite, mild protest, as if presenting just one opinion among many?

Myself being one who is sometimes accused of imitating Śrīla Prabhupāda, I do not hesitate to admit the obvious: I am not on the same plane as Śrīla Prabhupāda. I am nowhere near his level of purity and expertise. But Śrīla Prabhupāda exhorted his followers to come to the same standard as he, by being knowledgeable and accepting the preaching challenge:

> The servant should be as good as the master. That is servant. Because sometimes servants may be challenged. So that is the qualification of Kṛṣṇa's servant. Kṛṣṇa's servant must be always equipped because they have to meet so many opposing elements.... Practically the whole material world is full of *duṣkṛtām*. They want to create God. They don't want to become servant of God. That is their challenge.

---

* That preaching is especially meant for *madhyama-adhikārīs* is further discussed in ch. 12, "Learning How to Preach Strongly."

---

1 Śāstric injunction—See SB 11.2.46.

> Therefore anyone who is claiming to become servant of God, Kṛṣṇa, he must be well equipped to meet the challenging spirit of others.[1]

Preachers who aspire to represent Śrīla Prabhupāda should come to the standard of being like him, fully competent to challenge opponents. As Śrīla Prabhupāda told reporters from national newspapers upon his arrival in London in 1969:

> Some of you are saying there is no God, some of you are saying God is dead, and some of you are saying God is impersonal or void. These are all nonsense. I want to teach all these nonsense that there is God. That is my mission. Any nonsense can come to me—I shall prove that there is God. Any scientist, any philosopher and logician, may come and we shall prove that there is God and we have got eternal relationship with God. That is my Kṛṣṇa consciousness movement. It is a challenge to the atheistic people.[2]

Speaking strongly necessarily entails speaking knowledgeably. Considering that no one can know everything and that specialization in any field is generally for only a few, most devotees should focus on presenting śāstric understanding as Śrīla Prabhupāda did, in a manner suitable for the modern milieu and addressing the major challenges it faces. Sadhus are supposed to be proficient in spiritual knowledge, and should be able to present it authoritatively, not merely offer unsubstantiated or insipid opinions. Just as a doctor, electrician, or mechanic must possess requisite qualifications, so a sadhu—one whose life's focus is spiritual cultivation—should know his subject thoroughly and, on that basis, be able to impart unequivocal spiritual advice. What is the meaning of preaching if one cannot confidently and competently state and defend his position, explaining the knowledge of *śāstra* for the benefit of others?

It would be presumptuous for anyone to enter into debates on technical issues (for instance, the intricacies of evolutionary

1 Lecture, 19 Jul 1975.

2 Lecture, 11 Sep 1969.

theory) unless he is thoroughly knowledgeable in that field, up to date on its present nuances, and in all other ways meticulously prepared. Hari Śauri Dāsa noted:

> Despite his often humorous critiques and sometimes general condemnations of the modern materialistic scientists, Prabhupāda cautioned us that any attempt to preach on a scientific basis must be done expertly. When a devotee told him of plans to publish a magazine in Sweden with articles challenging the material scientists, Prabhupāda warned him. "Don't write anything nonsense. It must be very solid. Otherwise you'll be laughing stock. One must be confident before challenging others. In all stages he must be able to defend himself from the opposing elements. Then such challenge is alright. We are confident that this soul cannot be manufactured by any material combination. Therefore we can challenge. And we can defend ourselves in any stage."[1]

It may be said, "Only if one can speak strongly without upsetting others should he do so." Granted, if a preacher frequently causes uproars, he probably should be restrained. And generally, it may be said that a devotee is qualified to speak strongly if he is a good judge of what is appropriate to be stated straightforwardly according to the recipients and the situation. However, even the most prudent speakers of the truth cannot avoid sometimes inflaming others, simply because most people of this world harbor deep-seated antagonism toward the truth. It is impossible to predict how any individual will react to the outright words of even the most expert preacher. Some persons may acquiesce, while others may flare up.* Yet overall, devotees who aspire to follow Śrīla Prabhupāda's

* This also happened with Śrīla Prabhupāda. His calling a man a dog (see p. 11) could have occasioned a riot. Fortunately, instead the crowd gave a standing ovation and the man acquiesced by smiling. However, when in another public program Śrīla Prabhupāda had an onstage argument with a hippie, many in the crowd became disturbed and left (see p. 11).

1 *A Transcendental Diary*, vol. 1, pp. 74–75.

example of clearly distinguishing reality from illusion will, by his grace, be effective in doing so.

Therefore those who opine, "Although Śrīla Prabhupāda spoke strongly, others should not," not only disregard Śrīla Prabhupāda's instruction to speak strongly, but also indirectly fault Śrīla Prabhupāda, for his outspokenness sometimes caused the very outrage and adverse publicity that many devotees today are so anxious to avoid. Accepting that Śrīla Prabhupāda spoke only the truth, why not accept that same truth regardless of who utters it? Is it truth only when spoken by Śrīla Prabhupāda? Refusal to accept a statement that was originally made by Śrīla Prabhupāda merely because someone else has reiterated it is tantamount to rejecting what Śrīla Prabhupāda said. Moreover, the position that "Śrīla Prabhupāda said certain things that no one else can say" could be used to suppress any comment made by Śrīla Prabhupāda that one does not like, thus affording a tool for interpreting and redefining Śrīla Prabhupāda according to personal whims.

We have no right to censor Kṛṣṇa and His representatives. Kṛṣṇa says that those who do not surrender to Him are *mūḍhas*. Anyone who protests the re-utterance of this or similar statements simply proves himself to be in that same category of *mūḍhas*.*

---

* The question "Who is qualified to preach strongly?" is further dealt with throughout this book, especially in chs. 11 and 12.

NINE
A LONELY PATH

Undoubtedly, the path of boldly speaking the noncompromised truth is a lonely one. By following the example set by the predecessor Vaiṣṇava *ācāryas*, the straight-shooting preacher cannot expect to be popular. More likely, he will be rejected, insulted (sometimes even by persons presumed to be devotees), or physically assaulted. As Śrīla Prabhupāda sometimes quoted, *saccā bole to māre lāṭhā jhūṭhā jagat bhulāya:* "One who speaks the truth gets beaten with sticks, for all the world is deluded by lies."

The fighting preacher nurtures his love for Kṛṣṇa not by artificially cultivating remembrance of pastimes far beyond his eligibility to comprehend, but by serving the mission of the liberated *ācāryas*, who can grant admission into the transcendental realm. The resolute preacher places his life in Kṛṣṇa's hands, pledging to spend his whole life on the battlefield of preaching, combatting a *māyā* that will never cease. Without caring for comfort, safety, or personal reputation, he valiantly refuses to compromise the truth because he has full faith that Kṛṣṇa is the supreme controller and wants His message promulgated, and that He will surely protect His loyal servants.

> We have got Kṛṣṇa. We are not afraid in challenging anyone. I believe in that formula.[1]

---

1 Conversation, 14 Jun 1974.

As stated by Śrīla Bhaktisiddhānta Sarasvatī shortly before his passing away:

> I have most probably given many people troubles in the mind. Some of them might have thought that I am their enemy because I was obliged to speak the plain truth for service and devotion toward the Absolute Godhead. I have given them all those troubles only so that they may turn their face toward the Personality of Godhead without any desire for gain and with unalloyed devotion. I hope some day or other they may understand me rightly.[1]

Śrīla Prabhupāda made a similar apology in his final days, asking to be forgiven for his "offenses."[2] This should not be misconstrued to mean that Śrīla Prabhupāda was actually wrong and therefore his followers should not repeat the same "mistake." Such a misinterpretation regarding our *ācārya* is certainly rascaldom, for it seeks to cast Śrīla Prabhupāda as a conditioned soul and to negate his whole mission and strategy. Rather, those words of Śrīla Prabhupāda's should be understood as an expression of utmost humility, and an indication that when speaking forthrightly—as a genuine preacher must—even the purest and most expert of devotees cannot avoid alienating at least some people.

But others are saved. Strong preachers change lives. That is their ecstasy. They may initially have to fight. Yet they repeatedly relish the nectar of seeing apparently incorrigible materialists become convinced of Kṛṣṇa consciousness. There is no greater gratification for a battling preacher than to witness a vociferous adversary of Kṛṣṇa consciousness becoming a firm adherent. The pious compromiser can never know such transcendental pleasure, not even after decades of smiling and politeness.

Furthermore, strong preachers, although not many, can relish the company of other "purified men who are thoroughly honest."[3]

1 Quoted in BTG, vol. 1 (1944).
2 SPl ch. 54, "At Home in Vṛndāvana."
3 From Śrīla Prabhupāda's translation of SB 1.5.11.

For essence-seekers,[1] the association of even one such genuine, straightforward person is infinitely more desirable than that of legions of diplomatic types, whose words are not one with their heart and whose intentions can only be guessed at, who are duplicitious and untrustworthy due to pursuing a personal agenda.

Although the path of speaking out for Kṛṣṇa is a less-trodden one, it is a sure one that leads directly and swiftly to Kṛṣṇa.

1 SB 1.18.7.

TEN

ABSOLUTISM, RELATIVISM, CONSERVATIVISM, LIBERALISM

The contemporary Western psyche fosters deep suspicion of doctrines that claim unquestionable correctness. The effect of centuries of evil enacted in the name of religion and, more recently, the horrors of Nazism and the oppressiveness of Communism have been major factors in the rise of relativism in Western thought—nowadays so pronounced that many people unquestioningly reject any form of absolutism. In recent years, an upsurge of religious fundamentalism, ranging from inane evangelizing to terrorism in the name of God, has further spawned widespread distrust of religion, and especially in unbending religious doctrines. Particularly in America, society is becoming increasingly divided between "left-wing liberals" and "right-wing conservatives." But to simplistically package people according to a generalization overlooks the nuances and complexity of the issues over which they differ. For instance, within the current cultural context, to invoke the term "liberal" paints for some a picture of a reasonable, progressive intellectual who is aghast at the mutterings of close-minded zealots intent upon dragging mankind back to the Dark Ages, whereas for others the "liberal" is an unprincipled, godless supporter of depravity. And while some right-wing ultras are ready to kill over certain moral causes (such as countering abortion), it is inaccurate and unfair to identify all persons of traditionalist leaning as being supportive of such dangerous antisocial elements.

Certainly the designations of conservative and liberal are applicable even among devotees. But to overly emphasize such loaded terms—which reflect the contemporary materialistic outlook rather than that of *śāstra*—unnecessarily risks putting devotees at opposition, whereas all sincere devotees simply aspire to become conduits of the Lord's mercy upon the conditioned souls. Undoubtedly, some conflict between the two stances is inevitable, because devotees who have a more liberal, pragmatic approach aim primarily for immediate results, such as acceptability or impact that is relative to the world today, whereas devotees of more conservative, idealistic bent emphasize protecting the pristine, absolute values of Vaiṣṇavism and are concerned about the long-term consequences of introducing foreign elements into Vaiṣṇava culture.* But actually, Kṛṣṇa consciousness is both absolute, in recognizing Kṛṣṇa as the uncontestable supreme reality, and relative, in appreciating that "all are on Kṛṣṇa's path in all respects."[1] Śrīla Prabhupāda taught us to not narrow-mindedly tout Vaiṣṇavism as the sole manifestation of spirituality but to sensibly accept that God reveals Himself in varying degrees in contrasting cultures and climes.

However, Vaiṣṇavism is ultimately more absolutist than accommodating, and its acknowledgment of certain doctrines is not without caveats. While devotees do not claim a monopoly on God, they realistically uphold that Vaiṣṇavism alone offers thorough, perfect knowledge concerning God and how to approach Him, whereas others have only vague ideas and sentiments. Furthermore, Vaiṣṇavism condemns as sinful much of the behavior—such as animal slaughter and consumption of

* For a discussion of conservatism and liberality in preaching, see p. 179.

1 Bg 4.11.

alcohol—that is widely accepted, or even deemed sacred, within the world's "great religions."

From a Kṛṣṇa conscious perspective, the world's cultural polarization is between misplaced absolutism and misplaced relativism, both of which present the bound *jīva* with worldviews conducive for prolonged forgetfulness of Kṛṣṇa. Thoughtless absolutism either misrepresents the actual point or grasps the wrong point, thus being a zealous but misguided charge in the wrong direction. But relativism denies that there even is a specific point to be grasped, thus providing no direction. In rejecting the irrationality of blind absolutism, relativism is similarly irrationally dogmatic in insisting that there can be no absolute harmonizing principle. In its attempt to avoid the excesses of absolutism, relativism casts the individual as the arbiter of knowledge, experience, and morality. Although promoted as freedom of the spirit, relativism actually binds the *jīva* to material existence by obfuscating the inescapable fact of his eternal subordination to the Supreme Absolute, Śrī Kṛṣṇa, whose lotus feet are the only reliable shelter from all peril, whether spawned by relativism or incorrect absolutism.

Neither misguided absolutists nor relativists are seeking the truth. Misguided absolutists are convinced that they have already attained the truth, whereas relativists doubt that an ultimate truth exists. Among these two classes, generally only the relativists will give devotees a hearing, for they profess to be open-minded and willing to learn about what they consider to be others' views. The challenge for Vaiṣṇava preachers is to unambiguously and uncompromisingly communicate the message of Kṛṣṇa consciousness to all types of persons, yet to do so non-dogmatically, not simply making pronouncements but by explaining the philosophy in a cogent, reasonable manner—scientifically (i.e., rationally and logically), as Śrīla Prabhupāda did.

ELEVEN

FANATICISM AND FUNDAMENTALISM

Even among devotees, those who preach uncompromisingly are often labeled "extremists," "fanatics," or "fundamentalists"—which is itself an extreme indictment:

> Why should one be a fanatic? If one has got brain, one has got logic, why should he be a fanatic? Fanatic means dull-headed rascal.[1]

Śrīla Prabhupāda identified fanaticism as a manifestation of religion without philosophy: "Religion without philosophy is sentiment, or sometimes fanaticism."[2] A fanatic may be defined as a dogmatic numbskull who is convinced about something and, although he cannot reasonably explain why, expects others to accept his chosen doctrine with the same unquestioning zeal as himself. Thus it is a great injustice and a disservice to the preaching mission of Kṛṣṇa consciousness to inappropriately invoke pejoratives upon devotees for their staunch commitment to śāstric truth. If that which is dubbed as fanaticism is actually firm faith in guru and Kṛṣṇa—manifest as no compromise with karma, *jñāna*, yoga, atheism, or sense gratification, and as an unreserved resolve to serve the mission of the *ācāryas* in the manner that they have taught—then such an uncompromising attitude is desirable.

1 Conversation, 12 Dec 1976.

2 Bg 3.3, purport.

Śrīla Prabhupāda himself was sometimes so extreme—for instance, by arguing onstage before thousands—that any other member of ISKCON today would be liable to be labeled immature, inexpert, or fanatical for behaving similarly. But a preacher who faithfully and thoughtfully follows Śrīla Prabhupāda's example does not deserve to be labeled a fanatic (although he may be imitated by fanatics and denigrated by sentimentalists). Indeed, another form of fanaticism is to equate a mature devotee's intelligent commitment and candid preaching, born of genuine spiritual strength and realization, with the bluster of a neophyte. Similarly, it is dismissive chauvinism—an ignorant, biased, and haughty (i.e., fanatical) position—to deem as a fanatic anyone who speaks frankly or who has a strong outlook or conviction without considering the arguments they present.

Devotees who would vilify their forthright compatriots should consider the analysis of Śrīla Bhaktisiddhānta Sarasvatī:

> Those who are unwilling to show any duplicity, who desire to be frank and straightforward, or in other words, to exercise unambiguously the function of the soul—such really sincere individuals are called "sectarian" and "orthodox" by those who practice duplicity.[1]

Firm adherence to guru, sadhu, and *śāstra,* being the necessary foundation for rapid advancement in Kṛṣṇa consciousness, should not be equated with the fundamentalism epitomized by linear thinking, intolerance, and myopic triumphalism. A well-situated devotee might resemble a religious fundamentalist, inasmuch as both have deep faith and resolution. But religious systems without scientific knowledge of the nature of God and the *jīva,* and which therefore lack satisfactory answers to basic questions such as the cause of suffering, cannot but demand blind and unquestioning faith, and hence naturally tend toward fundamentalism. Only

---

1 *Harmonist* 28.243 (Jan 1931); SBV, vol. 1, p. 143.

devotees who are uneducated in or unmindful of the tremendous philosophical depth of Kṛṣṇa consciousness would fault a colleague as being fanatical because of his unwavering adherence to the perspective of reality that Kṛṣṇa consciousness offers.

Admittedly, the public cannot be expected to immediately differentiate between a knowledgeable, dedicated, enthusiastic preacher of Kṛṣṇa consciousness and those unmindful zealots who are rightly seen as dogmatic, obnoxious, insulting, puerile, and insubstantial. Therefore devotees should take care not to become misidentified with those blinkered fanatics whose "believe or burn" proselytization is rightly seen as dogmatic, obnoxious, insulting, puerile, and insubstantial. But rather than hiding behind the limp role of an all-inclusive moderate religionist, Vaiṣṇavas should aim to educate the public regarding the depth, universality, and scientific approach of Kṛṣṇa consciousness in contrast to myopic religious systems.

It is true that forwardness in preaching may be construed as or actually motivated by egoism, envy, or unnecessary anger toward others. And certainly a preacher should be devoid of fanatical behavior, such as vehemently presenting teachings which he has little knowledge or realization of, being more interested to defeat and denounce than to convince and uplift others, or adopting unfair means of argument (for instance, deliberately misrepresenting facts). Senior devotees should recognize and restrain all such instances of fanaticism; they should teach immature devotees that a preacher can be protected from succumbing to such baseness only if, while presenting the topmost truth to others, he is internally peaceful by considering himself an unworthy instrument and the servant of those to whom he ministers.

Despite all of these considerations, Śrīla Prabhupāda's mandate to "kick the rascals in the face with boots" remains. Many devotees today would be appalled if any of their contemporaries were to consider these celebrated words of Śrīla Prabhupāda anything but an idiosyncracy to be recited occasionally as a nostalgic remembrance; to take them seriously would risk being branded the egoistic antithesis of a sadhu. Yet there is no doubt that in pronouncing these words Śrīla Prabhupāda meant his disciples to earnestly accept his diktat to preach robustly and to (metaphorically, not literally) kick the rascals.* Śrīla Prabhupāda and all previous *ācāryas* rightly exhorted the rascals to give up their rascaldom, accept Kṛṣṇa, and become happy. So to label as fanatics those devotees who similarly speak contentiously implies that Śrīla Prabhupāda and the *ācāryas* also were fanatics.

Factually, the Vaiṣṇava *ācāryas*, by decisively repeating the message of *śāstra* though it be annoying to rascals, demonstrate total freedom from egoism. Even if seemingly intolerably strong in their preaching, their sole motive is compassionate desire for uplifting others. They do not consider personal loss or gain, or popular acceptance or rejection; they simply want to please Kṛṣṇa. They are the most broadminded personalities, for they wish to see everyone engaged in the service of Kṛṣṇa. Such is the exalted example to follow, which stands far above the fanaticism of one class of neophytes and the misplaced tolerance of another.

Misplaced tolerance means the socially acceptable version, i.e., acquiescence toward much behavior that traditional societies have always deemed unacceptable. But in Vaiṣṇava parlance, Śrī Caitanya Mahāprabhu's cardinal ordinance to be more forbearing than a tree refers to acceptance of the various difficulties that a devotee must undergo while serving Mahāprabhu's mission within this world.

---

* See the anecdote related by Girirāja Swami, p. 167.

TWELVE
LEARNING HOW TO PREACH STRONGLY

Preaching is especially meant for *madhyama-adhikārīs*, not for neophytes:

> Neophyte devotee does not know how to preach.[1]
>
> In the lower stage of devotional service, he cannot become preacher. When he's in a little upper, second stage, he can become preacher.[2]
>
> *Madhyama-adhikārī* means preacher. Unless one comes to the *madhyama-adhikāra*, he cannot preach.[3]
>
> First of all you become really preacher, then go to preach. Caitanya Mahāprabhu never sent neophytes to preach. For neophytes, preaching is not their business. Neophytes should stick to the worship of the Deity in the temple. And those who have understood the philosophy, applied the philosophy in his life, he should go for preaching. Otherwise he'll preach wrongly.[4]

However: "We should not remain as neophyte devotees."[5] "Those who are active in the Kṛṣṇa consciousness movement should not remain in the neophyte stage but should rise to the platform of preachers, the second platform of devotional service."[6]

---

1 Letter, 9 Apr 1968.

2 Lecture, 5 July 1976.

3 Lecture, 4 Nov 1972.

4 Conversation, 2 May 1976.

5 Letter, 9 Apr 1968.

6 Cc 2.24.205, purport.

It is expected and desirable that those who have newly discovered the treasure of Kṛṣṇa consciousness be bursting with zeal to share it with others. Such enthusiasm should be encouraged, not discouraged, even if it sometimes goes overboard:

> Neophytes may sometimes commit some offense. There is nothing surprising in this, but their ardent desire to convey the idea of Kṛṣṇa consciousness is always laudable.[1]

Still, the enthusiasm of neophytes must be refined and purified of tendencies toward fanaticism, lest they continue to unnecessarily offend. Fanaticism—manifested as lack of proper understanding, discrimination, and compassion—springs from the neophyte's dearth of knowledge. "One must know the science of Kṛṣṇa. Then he can preach to others."[2] Therefore the natural antidote to fanaticism is spiritual education. Newcomers should be trained to become effective members in the preaching mission of Śrīla Prabhupāda, who desired "many preachers who are soundly versed in the scriptures, to convince the world to take to Kṛṣṇa consciousness."[3]

Given that Śrīla Prabhupāda's mission is meant for preaching, its leaders should be expected to act on the platform of *madhyama-adhikāra* and to prepare beginners (*kaniṣṭha-adhikārīs*) to come to that platform. Everyone starts raw and commits mistakes, but through experience and by the careful guidance of concerned seniors, newcomers can learn how to speak clearly, incisively, and effectively while also remaining realistically humble, not imitatively posing themselves as more advanced than they are.

Just as a fighter must be trained in wielding weapons (*astra*), a devotee should be trained in the art of presenting *śāstra*. Regular participation in devotional programs, including hearing of

1 Letter, 31 Aug 1975.

2 Lecture, 27 Oct 1972.

3 Letter, 9 Nov 1970.

classes conducted in the spirit of Śrīla Prabhupāda, should help newcomers to absorb the teachings that they are expected to live by and propagate.* Also helpful for trainee preachers are question-and-answer sessions and mock debates aimed at preparing devotees for the actual challenges that they are likely to meet.

Gradually, newcomers can be introduced to the practical preaching field. Or in some cases, depending on the newcomer's attitude and maturity and the level of competence of those guiding them, recruits can, almost from their first day in devotional service, be inducted into preaching. And factually, often newcomers automatically preach from the moment they decide to take up Kṛṣṇa consciousness; being peppered with questions (and maybe also objections) from their relatives and acquaintances, they have no choice but to reply as best they can. And sometimes the unconsidered words of a beginner can be transformatory—as happened with Arnoldas, a sociology professor from Lithuania who was a self-confessed atheist and hedonist. A friend of his who had just begun devotional service warned him that he could end up taking his next birth as a monkey. Those words inspired in Arnoldas a fear and introspectiveness that some years later culminated in his taking to Kṛṣṇa consciousness in full seriousness.[1]

Śrīla Prabhupāda gave a formula that should be the motto of all preachers, by imbibing which even beginners can start to preach effectively:

> The real purpose of this movement? To teach people how he can surrender to Kṛṣṇa—that's all. That is the sum and substance of this movement. If one accepts this principle without any difficulty, he is immediately a preacher.[2]

---

* Classes in the spirit of Śrīla Prabhupāda are further discussed on p. 228.

1 Told by Arnoldas to Bhakti Vikāsa Swami.

2 Lecture, 7 Apr 1971.

However, preferably for at least the first few months, an apprentice preacher should accompany senior devotees, observe them in action, and start his preaching career in their presence—for instance, by assisting in manning a book table. Indeed, several years of book distribution provides a solid basis for a devotee to excel in preaching and indeed all areas of devotional service.

Self-study is also essential. Śrīla Prabhupāda particularly emphasized the importance of studying his books, and it is the duty of all who claim to be his followers—especially those who represent him as preachers—to become deeply acquainted with the teachings that he so painstakingly imparted therein. This requires regular, thorough, and prayerful perusal of those books:

> If you read, then you will be able to defend yourself from the opposing parties. That will help you in preaching, because in preaching you have to answer so many question, you have to meet so many opposing elements. So if you are strong in your position by reading books, Vedic literature, then you become very, very favorite to Kṛṣṇa.[1]

> Because you are on the field work, you have to meet so many opposite elements. And you have to satisfy them or fight with them with conclusive statements from *Bhagavad-gītā* and *Śrīmad-Bhāgavatam*, and as such, it is needed that you should be thoroughly conversant with the truth.[2]

Reading biographical works about Śrīla Prabhupāda and listening to recordings of his lectures and conversations is also very helpful for imbibing the sense of how Śrīla Prabhupāda personally preached among various types of people, including committed devotees, the curious, the apathetic, and the vociferously inimical. However, devotees should exercise discrimination, as not everything is meant for everyone. For instance, certain statements made by Śrīla Prabhupāda to individuals in letters or spoken to a few devotees in private settings were not intended to be widely broadcast.

1 Lecture, 15 Jul 1975.

2 Letter, 30 Sep 1968.

Until devotees become steeped in the transcendental knowledge delineated in Śrīla Prabhupāda's books and thus raised to the *madhyama* platform, their criticism of nondevotees, even if accurate, is likely to be tinged by dogmatism and sectarianism, and they are liable to appear foolish in proportion to the degree of their assertiveness. Therefore:

> All devotees, especially preachers, must know the philosophy of Kṛṣṇa consciousness so as not to be embarrassed and insulted when they preach.[1]

> Unless our men understand thoroughly the philosophy, how will they be able to preach?[2]

Attaining the competence required to preach need not be very difficult:

> Everyone can become a first-class speaker. Simply cram the purports of my books. The references are there, the philosophy is there. Everything is there. So if you do it, everyone will be pleased with your speaking.[3]

> If you chant and read, you will also be powerful to preach, and whoever will hear will be converted.[4]

> Simply read my books and repeat what I have written, then your preaching will be perfect.[5]

When a devotee asked how he could face South Indian *paṇḍitas* possessing extensive knowledge of *śāstra*, Śrīla Prabhupāda replied that if he could just memorize thirty key verses of *Bhagavad-gītā*, he would be able to defeat Māyāvādī arguments.[6] * Śrīla Prabhupāda

* Although Śrīla Prabhupāda did not specify what those key verses were, those that he most often cited may be understood as being the most important for his followers to quote when preaching.

1 SB 6.1.38, purport.

2 Letter, 7 Nov 1973.

3 Letter, 19 Sep 1974.

4 Letter, 15 Mar 1970.

5 Letter, 4 Sep 1975.

6 *Life with the Perfect Master*, ch. 5.

similarly instructed another disciple:

> So far the impersonalist rascal, you may simply challenge him by asking "What is your philosophy?" It is not very difficult to defeat these persons, because they haven't got any substance, simply big words. But we have got our books, *Bhagavad-gītā*—if you engage him in public debate, politely handle his statements with a cool head and reply from the authority of our books, that's all. Kṛṣṇa will give you all help to expose his lack of knowledge and his faulty understanding.[1]

Of course, it is also essential to study Śrīla Prabhupāda's books in their entirety, to gain deep understanding of the teachings therein. Neophytes who are unwilling to imbibe the philosophy of Kṛṣṇa consciousness in all its depth and subtlety should be restrained from attempting to present it forcefully. Those who attempt to speak strongly but lack the requisite knowledge, spiritual strength, and expertise are more likely to mangle the message of the absolute truth than to effectively communicate it. Such "preaching" is at best an embarrassment, and is liable to resemble the bigotry of fanatical religionists, who are a blight on true theism. Furthermore, controversial subjects about which a devotee is likely to be challenged—for instance, the subordinate social role of women in Vedic culture—are better broached by devotees who have sufficiently studied and understood, according to guru-sadhu-*śāstra*, the various issues involved. As Śrīla Prabhupāda once warned a group of disciples, "There is a great art to criticizing. Unfortunately, you do not know that art."[2]

To be most effective, preaching requires not only knowledge but also developed insight. While always stressing that the message should not be changed, Śrīla Prabhupāda expected devotees to come to the level of being able to convey that message in their own idiom:

---

1 Letter, 17 Dec 1971.

2 Told by Girirāja Swami to Bhakti Vikāsa Swami.

> You simply have to study carefully our books and then in your own words try to express what you have read. This will automatically make you a very successful preacher.[1]

> Study my books and reproduce the purports in your own language. You should instruct your temple presidents to preach like this. This is preaching. We haven't got to invent something by our fertile brain for preaching. Everything is there. One who is expert for presenting these things before the audience so they can conveniently understand, this is a successful preacher. You have only to speak what Kṛṣṇa has said. Then you become a preacher.[2]

A devotee should speak *yathā-mati yathā-śrutam,* "according to realization, based on what he has heard."[3]

> [A speaker] must have full confidence in the previous *ācārya,* and at the same time he must realize the subject matter so nicely that he can present the matter for the particular circumstances in a suitable manner. *The original purpose of the text must be maintained.* No obscure meaning should be screwed out of it, yet it should be presented in an interesting manner for the understanding of the audience. This is called realization.[4]

Such realization arises from serious hearing:

> Because I was serious for hearing, therefore now I am serious about *kīrtana,* means speaking, or preaching. One who is serious about hearing, he can become a future nice preacher. *Śravaṇaṁ kīrtanam.* Next stage is developed. If one has actually heard nicely, then he will speak nicely. *Śravaṇaṁ kīrtanaṁ smaraṇam.* Then consciousness will automatically develop because when you speak or you hear, unless your mind is concentrated, your consciousness is right, you cannot rightly hear or speak.[5]

---

1 Letter, 13 May 1977.

2 Letter, 9 Nov 1975.

3 The Sanskrit quoted is from SB 3.6.36.

4 SB 1.4.1, purport.

5 Conversation, 10 May 1969.

Notwithstanding various caveats for restraining neophyte devotees who themselves are not very sure about what they are meant to be preaching, there is really no substitute for "taking the plunge." Sincerity is the key, and association with proficient preachers is the classroom, but ultimately a devotee who desires to speak strongly in service to Śrīla Prabhupāda has to get out and do it. Actually attempting to present the Kṛṣṇa conscious message as it is to nondevotees constitutes a crash course in gaining insightful knowledge. A devotee out in the fray is liable to be challenged at every moment, without forewarning, on any one of a galaxy of possible objections. By definition, a neophyte's faith is pliable and uncertain, and his knowledge of devotional lore meager. Yet even a neophyte can sense the inherent error in the words of nondevotees, even if he is unable to rebutt them. Preaching gives impetus to the neophyte to deepen his knowledge and hone his skills, and to pray to Kṛṣṇa for the ability to comprehend and effectively present śāstric teachings. In short, a neophyte's beginning attempts to preach are the very means by which he can quickly become convinced and thus rise to the level of a competent preacher, a *madhyama-adhikārī*.

Time and practice are also required. With regard to speaking the truth in a manner so that it will be accepted, Śrīla Prabhupāda wrote: "To perfect this art takes practice, so practice preaching from this understanding and gradually you will develop it more and more."[1] *

> For those who engage in the preaching of these two Vedic literatures [*Bhagavad-gītā* and *Śrīmad-Bhāgavatam*] it is very easy to get out of the illusory conditional life imposed upon us by *māyā*.[2]

* For context, see the quotation beginning "The highest development… " p. 193.

1 Letter, 31 Dec 1972.

2 SB 4.7.44, purport.

Preaching is the very means of purification, and thus neophyte devotees (unless they are extraordinarily disqualified, e.g. highly socially incompetent or mentally disordered) should by all means be encouraged to qualify as a preacher. If even an inexperienced devotee has at least a basic grasp of *śāstric* lore, then by sincerely repeating Kṛṣṇa's teachings he not only benefits others but also preaches to himself. By railing against all that is wrong in the world and in other people, he must (unless he is a hypocrite) likewise confront the wrong within himself. Knowing himself to be susceptible to the influence of *māyā*, he nonetheless seriously endeavors to surrender to Kṛṣṇa and to forsake *māyā* forever, and exhorts others to do so. Thus his conviction increases, and undesirable traits within him diminish. Gradually or even quickly, by his absorption in the preaching struggle, the aspiring devotee imbibes a deep desire to benefit others. As he continues to speak the unadulterated truth, notwithstanding the inevitable difficulties in so doing, Kṛṣṇa increasingly bestows upon him the necessary intelligence, purity, and skill for preaching effectively, and thus he becomes surcharged with spiritual energy.

Over and above all other considerations, the most important factor in becoming an effective preacher is to always consider oneself an insignificant servant, and to constantly pray for the blessings of Śrīla Prabhupāda, all the *ācāryas*, and Lord Kṛṣṇa that one may become an instrument in fulfilling their desires for injecting pure love of Godhead into the heart of every *jīva* in existence.

THIRTEEN
SCIENTIFIC, NOT DOGMATIC

> Our propaganda should be—by reasoning, by philosophy, by science, by argument—how to convince him that he is in the illusory stage.[1]

> The approach shall be and must be authoritative, scientific, and universal.[2]

> You should present Kṛṣṇa consciousness not as a religion, but a science of God realization. Try to convince them that it is not just a kind of faith. It is a chance to understand God. In every religion there is a glimpse of the idea of God. This movement is explaining what God is. The educated persons should be convinced about this fact. Every sane man should be interested to know God and then love Him.[3]

> You have to introduce the matter of God scientifically, and that will be appreciated by any reasonable man.[4]

Prominent symptoms of the confusion and arrogance of the modern age are that few people accept *śāstra* as incontrovertible and that calls to scriptural authority are largely deemed sectarian and dogmatic. Indeed, even many persons who are somewhat sympathetic to Kṛṣṇa consciousness tend to consider it just one opinion among many. Therefore Śrīla Prabhupāda often stressed the scientific, non-dogmatic nature of his presentation:

---

1 Conversation, 24 Dec 1969.

2 Letter, 13 Jul 1947.

3 Letter, 2 Nov 1976.

4 Letter, 13 Jul 1971.

> The Kṛṣṇa consciousness movement is trying to teach this science of the soul, not in any dogmatic way, but through complete scientific and philosophical understanding.[1]

> We are presenting religion on the basis of philosophy and logic. We are not blindly following. We are not dogmatic. We have got reason, philosophy, and science, everything. If you want to understand this Kṛṣṇa consciousness on the basis of philosophy, logic, and science, we are prepared to present to you.[2]

Religion is generally considered to be an unverifiable belief system, regarded by detractors (and also by many proponents) as being inherently indefinable and vague. But vagueness naturally tends toward affectiveness, which simply nourishes the disgust that materially intelligent skeptics feel toward religion as being (in their view) irrelevant fluff, a psychological crutch, or a deliberately misleading scourge upon mankind. The present deluge of atheism is an inevitable response to religion as propagated in the world today, and only devotees who have been trained in *bhāgavata-siddhānta* can offer an appropriate and sensible understanding of God that can deliver the world from both outrageous theism and outraged atheism.

Therefore Śrīla Prabhupāda wanted to establish Kṛṣṇa consciousness as being scientific, inasmuch as every person is capable of experiencing its reality if he but applies himself to the process,* and also because the basic principles of Kṛṣṇa consciousness as stated in *śāstra* are not mere doctrinal pronouncements but are facts that can be established by intelligent analysis, and thus should be accepted by anyone who is actually

* See Bg 9.2, *pratyakṣāvagamaṁ dharmyam* (directly experienced religion).

1 *Journey of Self-Discovery*, 1.2.

2 Lecture excerpt, 20 Jul 1968.

scientific in the true sense of the term.*

Whenever asked what he believed, Śrīla Prabhupāda would correct the questioner:

> [Mike Robinson:] Can you tell me what you believe—what the philosophy of the Hare Kṛṣṇa movement is?
>
> [Śrīla Prabhupāda:] Yes. Kṛṣṇa consciousness is not a question of belief; it is a science. The first step is to know the difference between a living body and a dead body...
>
> [Mike Robinson:] So we are free to choose what we believe to be important? Religion is important, because if we believe in God and lead a good life...
>
> [Śrīla Prabhupāda:] It is not a question of belief. Do not bring in this question of belief. It is law. For instance, there is a government. You may believe or not believe, but if you break the law, you'll be punished by the government. Similarly, whether you believe or don't believe, there is a God. If you don't believe in God and you independently do whatever you like, then you'll be punished by the laws of nature.
>
> [Mike Robinson:] I see. Does it matter what religion you believe? Would it matter if one was a devotee of Kṛṣṇa?
>
> [Śrīla Prabhupāda:] It is not a question of religion. It is a question of science. You are a spiritual being, but because you are materially conditioned, you are under the laws of material nature. So you may believe in the Christian religion, and I may believe in the Hindu religion, but that does not mean that you are going to become an old man and I am not. We're talking of the science of growing old. This is natural law. It is not that because you are Christian you are becoming old or because I am Hindu I am not becoming old. Everyone is becoming old. So, similarly, all the laws of nature are applicable

---

* While opposing the scientific orthodoxy that promotes atheism and materialism, devotees should take care to not be identified with the type of pseudo-science that purports to prove, for instance, Biblical claims that the world was created 6,000 years ago.

> to everyone. Whether you believe this religion or that religion, it doesn't matter.[1]

A major challenge for devotees in the modern world is to present the message of *śāstra* (as Śrīla Prabhupāda did) in a format meant to appeal to persons without faith in *śāstra*, who believe in analysis and reasoning:

> Those who are preachers in ISKCON will certainly meet many people who believe in intellectual arguments. Most of these people do not believe in the authority of the *Vedas*. Nevertheless, they accept intellectual speculation and argument. Therefore the preachers of Kṛṣṇa consciousness should be prepared to defeat others by argument, just as Śrī Caitanya Mahāprabhu did.[2]

Generally, whenever Śrīla Prabhupāda spoke to people who lacked faith in Vedic pronouncements (which broadly means persons who were neither Hindus nor his disciples), he would argue certain basic principles. Knowing that Kṛṣṇa consciousness is largely unintelligible to persons whose brains are muddled by modern education, Śrīla Prabhupāda nevertheless set about the task of making it intelligible to them. Repeatedly and untiringly, he presented reasons for acknowledging that the living force is distinct from the body, and that no one can honestly deny being controlled by superior powers. To listeners who were sufficiently intelligent and sincere to accept such existential facts, and thereby also to accept him as superior in knowledge, Śrīla Prabhupāda would provide specific information from *śāstra* on those topics and would also explain the relevance of those truths in people's lives.

Following Śrīla Prabhupāda's example, preachers of Kṛṣṇa consciousness seek to disabuse materialistic persons of the multiple misconceptions they are attached to—not an easy task, for the

1 *The Science of Self-realization*, ch. 1 (d).

2 Cc 2.9.49.

Vaiṣṇava understanding directly contradicts all dogmas cherished by materialists. For instance, almost everyone who prides himself on a scientific outlook is unknowingly attached to materialistic credos, beginning with implicit faith in the (supposedly) scientific method and in certain unprovable theorems, such as biological evolution of species. Another widespread error, popular among both materialistic and pseudo-spiritual egalitarians, is the notion that everyone is entitled to his own opinion. Concomitant with this is widespread revulsion against proselytizing and strong persuasion, on the grounds that it is arrogant to consider one's own doctrine superior, for "all opinions are equally valid." Critics uphold that people should be allowed to do as they like, without being bothered by any preaching or proselytizing—based on the myth that everyone is sufficiently intelligent and unbiased to decide what is best for them, and therefore they may impartially be given information and ideas and then themselves decide how to accept it. Of course, such detractors of proselytization contradict themselves by proselytizing against proselytizing.

The taboo against proselytizing is further hypocritical because the educational system, the mass media, and indeed the whole materialistic culture all indoctrinate people from their very birth to fully identify themselves as their bodies, and to unquestioningly believe that life comes from chemicals and that the goal of life is to acquire money for indulgence in sense gratification. When charged with proselytizing, devotees should respond that to urge people to admit that they are facing a dire reality, and to thus exhort them to consider a wholly different approach to life, should not be deemed antisocial, especially when both ribald materialism and standard religious processes have failed to create happiness and peace within human society.*

---

* In this regard, the analogy of the kite-flyer (p. 62) is also relevant.

The task of devotee preachers is to demonstrate how Kṛṣṇa consciousness is factually superior to the tangle of false concepts that people of stultified intelligence accept as their template of reality. Vaiṣṇavas must scientifically establish Kṛṣṇa consciousness as being categorically distinct from both ordinary religious faith (which is changeable*) and all anthropocentric efforts to understand the nature of actuality. Unless devotees present Kṛṣṇa consciousness as *sanātana-dharma*—the eternal, intrinsic characteristic of every living being—people cannot but consider it merely another dogma. This misunderstanding was refuted by Śrīla Prabhupāda:

> [Prof. Hopkins:] Some people see your writings as dogmatic.
>
> [Prabhupāda:] No. You find out any passage in my books that is dogmatic, then you say that it is dogmatic. Any page you open, where is it dogmatic?
>
> [Prof. Hopkins:] Well, dogmatic—to call someone else dogmatic means to start with that you don't agree with what they are saying. If I agree with you and you…
>
> [Prabhupāda:] No, you have to agree. You open any passage of my book.
>
> [Prof. Hopkins:] Well, some people would say to insist that Kṛṣṇa is the only way, that Kṛṣṇa consciousness is the only way…
>
> [Prabhupāda:] No, no. The only thing is that God is one—that you have to accept. God cannot be many. If God has got competitor, then He is not God.
>
> [Prof. Hopkins:] OK.
>
> [Prabhupāda:] So if we don't admit Kṛṣṇa is the only God, then you present who is the only God. You tell me. Either you have to learn from me or I have to learn from you. If you do not know what is God,

---

* Śrīla Prabhupāda succinctly and lucidly establishes this in his introduction to *Bhagavad-gītā As It Is*.

you cannot say, "Kṛṣṇa is not God." As soon as you say, "Kṛṣṇa is not God," that means you must know what is God. You present. But if you cannot present, you say, "No, I do not know God." Then you cannot say, "Kṛṣṇa is not God."

[Prof. Hopkins:] Alright.

[Prabhupāda:] So *they* are dogmatic. Dogmatically they are saying, "Kṛṣṇa is not God." He does not know God and he says, "Kṛṣṇa is not God." So what is this nonsense? You do not know God. How can you say Kṛṣṇa is not God?[1]

In this confrontational dialectic style, Śrīla Prabhupāda revealed all doctrines other than the pure Vaiṣṇava-*siddhānta* as dogmatic, humdrum, ignorant, and unscientific. Devotees must submissively hear from Śrīla Prabhupāda to become convinced that nondevotees are awash in an ocean of unfounded beliefs, having been cheated by deluded intellectuals, scientists, and religionists, all of whose theories are based on disastrously misconceived propositions. Fortified by the pure knowledge of Kṛṣṇa consciousness, particularly as given by Śrīla Prabhupāda in reference to the modern context, devotees can (as did Śrīla Prabhupāda) boldly, clearly, and provocatively challenge the sick status quo. All types of demonic misleaders—religious, political, intellectual, and the rest—should come to fear the Kṛṣṇa consciousness movement as a determined enemy sworn to counter at every step their chronic espousing of deceitful speculations.

1 Conversation, 13 Jul 1975.

FOURTEEN

THE DECLINE OF STRONG SPEAKING IN ISKCON

That which some perceive as fanaticism within our movement originated from Śrīla Prabhupāda himself. Śrīla Prabhupāda was confrontational, and he inculcated an aggressive mood in his disciples. He often spoke of "defeating" others, and particularly liked to meet famous men, to "corner them and defeat them."[1] He regularly railed at the "*karmīs*," whose "nonsense" he never tired of scorning. The black-and-white distinction he made between *karmīs* and devotees helped to keep his disciples alert to the dangers of *māyā*. "Godhead is light. Nescience is darkness. Where there is Godhead there is no nescience."[2] Painting Kṛṣṇa consciousness as white (which it is) and *māyā* as black (which it is) created an atmosphere in ISKCON that was conducive for accepting everything favorable and rejecting everything unfavorable for advancing in Kṛṣṇa consciousness. The original outlook in ISKCON was "Kṛṣṇa consciousness is all there is. Everything else is madness. We have to surrender to Kṛṣṇa and go out preaching to save the *mūḍhas*."

In the years subsequent to Śrīla Prabhupāda's departure from this world, several devotees, observing that our movement's members were generally young, passionate, and immature, decided that

1 *ISKCON in the 1970s*, vol. 1, p. 29.

2 Motto of BTG, derived from Cc 2.22.31.

we should be more mature and balanced. Disturbed by "public disapproval" resulting from "excesses of neophyte proselytising zeal,"[1] such reformers sought to defuse the combative mood and the holier-than-thou mentality. They considered that the bandying of words like *karmīs, mūḍhas, demons,* and *animals* by their compatriots—who themselves were prone to fall back into the very activities they so fiercely vociferated against—was simply the sloganeering of fanatics. These less-militant devotees opined that if ISKCON members are boorish and dismissive of those whom they are supposed to be communicating with—if we so vehemently reject the *karmīs*—then *karmīs* will reciprocally reject us as a cult of moronic, blinkered zombies. Therefore an endeavor was made to instill a more mature, empathic ethos in ISKCON, and to present Kṛṣṇa consciousness in a manner deemed respectable by the *mūḍhas.*

Arguably, in nontraditional climes it makes sense to repackage our message according to the prevailing social milieu and via secular topical issues. Śrīla Prabhupāda himself did so in *Easy Journey to Other Planets,* by using scientific themes and terms for presenting the teachings of the *Bhagavad-gītā.* Śrīla Prabhupāda described the rationale behind that technique:

> The world is most sorely in need of education in Kṛṣṇa consciousness, but due to the ignorance of the age they are not interested in knowledge of the self. So if by labeling the bottle in some way more to attract them we are still able to teach Kṛṣṇa consciousness, let us do it.[2]

Thus it is acceptable to change the packaging, but not the content. Nonetheless, adjustment or understatement of the philosophical content seems to be widespread in ISKCON today. And devotees

1 *The Hare Krishna Movement—The Postcharismatic Fate Of A Religious Transplant,* ed. Edwin F. Bryant and Maria L. Ekstrand (Columbia University Press, 2004), p. 4.

2 Letter, 2 May 1974.

who aspire to follow Śrīla Prabhupāda in the unequivocal manner that he taught are often labeled fanatics or dinosaurs for attempting to do so. Devotees aspire for sophistication and social integration, and all-out attacks on material life have become unfashionable. Controversial topics are tactfully sidestepped, or explained largely in terms of contemporary psychology or political theory rather than via Śrīla Prabhupāda's teachings. Many verses that Śrīla Prabhupāda regularly quoted are rarely heard.* Śrīla Prabhupāda's style of lecturing—didactic, intense, and aimed at educating and convincing the hearers—is now uncommon. Classes by devotees are often hardly what might be expected in a mission meant for ushering in a spiritual revolution for saving the world. Too many discourses consist mostly of stories and jokes, seemingly meant to make the audience feel good rather than offer them vital instruction, more to entertain than to convey the grave message of the *paramparā*. Lectures that previously would have been considered normal are now frowned on as fundamentalist and overbearing. Our movement has become reoriented, publicly acceptable, and staid—no longer a threat to the sinful culture, as it was perceived in the late seventies:

> They are now feeling the weight of this movement. Formerly they thought, "These people come and go," but now they see we are staying. Now we have set fire. It will go on; it cannot be stopped. You can bring big, big fire brigades but the fire will act. The brainwash books are already there. Even if they stop externally, internally it will go on. Our first-class campaign is book distribution. Go house to house. The real fighting is now. Kṛṣṇa will give you all protection. So chant Hare Kṛṣṇa and fight. By propaganda you cannot suppress the truth. You cannot suppress fire by propaganda. Now we have to become strong to defend. The fighting has become acute, but if you stick to the regulative principles, Kṛṣṇa will give all strength. Whatever is

---

* For examples, see pp. 48 and 49.

> done is by Kṛṣṇa's mercy. They are afraid that a different culture is conquering over their culture.[1]

> Men of Kaṁsa's class are very much afraid and are busy trying to stop this movement, especially in the Western countries. One politician has remarked that the Kṛṣṇa consciousness movement is spreading like an epidemic and that if not checked immediately, within ten years it may capture governmental power.[2]

Have we thrown out the baby with the bath water? By overadjusting our former tirade against materialism, we have again become influenced by the superficially broadminded humanistic ethos that we previously rejected, wherein assertiveness and certainty are seen as faults and everyone is entitled to his own view, according to the understanding that there is no fixed reality,* no absolute black or white, just innumerable poorly defined shades of gray. By our becoming a part of society instead of remaining a brave alternative to it, public appreciation of Kṛṣṇa consciousness has not dramatically increased. Rather, in the Western world the Hare Kṛṣṇa movement has largely merged into insignificance.

Although many elements have contributed to the Hare Kṛṣṇa implosion in the West, clearly a major difference between the ISKCON of then and the ISKCON of today is that the daring spirit of challenging the materialistic civilization is now largely absent. But the less we speak our distinct message, the more we lose our distinct identity; the less that there is straightforward scientific delineation of the philosophy of Kṛṣṇa consciousness, the more our movement moves toward the sentimental type of *bhakti* presented by innumerable deviant Hindu groups and gurus, with all their attendant cheapness. Considering that our departure from Śrīla Prabhupāda is already so obvious that several academic scholars

* This understanding is actually demonic. (See Bg 16.8)

1 Letter, 30 Oct 1976.

2 SB 10.2.20, purport.

have written entire books about it,[1] we as a society must decide how serious our commitment is to following Śrīla Prabhupāda in word and deed, and whether our practice of not speaking strongly (as did Śrīla Prabhupāda) is actually the best way to serve him.

---

1 See *Hare Krishna Transformed*, E. Burke Rochford, Jr. (New York University Press, 2007), ch. 6. See also *The Hare Krishna Movement: Forty Years of Chant and Change*, Graham Dwyer and Richard Cole (I.B. Taurus & Co., 2007).

FIFTEEN
DISTURBING OTHERS IS INEVITABLE

প্রাণি-মাত্রে মনো-বাক্যে উদ্বেগ না দিব ।

prāṇi-mātre mano-vākye udvega nā diba

> Neither by mind nor words should a devotee cause anxiety to any living entity.[1]

Devotees in the *sampradāya* of Śrī Caitanya Mahāprabhu certainly respect this order of His, and thus they avoid harming even plants and insects. Yet they more emphasize His instruction to preach the truth of Kṛṣṇa consciousness, so that people may be entirely and eternally relieved of the inevitable disturbances of material existence. And in the course of propagating that truth, sometimes disturbing others becomes unavoidable.

But why (it may be postulated) should we trouble people if they do not trouble us? We do not expect that many will accept our message, so why not just be friendly with people so that they will be friendly with us? If they do not like the truth, why thrust it on them? Why unnecessarily make enemies? Indeed, Kṛṣṇa Himself states that the wise should not unsettle the ignorant.[2] However, Śrīla Prabhupāda has revealed Kṛṣṇa's inner intention:

> Men who are ignorant cannot appreciate activities in Kṛṣṇa consciousness, and therefore Lord Kṛṣṇa advises us not to disturb

1 Cc 2.22.120.

2 Bg 3.29.

> them and simply waste valuable time. But the devotees of the Lord are more kind than the Lord because they understand the purpose of the Lord. Consequently they undertake all kinds of risks, even to the point of approaching ignorant men to try to engage them in the acts of Kṛṣṇa consciousness, which are absolutely necessary for the human being.[1]

The general injunction for *madhyama-adhikārīs* is to preach among favorable people and to avoid inimical persons:

ईश्वरे तदधीनेषु बालिशेषु द्विषत्सु च ।
प्रेममैत्रीकृपोपेक्षा यः करोति स मध्यमः ॥

īśvare tad-adhīneṣu
bāliśeṣu dviṣatsu ca
prema-maitrī-kṛpopekṣā
yaḥ karoti sa madhyamaḥ

> An intermediate, second-class devotee shows love for the Supreme Personality of Godhead, is friendly to all devotees, and is very merciful to neophytes and ignorant people. The intermediate devotee neglects those who are envious of devotional service.[2]

However, Śrīla Prabhupāda once gave a more radical interpretation of this last phrase, explaining it to mean that a preacher should "kick on the face of the atheist."[3] * Similarly, when asked, "Is it alright to disturb the mind of the envious?" Śrīla Prabhupāda replied:

> Everyone is envious. This world is envious. So we have to disturb these envious persons: "Hare Kṛṣṇa!" That is our duty, to disturb

* This is in accord with the dictionary definition of *upekṣā,* which describes the attitude of *madhyama-adhikārīs* toward envious persons: *overlooking, disregard, negligence, indifference, contempt,* or *abandonment.*

1 Bg 3.29, purport.

2 SB 11.2.46, as cited in Cc 2.22.73, purport.

3 Conversation, 7 Oct 1975.

> them. And that is the greatest service. Just like a man is sleeping and somebody is coming to kill him, and other friend: "Mr. Such-and-such! Wake up! Wake up! Wake up!" So he may say, "Why you are disturbing me?" But that is the greatest service; he'll be saved. *Māyā* is coming to kill him, to send him to the darkest region of hell, and you are saving him: "Chant Hare Kṛṣṇa and be saved."[1]

Of course, devotees should not needlessly alienate persons who are neutral and potentially appreciative. Not everyone is an arrant scoundrel, and sincere inquirers deserve personal attention and sympathetic treatment. But what should we do when, for instance, rogues are making a business of cheating innocent spiritual novices and do not honestly respond to fair questioning? We could politely withdraw (and perhaps the neophyte devotee should be advised to do so), but Śrīla Prabhupāda unmistakably wanted better-trained devotees to face up to that type of pseudo-spiritual garbage and to expose such rascals for what they are. Or is there no longer any scope for "kicking the rascals on their face"—as Śrīla Prabhupāda prescribed for the proud, defiant, speculative impersonalists and others who mislead uncounted naive souls? Sometimes a preacher is obliged to disturb others—just as a doctor disturbs a cancer patient by telling him the unwelcome truth of his condition:

> Often persons afflicted with ghastly diseases undergo inconceivable suffering, which ends in death. If a sincere well-wisher points these facts out to them, trying to inform them of the reality, they become angry and accuse him of being a pessimist or a religious fanatic.[2]

> Certainly a [spiritually] diseased person, disturbed by material pangs and devoid of discrimination between the beneficial and the harmful, condemns the medicine and spurns the prescribed diet. Yet it should be known that observance of these is the only means for him to become free from the material pangs and attain pure devotional service.[3]

---

1 Lecture, 30 Dec 1968.

2 SB 11.2.2, purport.

3 Śrīla Bhaktisiddhānta Sarasvatī (*Sajjana-toṣaṇī* 19.452).

The devotees' missionary fervor and persistence are necessary for spreading Kṛṣṇa consciousness, but not everyone will appreciate it:

> They will say, "Why do you bother us? You do your own business. Let us do our own business." But why we are bothering? Because we are servant of Kṛṣṇa. Kṛṣṇa wants that these rascals should be informed. These rascals should be raised from this status of ignorance. That is our mission.[1]

The unmixed approach will inescapably sometimes lead to confrontation:

> We have no business creating enemies, but the process is such that nondevotees will always be inimical toward us. Devotees engaged in preaching should be prepared to be accused by ignorant persons.[2]

> If you become Kṛṣṇa conscious, the whole world will be your enemy. You must be prepared for that.[3]

> [Nondevotees] are simply wasting their time and misleading their followers. When we point this out very plainly to an audience, members of opposing groups become angry at us. But according to the injunctions of the *śāstras*, we cannot make compromises with these so-called *jñānīs, yogīs, karmīs,* and *tapasvīs*.[4]

Devotees need not become upset if in the attempt to present Kṛṣṇa consciousness nondevotees become upset. Those who are actually preachers know that there will always be antagonists and that to pacify them is not always possible. However discreetly or expertly a preacher may present his case, if he is uncompromising then inevitably someone will protest. As Śrīla Bhaktisiddhānta Sarasvatī noted, "An envious person will resent strong preaching by a Vaiṣṇava and disrespect him, considering the devotee to be

1 Lecture, 11 Mar 1975.
2 SB 6.5.39, purport.
3 Lecture, 2 Aug 1974.
4 Cc 1.17.24, purport.

unnecessarily criticizing others."[1] Demons like Śiśupāla (who could not tolerate hearing glorification of Kṛṣṇa) are determined to not become Kṛṣṇa conscious under any circumstances, and they always become agitated whenever the message of *śāstra* is presented without euphemism or embellishment.* In this vein, Śrīla Bhaktisiddhānta Sarasvatī stated:

> In rejecting sense indulgence and instead talking of satisfying Kṛṣṇa's senses, I have become a source of disgruntlement for many. One cannot help becoming the butt of dislike for people absorbed in greed, egoism, prestige, and duplicity.[2]

Unavoidably, candid exposition of the truth necessitates the debunking of all speciousness, and thus tends to create enemies. And the stronger the presentation, the more likelihood of arousing opposition. "As soon as you introduce something strong, there will be fight."[3] The only way to minimize the risk of unfavorable responses is to dilute the message—which under some circumstances might be acceptable,† but which true followers of Śrīla Prabhupāda cannot adopt as a general policy:

> If I criticize them, they become angry. So what can I do? I have to speak the truth. I cannot amalgamate real and nonreal. That is not possible.[4]

> If you call a thief a thief, he will feel insulted. But does it mean that I shall say that "You are very honest?" A thief shall be called thief.[5]

---

* Persons who are determined not to become Kṛṣṇa conscious are described in SB 7.5.30 (quoted on p. 67).

† For examples of circumstances under which prudence and diplomacy might be advisable, see ch. 26, "Discretion and Tact," end of second paragraph.

---

1 SB 11.2.46, commentary.

2 SBV, vol. 1, p. 150.

3 Conversation, 2 Nov 1976.

4 Lecture, 15 Mar 1974.

5 Conversation, 9 Jul 1975.

> We say plainly, "You are all rascals—that's all. You have no discrimination." Anyone who does not believe as it is, he's a rascal, that's all. He may be happy or sorry, you don't mind. You don't make compromise.[1]

> We have to point out their foolishness. That is our business.[2]

Devotees follow the example of Prahlāda, who did not refrain from benefiting Hiraṇyakaśipu, the archetypal materialist, by informing him that he was a misdirected fool and rascal, even though doing so was sure to severely disturb Hiraṇyakaśipu. That inevitably some people will become upset is no grounds for gagging the message of the *paramparā*. Devotees should know that—whatever supposedly altruistic reasons opponents proffer for opposing Kṛṣṇa consciousness—such persons are actually demons whose agenda is to exploit others:

> Rascals and fools ... are trying to obstruct us because if everyone becomes Kṛṣṇa conscious then they can't cheat anyone.[3]

Thus, notwithstanding the ire of the envious, devotees must continue to disturb others by preaching the truth:

> A child is also irritated when he is given instructions, but that does not mean that we should stop.[4]

Even if bluntness will make devotees unpopular, to be unpopular among fools is not bad. What is bad is to acquiesce with foolishness by not speaking against it. After all, nondevotees are certified by *śāstra* to be madmen.[5] However much we try to please such deluded people, we will never be able to satisfy them, for as long as they are not Kṛṣṇa conscious, they must remain dissatisfied.

---

1 Lecture, 23 Mar 1975.

2 Conversation, 10 May 1975.

3 Conversation, 27 Jan 1975.

4 Letter, 30 Sep 1972.

5 SB 5.5.4.

ভুক্তি-মুক্তি-সিদ্ধি-কামী—সকলি 'অশান্ত' ।
bhukti-mukti-siddhi-kāmī—sakali 'aśānta'

> All varieties of nondevotees have material desires and thus cannot be peaceful.[1]

If, in their madness, conditioned souls consider a devotee their worst foe, a dutiful devotee still continues to act as their best friend by unfailingly delivering to them spiritual knowledge as it is. Only devotees can understand that without the liberating knowledge of *śāstra*, madmen are doomed to consider themselves sane and will continue to foist their insanity on others. Therefore devotees must try to save the madmen, notwithstanding their opposition:

> You cannot expect a favorable situation. And still you have to preach. That is preaching. They will speak like madmen, so many things. They are mad, after all. *Nūnaṁ pramattaḥ kurute vikarma yad indriya-prītaya āpṛṇoti.* They have no sense. All materialistic persons are madmen. Still, by the order of superior, Caitanya Mahāprabhu, we have to do this preaching work. Actually, the American boys are fighting against so many unfavorable situations. They are sometimes beaten in the airport—do you know that? Still they are preaching. That is preaching.[2]

Only persons who are not straightforward become perturbed by straightforward delineation of the truth.* Those who become disturbed reveal themselves to be egoistic rascals.

पयःपानं भुजङ्गानां केवलं विषवर्धनम् ।
उपदेशो हि मूर्खाणां प्रकोपाय न शान्तये ॥

* My experience throughout many years of straightforward speaking is that devotees within ISKCON, on the grounds that the general populace will become disturbed, are more likely to become irritated by strong words than are nondevotees. In fact, that very observation was a major factor in prompting me to write this book.

1 Cc 2.19.149.

2 Conversation, 8 Aug 1976.

payaḥ-pānaṁ bhujaṅgānāṁ
kevalaṁ viṣa-vardhanam
upadeśo hi mūrkhāṇāṁ
prakopāya na śāntaye

Just as feeding milk to a snake only increases its venomous poison, to give good counsel to a foolish person causes him to become more angry.[1]

Let the rascals become angry. The so-called leaders and experts are simply bluffing and cheating people. They should be exposed by challenging them with the sword of śāstric knowledge.

1 *Hitopadeśa.*

SIXTEEN

PUBLIC OPINION: OPPOSITION IS OUR VICTORY

> Why do you bother about people who are against us? As there are some people against us, there are many people for us. That is the position in every field of activity. If somebody is against us, why should we bother about it?[1]

Many devotees today apparently believe that the main goal of ISKCON's "outreach" (a word that in some quarters has largely superseded the word *preaching*) is to create a good impression. It is indeed preferable that the public should come to consider devotees as being genial and friendly. However, those who claim to be followers of Śrīla Prabhupāda should actually follow him by following his example of interacting with others not simply to leave a good impression, but to effect a change in their consciousness.

Obviously, the full, undiluted message of Kṛṣṇa consciousness will not be easily accepted. But without the earnest attempt to instill it in others, there is no meaning to preaching:

> Why do you expect that every man will immediately agree with you? That is foolishness. You must know that everybody will disagree with you, and it is your preaching work that you will make him agree with you. We do not expect that everyone will agree. Everybody will disagree. Just like our books—four, five years ago, nobody knew these

1 Conversation, 13 Jul 1975.

> books. So there was no market. But we have created our market. That is preaching. We have created our market. Nobody was dying for want of these books. So that is preaching. Preaching does not mean everyone is ready to accept your theories. You must expect that everyone will not accept it. Now it is your power to convince him, "Yes, you must accept." That is preaching.[1]

Simply to make people generally favorable is insufficient; they must be given our message. Better to convey the message and become unpopular, rather than be popular for superficial reasons but with our teachings not communicated.

> Our Kṛṣṇa consciousness movement is a protest against all this nonsense, and therefore we are unpopular. But we don't care for that. Popular or unpopular, we must go on with our business.[2]

Indeed, if demons become annoyed it is likely a sign that our preaching is to the point. As Śrīla Prabhupāda pronounced, "Opposition is our victory."[3]

Considering that the Kṛṣṇa consciousness movement is meant to oppose everything held dear by the demons (beginning with meat-eating, gambling, illicit sex, intoxication, and all forms of impersonalism and cheating religiosity), if demons do not oppose us it indicates that they deem us insignificant and unthreatening—which means that we are not doing our job properly.*

It is nothing new that many people consider the lifestyle and practices of devotees to be radical and extreme. In all times, places,

* Devotees have also come under public scrutiny for genuine deviations from proper behavioral norms. For instance, in recent times devotees have sensibly acknowledged that widespread concern about child abuse within ISKCON schools was not simply the ranting of oppositional voices but a serious call for devotees to expunge demonic activities within their own ranks.

1 Conversation, 11 Dec 1973.

2 Lecture, 13 Dec 1970.

3 Conversation, 9 Jan 1977.

and circumstances throughout human history, the path of utter surrender to Kṛṣṇa has been in opposition to those of materialists, renouncers, and pseudodevotees. Tension between devotees and nondevotees existed at the time of Prahlāda Mahārāja, existed at the time of Śrī Caitanya Mahāprabhu, and will always exist if devotees actually live as devotees.

> When Lord Caitanya Mahāprabhu started the *saṅkīrtana* movement, even He was unnecessarily criticized by Māyāvādīs, atheists, and fools. Naturally we are also criticized by such men. They will always remain and will always criticize anything that is actually good for human society. But the preachers of the *saṅkīrtana* movement should not be deterred by such criticism.[1]

Even devotees who do not preach will be harrassed by demons, who cannot tolerate seeing others "spoil their lives" by abjuring sense gratification and worshiping a God whom the atheists deem to be mythical. So devotees who wish to stick to their principles may have to tolerate being viewed as odd or antisocial.

However, that people react to devotees, even negatively, means that devotees are making an impression. Indeed, the more that others are upset, the more they indirectly acknowledge the significance of the devotees and their teachings. Although opponents are unlikely to admit it, their strongly adverse responses show that they cannot ignore the devotees, and also suggest that they fear the devotees' message and very existence as a severe challenge to all the falsity in which nondevotees have invested.

In the sixties, Śrīla Prabhupāda was pleased to hear that Alan Watts, a prominent atheistic author, had become indignant when asked to review Śrīla Prabhupāda's original *Bhagavad-gītā* manuscript. Śrīla Prabhupāda commented, "Our preaching is proved successful when the demons are disturbed."[2]

---

1 Cc 1.9.53, purport.

2 *My Glorious Master*, p. 353.

We must remember that such incidents [as Chand Kazi's objections to *saṅkīrtana*] took place in the past, five hundred years ago, and the fact that they are still going on indicates that our *saṅkīrtana* movement is really authorized, for if *saṅkīrtana* were an insignificant material affair, demons would not object to it. The demons of the time tried to obstruct the *saṅkīrtana* movement started by Śrī Caitanya Mahāprabhu. Similar demons are trying to obstruct the *saṅkīrtana* movement we are executing all over the world, and this proves that our *saṅkīrtana* movement is still pure and genuine, following in the footsteps of Śrī Caitanya Mahāprabhu.[1]

As soon as you become successful, there will be many enemies. That is natural. That is the sign of success.[2]

Unless there is opposition it is not genuine. It is not genuine or it is not serious. Opposition must be there.[3]

When asked, "What if people don't want to hear our message?" Śrīla Prabhupāda replied:

The people might not understand our message, but Kṛṣṇa will be pleased. And that is our mission. They thought Jesus Christ's mission was stopped. They killed him. But his mission was attained. He preached three years only, but so many followers. He pleased Kṛṣṇa. We must not be disappointed that no one is hearing Kṛṣṇa consciousness. We will say it to the moon and stars and all directions. We will cry in the wilderness, because Kṛṣṇa is everywhere. We want to get a certificate from Kṛṣṇa, that "This man has done something for Me." Not popularity. If a pack of asses says you are good, what is that? We have to please Kṛṣṇa's senses with purified senses.[4]

Our mission is to see that Lord Caitanya is satisfied, never mind if we could not turn many of them to this cult. By the order of Caitanya Mahāprabhu, we shall try to teach people about the *Bhagavad-gītā* and *Śrīmad-Bhāgavatam*, etc., without being depressed whether

1 Cc 1.17.127, purport.

2 Conversation, 3 Nov 1973.

3 Conversation, 9 Jan 1977.

4 *Prabhupāda-līlā*, 7-3: "A Visit to Boston, 1968."

> people are accepting them or not. This is our credit. We shall be judged by the quality of our work and not by the material return.[1]

Certainly, the aim of preaching is to bring people to devotional service, not to deliberately drive them away. And the knowledge that people need to hear is unlikely to be as well-received as the nonsense that they prefer to hear. Still, the truth must be spoken even though demons will become angry and the insincere will melt away upon being confronted with the truth. But the gain, which makes worthwhile all the difficulties that are inevitable in straightforward preaching, is that sincere people come forward and accept Kṛṣṇa consciousness as it is. Real preaching polarizes. Just as the appearance of Kṛṣṇa in this world instigates the demons to harrass the devotees, until Kṛṣṇa intervenes and renders His devotees victorious, so also do demons become riled upon His appearance in the form of the pure Hari-*kīrtana* of uncompromised propagation of His glories. Such polarization forces genuine devotees to walk the walk by increasing their surrender to Kṛṣṇa, being confident that Kṛṣṇa will protect them. Devotees who are not fully surrendered prefer to live more comfortably by deliberately not invoking opposition, but such comfort is their downfall. Better is to accept the challenges that compel one to surrender.

It may be postulated that if by going with the flow of public opinion—adjusting to, rather than challenging, popular sentiments—numerous people start to chant Hare Kṛṣṇa, is that not successful preaching? Is it not better to try to encourage many individuals to practice devotional service at some level rather than to remain an obscure sect preoccupied with its own little world? However, to accommodate the worldliness of nondevotees was not the policy of those great *ācāryas* who were most succesful in widely propagating Kṛṣṇa consciousness. As was said of Śrīla Bhaktisiddhānta Sarasvatī:

---

1 Letter, 21 May 1973.

> If he would just be a little more sensitive to public opinion and more positive in his outlook, if he would look for the good in others and not grouse so much, and not be so insistent on always speaking the straight facts, then surely today no other religious leader would have as many supporters as he.[1]

Undoubtedly, the pristine message of the *ācāryas* is a tough one to market. Remove the bite—those aspects that make people feel uncomfortable—and preaching becomes so much easier. But there is little meaning in propagating a message so denatured that it has negligible spiritual impact. Faithful servants of the *ācāryas* never consider tweaking their instructions to gain widespread acceptance.

Even if millions of people were to start chanting Hare Kṛṣṇa, if whole nations were to declare allegiance to Śrīla Prabhupāda, if the world's richest people were to dedicate their resources in the service of ISKCON, we still will have failed in our duty if our presentation was not fully in accord with guru, sadhu, and *śāstra*—just as several *apa-sampradāyas* are constituted of numerous members who chant the holy names and claim to be followers of Śrī Caitanya Mahāprabhu yet, due to their being philosophically and behaviorally deviant, are rejected as bogus by genuine devotees of Mahāprabhu. Hence, if like the *apa-sampradāyas* we do not clearly distinguish pure devotional service from karma, *jñāna*, and yoga, then widespread acceptance of Kṛṣṇa consciousness is not success but failure. For instance, we can expect to gain public approval by emphasizing bodily and social welfare work, or by portraying Kṛṣṇa consciousness not as the ultimate truth but as one path among many (which smacks of Māyāvāda). But better that we adhere to the spirit of the *paramparā*. As Śrīla Prabhupāda repeatedly emphasized, preaching is to be judged by quality, not merely quantity.[2] He would compare the preaching of Kṛṣṇa consciousness to selling diamonds: "When you are selling

1 SBV, vol. 1, p. 151.

2 E.g.: Conversation, 9 Jun 1974.

diamonds, you don't expect many customers. But if you are giving cut glass, the fools will come. We have a very precious thing—this Kṛṣṇa consciousness movement. Don't expect that all the foolish people will take to it."[1] Śrīla Prabhupāda also often quoted, *ekaś candras tamo hanti na ca tārāḥ sahasraśaḥ:* "Darkness is dissipated, not by thousands of stars, but by one moon."[2] Thus:

> It is not that we should compromise to attract the mass—we are after the class.[3]
>
> We have not very many followers because we disagree with all rascals. We are not rascals.[4]
>
> Stop all this rascaldom. That is our challenge. We may not have many followers. We don't care for that. We don't want these nonsense followers, many thousands. What they will do? But if we can turn one man into Kṛṣṇa consciousness perfectly, he can do tremendous work in the world. That is our principle. We don't want nonsense.[5]
>
> We want a few selected men, not a big crowd.[6]
>
> Don't be misled by the bogus. Stick to your own principles. People may come or may not come. We don't care for them. We must speak the right truth.[7]

Referring to Śrīla Prabhupāda's public lectures in Mumbai in 1975, Girirāja Swami observed:

> Prabhupāda was speaking so powerfully that I knew that what he was saying would be hard for many of the audience to accept. If Prabhupāda had wanted to flatter the audience or compromise his philosophy, he could have attracted millions of followers. But because he was preaching so boldly and forcefully without compromise, many

---

1 SPl ch. 30, "London: A Dream Fulfilled."

2 Cāṇakya's *Nīti-śāstra.*

3 Letter, 15 Nov 1971.

4 Conversation, 18 Sep 1973.

5 Lecture, 23 Nov 1968.

6 *TKG's Diary,* 16 May.

7 Conversation, 20 May 1975.

of the audience did not like it, because it was a challenge to their sense gratification and to their sentiment.[1]

Considering that Śrīla Prabhupāda's whole purpose was to bring people to Kṛṣṇa consciousness, why did he not take this opportunity to enroll as his followers many of that large group of people, who had come to hear him (presumably) because they were favorable to his mission and ready to accept his teachings, at least to some extent? It appears, as Girirāja Swami has hinted, that Śrīla Prabhupāda wanted to raise the audience beyond a sentimental, compromised acceptance of Kṛṣṇa consciousness and bring them to the level of pure devotional service, and for that purpose he attempted to expose and eliminate their deep-rooted mundane attachments and misconceptions.

Śrīla Prabhupāda never accepted the policy of becoming acceptable to the public by not disturbing them, which converts the devotee into a servant of popular opinion rather than a servant of Kṛṣṇa. Materialistic people may occasionally offer such compromised devotees a pat on the head, while mostly ignoring them. Better to be disliked than unknown. When once informed of negative news articles, Śrīla Prabhupāda said they were a good sign that the public was feeling pressure from us. When then asked if we should not worry about bad publicity, Śrīla Prabhupāda replied, "Why worry about news articles? The day will come when they will fire on you. You have to be prepared."[2]

Following Śrīla Prabhupāda's example, bold preachers are fearless in the face of opposition; far from being intimidated, they thrive on it. Contrary to those devotees who scrupulously try to escape controversy, Śrīla Prabhupāda often courted it. He sometimes made his point in a manner practically guaranteed to alienate

1 SPl ch. 33, "A Lot of Ground to Be Covered."

2 *ISKCON in the 1970s*, vol. 1, p. 162.

large sections of the public, as in his condemnation of feminism and his quarreling onstage with a hippie. After the interview in which a female reporter left in disgust, Satsvarūpa Dāsa Goswami asked Śrīla Prabhupāda, "If we speak these things on television and the newspapers and people become angry, if all the people become angry like she does, is it still good propaganda for us?" Śrīla Prabhupāda replied:

> No, then we chant Hare Kṛṣṇa. We don't make disturbance. But in the *Bhagavad-gītā* everything is discussed, this *varṇa-saṅkara* and the first-class man, second-class man.* If we have to push on the Kṛṣṇa consciousness movement, then we have to discuss. But if they do not like, better chant Hare Kṛṣṇa and don't discuss anything. But these things are discussed. If you are not agreeable to hear from *Bhagavad-gītā,* then let us chant together Hare Kṛṣṇa, that's all. But these things are discussed in the *Bhagavad-gītā,* about *varṇa-saṅkara.* If the *varṇa-saṅkara* population is increased, then it becomes hell. So if you want to increase the hellish person, then don't discuss. But if you think it is a problem, then discuss.[1]

This response might seem ambiguous. In essence, Śrīla Prabhupāda stated, "We do not want to disturb you if you do not want to consider these points, but to push on the Kṛṣṇa consciousness movement we have to discuss them, and actually you should also be sensible enough to understand the need to examine these topics."

Thus it is understood that Śrīla Prabhupāda did not want to become controversial simply to attract publicity, or for other wrong reasons. His criterion was whatever is best to spread and establish Kṛṣṇa's message within the world. Śrīla Prabhupāda chose his controversies carefully, and sometimes deliberately

---

* *Varṇa-saṅkara*—children conceived without regard for Vedic religious principles, and thus of sinful inclination.

---

1 Conversation, 9 Jul 1975.

downplayed contentious issues.* When informed of widespread public dissatisfaction with devotees' collection techniques, he instructed:

> Everyone should adore our members as honest. If we do something which is deteriorating to the popular sentiments of the public in favor of our movement, that is not good. Somehow or other we should not become unpopular in the public eye.[1]

Clearly, Śrīla Prabhupāda was not wholly insensitive to public opinion. Yet it was not his guiding principle:

> Our process is to show Kṛṣṇa consciousness as it is, not as others want to see it. By showing Kṛṣṇa consciousness in this way, you are making the thing less important.[2]

Śrīla Prabhupāda advocated gaining public acceptance by another, radical method:

> I am not much fond of the idea of changing things to accommodate the public—better to change the public to accommodate us.[3]

The path of satisfying God and that of gratifying the public rarely converge, and usually they are opposed. Those who serve public opinion can never properly serve Kṛṣṇa. Those who are too anxious about being accepted by the misguided general populace cannot offer it any real welfare. Hence Śrīla Prabhupāda sharply criticized the predilection for being concerned about vox populi:

> What is the value of opinion if the people are all asses? There is no opinion. One should take as it is enjoined in the *śāstra*—no opinion. What is the use of taking opinion of an ass? So the people are trained up just like dogs and asses, then what is the use of their

* For instance, see his response to a letter of protest from Sumati Morarji, p. 189.

1 Letter, 9 Jan 1975.

2 Letter, 28 Dec 1971.

3 Letter, 28 Dec 1971.

> opinion? If you are to enforce, you must do like this. Just like when we introduced this "No illicit sex," I never cared for their opinion. The opinion, immediately there will be discussion. And what is the use of taking their opinion? It must be done. That is the defect of Western civilization. Vox populi, taking opinion of the public. But what is the value of this public? Drunkards, smokers, meat-eaters, woman-hunters. They are not first-class men. So what is the use of such third-class, fourth-class men's opinion? We do not advocate such opinion. What Kṛṣṇa said, that is standard—that's all. Kṛṣṇa is the Supreme, and His version is final.[1]

It is the duty of the genuine devotee to always choose the path of satisfying God, even by passing his whole life battling the relentless waves of popular opinion. A real devotee lives by the conviction that it is better to present the unadulterated truth—even if no one accepts it or he becomes the object of scorn for doing so—than to dispense a diluted message that many respond favorably toward:

> We are not after vox populi. That is not our concern. We have got our standard method. That is making us successful. We do not make any compromise. This is our method. If you like, you take it. If you don't like, you go away.[2]

An anecdote from New York, 1966:

> To speak ill of sexual pleasure was certainly not a strategic move for one who wanted to create followers among the Lower East Side hippies. But Prabhupāda never considered changing his message. In fact, when Umāpati had mentioned that Americans didn't like to hear that sex was only for conceiving children, Prabhupāda had replied, "I cannot change the philosophy to please the Americans."[3]

Śrīla Prabhupāda often quoted the following prayer of Prahlāda Mahārāja to Nṛsiṁha-deva:

---

1 Conversation, 21 May 1975.

2 Ibid.

3 SPl ch. 21, "Beyond the Lower East Side."

एवं जनं निपतितं प्रभवाहिकूपे
कामाभिकाममनु यः प्रपतन् प्रसङ्गात् ।
कृत्वात्मसात्सुरर्षिणा भगवन् गृहीतः
सोऽहं कथं नु विसृजे तव भृत्यसेवाम् ॥

evaṁ janaṁ nipatitaṁ prabhavāhi-kūpe
kāmābhikāmam anu yaḥ prapatan prasaṅgāt
kṛtvātmasāt surarṣiṇā bhagavan gṛhītaḥ
so 'haṁ kathaṁ nu visṛje tava bhṛtya-sevām

My dear Lord, O Supreme Personality of Godhead, because of my association with material desires, one after another, I was gradually falling into a blind well full of snakes, following the general populace. But Your servant Nārada Muni kindly accepted me as his disciple and instructed me how to achieve this transcendental position. Therefore, my first duty is to serve him. How could I leave his service?[1]

It is most regrettable that some devotees, having once been saved by Śrīla Prabhupāda from following the general populace, have become reconverted into mediocre members of the public and are no longer surrendered servants of the Vaiṣṇavas. The goal of a committed devotee is not to satisfy people whose minds are distorted by material desires and misconceptions. Rather, he attempts to remove those impurities by hacking at their root: envy of Kṛṣṇa. It is farcical if, on the plea of making others favorable, devotees adopt a policy of suppressing the teachings of Kṛṣṇa consciousness or if they act contrarily to its principles. Those who thus pander to the imbecility of envious persons are not actual devotees, but traitors.

1 SB 7.9.28.

SEVENTEEN

CRITICISM, FAULTFINDING, AND JUDGMENTALISM

A devotee never tries to agitate others or criticize them unnecessarily.

This was stated by Śrīla Bhaktisiddhānta Sarasvatī in his commentary on verses 11.11.29–32 of *Śrīmad-Bhāgavatam*. The word *unnecessarily* implies that criticism is sometimes necessary. Blanket application of the principle of non-criticism would not only be impractical but also dangerous, for it would obfuscate distinctions between good and bad, right and wrong. Moreover, to suspend appropriate discrimination would mean that no standards could be set, thus rendering our preaching mission ineffectual. For instance, there would be no criteria for judging who is fit or unfit for initiation or for living in an ashram. Thus in this context *unnecessarily* can be understood to mean that a devotee should not criticize others or risk agitating them unless they or yet others can be benefited by so doing.

In his commentary on those verses (SB 11.11.29–32), Śrīla Bhaktisiddhānta Sarasvatī also stated: "A devotee, unable to tolerate seeing how the world populace is merged in ignorance and is suffering the whiplashes of *māyā*, busily engages in distributing Kṛṣṇa consciousness." Such preaching necessarily entails pointing out all that is errant and all that should be given up, as well as exposing cheaters and their cheating. Indeed, it is the duty of a devotee to discriminate between proper and improper, just as a swan extracts milk from a mixture of milk and water. Śrīla

Prabhupāda warned against suspending one's discrimination so as to appear mild and moderate:

> A good man or woman accepts anything very easily, but a man of average intelligence does not do so. But, anyway, we should not give up our reason and discriminatory power just to be gentle. One must have good discriminatory power to judge a thing on its merit. We should not follow the mild nature of a woman and thereby accept that which is not genuine.[1]

Although it might appear to be lofty, non-judgmentalism is actually a high-sounding cover for condoning rascaldom. Although to refrain from making "value judgments" is considered nigh sacrosanct by modern pluralistic man, Kṛṣṇa describes as demonic those persons who do not distinguish between proper and improper action.[2] Non-judgmentalism is actually compounded rascality, for it lends to rascality a false aura of acceptability and even nobility. In secular society, (and sometimes also among devotees), non-judgmentalism is an excuse to gloss over a host of sins, as is apparent in today's widespread sanction of social evils such as illicit sex, abortion, and divorce.

Various demons adopt this so-called non-judgmentalism because they want to redefine morality in terms of gratifying every illicit bodily and mental urge that they are addicted to. As humanists, they believe there is nothing higher than themselves and accordingly that there cannot be anything terribly wrong with their own vices. Most putative non-judgmentalists are non-judgmental only of others who tolerate their hypocrisy, and they will lambast anyone who opposes them.

Actually, non-judgmentalism is an absurd proposition, for no one in this world can live for a moment without constantly evaluating everything that he comes in contact with or hears about. Absolute non-judgmentalism would require the suspension of all legal

1 SB 1.7.42, purport.

2 Bg 16.7.

systems, thus extending a carte blanche to reprobate criminals. Clearly, the line must be drawn somewhere, and to delineate exactly where requires making value judgments. Actually, the plea for non-judgmentalism is actuated by a misconceived sense of fairness born of intellectual and ethical laziness. Certainly one should be fair to others, but that should be in accordance with the standards of right and wrong prescribed by *śāstra*, not those of humanists, atheists, and other relativists who—impelled by the Māyāvāda of not admitting any distinctions—recognize no ultimate right or wrong. Thus they tend to blur the distinction between vice and virtue, or wholly redefine them—for instance, by insisting that sexual promiscuity is a natural right and that opposition to it is an injustice.

Devotees who are enthralled by the fallacy of non-judgmentalism cite it to illegitimately legitimize certain behavior (such as mixing loosely with the opposite sex, or eating food cooked by nondevotees) that by proper Vaiṣṇava judgment should be considered illegitimate. Overlooking the fact that non-judgmentalism is entirely contrary to Śrīla Prabhupāda's teachings and praxis, some who tout it claim support from *Śrīmad-Bhāgavatam* (11.28.1–2):

श्रीभगवानुवाच
परस्वभावकर्माणि न प्रशंसेन्न गर्हयेत् ।
विश्वमेकात्मकं पश्यन् प्रकृत्या पुरुषेण च ॥

śrī-bhagavān uvāca
para-svabhāva-karmāṇi
na praśaṁsen na garhayet
viśvam ekātmakaṁ paśyan
prakṛtyā puruṣeṇa ca

The Supreme Personality of Godhead said: One should neither praise nor blame the conditioned nature and activities of other persons. Rather, one should see this world as simply the combination of material nature and the enjoying souls, all based on the one Absolute Truth.*

परस्वभावकर्माणि यः प्रशंसति निन्दति ।
स आशु भ्रश्यते स्वार्थादसत्यभिनिवेशतः ॥

para-svabhāva-karmāṇi
yaḥ praśaṁsati nindati
sa āśu bhraśyate svārthād
asaty abhiniveśataḥ

The *jñānī* who indulges in praising or criticizing the qualities and behavior of others will quickly fall from his position of *jñāna* by his entanglement in illusory dualities.†

Śrīla Viśvanātha Cakravartī explains that these verses explain *jñāna-yoga* of the Advaita (Māyāvāda) philosophy and are particularly aimed at adherents of that path. Nevertheless, Śrīla Bhaktisiddhānta Sarasvatī has cited the first of the above-cited verses to warn against blasphemy of devotees.[1] Of the two injunctions, the one proscribing criticism is more important than that proscribing praise.[2] Thus non-judgmentalism is valid in the sense that one should not be quick to condemn, but rather, with a generous and unbiased heart one should evaluate all sides of an issue before coming to a conclusion about any alleged wrong.

And of course, a devotee should glorify Vaiṣṇavas and be cautious not to unnecessarily criticize them. But these verses should be understood in context, for the overall message of *Śrīmad-Bhāgavatam* and of all Vaiṣṇava *ācāryas* is highly critical of all

* This is the BBT translation, except that *garhayet* (translated as criticize) is herein rendered as the stronger and more accurate word blame.

† This translation, by Bhānu Swami, is based on Śrīla Viśvanātha Cakravartī's commentary.

1 *Śrī Caitanya-bhāgavata* 2.13.43, commentary.

2 Cc 3.8.79.

that is nondevotional and pseudo-devotional.* Therefore this injunction should be accepted as a proscription of criticism enacted from the mundane platform:

'দ্বৈতে' ভদ্রাভদ্র-জ্ঞান, সব-'মনোধর্ম' ।
'এই ভাল, এই মন্দ'—এই সব 'ভ্রম' ॥

'dvaite' bhadrābhadra-jñāna, saba—'manodharma'
'ei bhāla, ei manda',—ei saba 'bhrama'

> In the material world, conceptions of good and bad are all mental speculations. Therefore, saying "This is good" and "This is bad" is all a mistake.[1]

In other words, a transcendentalist should not make distinctions based on notions of material sense enjoyment, such as considering one woman to be beautiful and therefore desirable, and another woman to be ugly and therefore undesirable. As Śrīla Prabhupāda explained in his purport to the above verse:

> When one is absorbed in the illusory energy of Kṛṣṇa and cannot understand Kṛṣṇa, one cannot ascertain what is good for him and what is bad. Conceptions of good and bad are all imaginations or mental speculations. When one forgets that he is an eternal servant of Kṛṣṇa, he wants to enjoy the material world through different plans. At that time he distinguishes between material plans that are good and those that are bad. Actually, however, they are all false.

So it is not that criticism is wholly prohibited, but one should know what and how to criticize, in terms of śāstric injunctions. As stated by Śrīla Bhaktivinoda Ṭhākura:

> The faults of others can be deliberated upon if one has a virtuous motive. We should consider that, without the right motive, it is inappropriate to reflect, even impartially, upon the faults of any living

* See Cc 3.8.79, purport. See also the sentence beginning "A true devotee's praise ..." p. 141.

1 Cc 3.4.176.

being, what to speak of Vaiṣṇavas. To blaspheme pure Vaiṣṇavas is an offense, but even blaspheming other *jīvas* is a sin. Vaiṣṇavas have no interest in performing such a sinful act. However, provided one has the right motive, the scriptures have not condemned a careful critique of someone's faults. Proper motive is of three types: desiring the welfare of the person criticized, desiring the welfare of the world and desiring one's own welfare. There are three types of proper motive:

(1) If the intention in analyzing someone's sins is to ensure that he attains his ultimate welfare, then such reflection is auspicious.

(2) If the motive behind reflecting on someone's sins is to benefit the entire world, then this is to be counted as an auspicious act.

(3) If such reflection is undertaken for one's own spiritual welfare, then also it is auspicious. There is no fault in such reflection.

When a disciple humbly asks his spiritual master to instruct him on how to identify a Vaiṣṇava, the spiritual master, desiring the welfare of his disciple and of the whole world, explains that those who exhibit unholy behaviour are non-Vaiṣṇavas. He thus points out how to identify true Vaiṣṇavas through antithesis. With the motive of encouraging one to accept the shelter of the lotus feet of a true Vaiṣṇava by abandoning false, so-called preachers of religion, one neither risks committing blasphemy of saints (*sādhu-nindā*) nor Vaiṣṇava-*aparādha*. In such cases, even criticism directed at a specific person is free from fault. These are all examples of criticizing with the proper motive.[1]

Considering all these points, it is impertinent, if not mendacious, to claim, on the basis of skewed assumptions derived from verses such as the above (SB 11.28.1–2), that the message of *śāstra* is one of unqualified non-criticism. In Vedic culture, no one would dare broadcast a conclusion without first having assiduously performed *śravaṇa-manana-nididhyāsana*—hearing the purport of *śāstra* explained by a qualified guru, endeavoring to comprehend that

---

1 *Sajjana-toṣaṇī*, 5.5.

instruction, and deeply reflecting on it over a prolonged period.* However, it is yet another curse of this accursed age that persons who were raised on cartoons and popcorn, who are ignorant of the depth and profundity of *śāstra* and the explications of the *ācāryas*, mindlessly mask their own shallowness under the guise of sacred authority.

Non-judgmentalism is often upheld by an analogy common in the modern West, and a favorite of some devotees: "When you point your finger, there's always three pointed back at you."[1]

> A lot of times what happens when we condemn other people is that we're condemning precisely what's wrong with ourselves. That's why it's said that when you point your finger at someone, three fingers of your hand are pointing right back at you.[2]

In contemporary psychology, such a mindset is called "projection," by which hypercritical persons ascribe their own inadequacies to others. This is redolent of the Sanskrit saying *ātmavan manyate jagat:* thinking everyone else to be like oneself. Yet it would be ridiculous to attribute this supposed syndrome to every person who draws attention to others' errors, as if only those who point out faults are at fault. Certainly it is wrong to criticize that which should not be criticized, but it is also wrong to fail to criticize that which should be criticized. Indeed, the preacher of Kṛṣṇa consciousness, whom Kṛṣṇa considers the best of all people, is obliged to point out defects:[3]

> [Prabhupāda:] The position of the preacher is *madhyama-adhikārī*. Therefore they have to point out, "Here is a jealous man, envious man." But people do not want it. They say, "Why you are pointing

* *Śravaṇa, manana,* and *nididhyāsana* are common terms in Vedantic discourse, derived from *Bṛhad-āraṇyaka Upaniṣad* (6.5.6).

1 Verbatim quotation from BTG 35-03 (2001).

2 BTG 25-06 (1991).

3 "The preacher ... people"—See Bg 18.69.

out?" But this is business of the preacher; otherwise how will he preach?

[Girirāja:] They want to be artificially the *uttama-adhikārī*, to see everyone as nice.

[Prabhupāda:] Yes, everyone as nice, except himself. [That is] *uttama-adhikārī* vision, that everyone is nice. Then [you should accept that] the preacher is also nice. Why do you find fault with the preacher? Imitation *uttama-adhikārī* will not help.[1]

By *uttama-adhikārī* vision, Śrīla Prabhupāda refers to that whereby an "advanced devotee sees that everyone is a devotee except himself. The advanced devotee sees that he is not a devotee, but all others are devotees."[2] To be uncritical and to see only the good in others is the natural decoration of a *paramahaṁsa*, who is above all distinctions and is aloof from the world:

It is a qualification of a Vaiṣṇava that he is *adoṣa-darśī:* he never sees others' faults. Of course, every human being has both good qualities and faults. Therefore it is said, *saj-janā guṇam icchanti doṣam icchanti pāmarāḥ:* everyone has a combination of faults and glories. But a Vaiṣṇava, a sober man, accepts only a man's glories and not his faults, for flies seek sores whereas honeybees seek honey.[3]

A devotee never finds fault with others, but tries to find his own and thus rectify them as far as possible.[4]

These statements, although apparently unequivocally proscribing faultfinding, have to be taken in context and reconciled with the many seemingly opposite instructions. It is not a devotee's nature to look for faults (to "seek sores") or to wrongly ascribe faults to others, but still it is his duty to point out genuine faults wherever

---

1 Conversation, 7 Apr 1974.

2 Lecture, 5 Dec 1974 (derived from SB 11.2.45).

3 Cc 1.8.62, purport.

4 SB 1.13.33, purport.

they exist.* It is also necessary that more advanced devotees criticize neophytes, to reveal and dismantle their anarthas. Particularly, those who have taken the responsibility of acting as guru show "no mercy" toward their disciples' mundane attachments:

> To cut something, a sharp instrument is required; and to cut the mind from its attachments, sharp words are often required. The *sādhu* or teacher shows no mercy in using sharp words to sever the student's mind from material attractions. By speaking the truth uncompromisingly, he is able to sever the bondage. For example, at the very beginning of *Bhagavad-gītā* Kṛṣṇa speaks sharply to Arjuna by telling him that although he speaks like a learned man, he is actually fool number one. If we actually want detachment from this material world, we should be prepared to accept such cutting words from the spiritual master.[1]

This poses a dilemma, for faultfinding is direly warned against in Vaiṣṇava *śāstras*. Faultfinding vitiates the atmosphere within Vaiṣṇava society and can swiftly destroy an aspiring devotee's spiritual advancement. Thus all devotees, and especially neophytes (many of whom are particularly prone to this dangerous tendency), need to be gravely cautioned against it. But to overly emphasize non-criticism—to the extent of stating that devotees should never, under any circumstances, see wrong in anyone—means to forever keep devotees as blind, unthinking (and thus easily manipulated) *kaniṣṭha-adhikārīs*. On the one hand, devotees are not to find faults in other Vaiṣṇavas (particularly seniors), and on the other hand, they are not to stand by idly and watch speculations and deviations cause defilement of the *paramparā*. Vaiṣṇava etiquette is misunderstood and misapplied if the principle of not finding fault is overstressed to the extent of violating another essential principle—that of trying to enlighten people who are on a wrong

* The reasoning for this parallels the discussion on unnecessary criticism that opens this chapter and continues throughout it.

1 *Perfection of Yoga*, ch. 4.

path. This is similar to not trying to prevent a blind man from falling into a ditch on the plea of not interfering with his right to walk wherever he pleases. If the śāstric injunction against finding fault is overemphasized to the degree that it becomes impossible to question whether a person or group is acting against the tenets of *śāstra*, then devotees are no longer seeing through the eyes of *śāstra*, for they have accepted only one teaching of *śāstra* while disregarding another. This is *ardha-kukkuṭī-nyāya* (half-hen logic), analogous to decapitating a chicken so as to not have to feed it yet vainly expecting to still procure eggs from its rear—a maxim that portrays the futility in accepting some scriptural teachings while whimsically rejecting others.

Similarly, unity is not desirable if it requires compromising the basic tenets of Śrīla Prabhupāda's teachings. A realistic approach is required, to distinguish malicious faultfinding from the *śāstra*-based discrimination whereby one is able to see and understand—not to simply ignore—certain observed shortcomings of others, and to discern in which instances and by what means one should attempt to rectify the situation. (To publicly expose such errors should usually be among the last of options.)

Some detractors question how a person who calls others fools and rascals can be considered saintly, when in normal respectable society to do so, especially habitually, is considered most uncouth. Do devotees who utter such damning epithets not violate Kṛṣṇa's description of a devotee as being *adveṣṭā sarva-bhūtānāṁ maitraḥ karuṇa eva ca*, "kind and friendly to all, with malice toward none"?[1] Śrīla Prabhupāda responded to such a claim:

> [Hṛdayānanda:] Sometimes, Prabhupāda, when we expose them, their argument is, "Oh, you are a saintly person. Why are you criticizing me?"

---

1 Bg 12.13.

> [Prabhupāda:] No, it is not criticizing. It is opening your eyes. You are blind with ignorance, so we are trying to open your eyes. See things as they are. It is favoring you. It is not criticizing you.[1]

Just as "to call a thief a thief is not faultfinding,"[2] to state that a person whose intention is to cheat and exploit others is a rascal is not malice, but realism. And it is also realism to recognize that the sociability of normal, respectable society is largely a sophisticated facade over ubiquitous cheating and exploitation. To point this out by calling a rascal a rascal is meant to check the rascal's nefarious activities and thereby benefit not only those whom he intended to cheat, but also the rascal himself, by curbing his incurrance of ever more severe sinful reactions. In this way, devotees exhibit actual goodwill and kindness toward the entire society of rascals by pointing out that they are indeed rascals—although rascals will never agree that they are anything less than saints. Among rascals it is deemed saintly to praise each other as magnanimous personalities, and thus, within the society of rascals (most of today's population) it has become reprehensible to state that rascals who defy Kṛṣṇa are indeed nothing but rascals. If someone describes a rascal as a saint, the rascal will surely believe himself to be so, and moreover, he will avail of that apellation to suavely further his criminal activities. But devotees should not be fooled by the rascals into joining the social convention of not calling rascals rascals, for in so doing they identify with the rascals and themselves become rascals. Thus Śrīla Prabhupāda warned, "Preaching means we have to preach amongst the rascals—but you do not become rascal."[3]

The currently prevalent idea that it is wrong to call others wrong is itself wrong. Rather, it is the duty of those who know what is right to inform others that all they are doing is wrong. Those who discharge this duty are liable to be criticized(!) as being egoistic. But actually,

1 Conversation, 6 Feb 1976.

2 Bg 16.1–3, purport.

3 Conversation, 20 Apr 1974.

failure to criticize that which should be criticized is false egoism, for it deviates from the soul's pure function to always adhere to the truth. A roundabout, non-critical approach is certainly likely to be better received by insincere people than would the truth—which they avoid—but for devotees to persistently neglect to present the truth to nondevotees means acquiescing with and reinforcing the insincerity of the insincere. Actually, a true devotee's praise or censure demonstrates his saintliness as much as insincere persons' praise or censure reveals their insincerity. Devotees praise or censure others to benefit them; the insincere do so to further their selfish ends, or to bolster their ego.

In the *Bhagavad-gītā* (16.2) Lord Kṛṣṇa declares that *apaiśunam* (aversion to faultfinding) is a godly quality. The full import of this term may be understood from its standard translation, "non-calumny." *Calumny* is defined as "a false and malicious statement designed to injure the reputation of someone or something; slander, defamation."[1] Thus the didactic criticism levied by great souls who are dedicated to the uplift of others, or by persons sincerely attempting to serve the mission of such great souls, should not be equated with the spiteful, egoistic faultfinding of petty persons, but as meant to mercifully waken people to their plight. Being true friends of everyone, pure devotees harbor no grudges or intrinsic bad feelings with even the worst of rascals. As did Lord Nityānanda with Jagāi and Mādhāi, genuine devotees will gladly excuse any rascal who is ready to reform—but they do not sentimentally fail to distinguish between rascals and non-rascals, or desist from informing rascals that they are indeed rascals.

Particularly *madhyama-adhikārīs*, as well as those *paramahaṁsas* who out of compassion accept the *madhyama-adhikārī* platform for preaching to and uplifting fallen souls, are required to be judgmental of everything and everyone not Kṛṣṇa conscious. The

1 *Random House Webster's Unabridged Dictionary* version 3.0 (1999).

madhyama-adhikārī incessantly distinguishes reality from illusion for the welfare of all persons rotting in ignorance and headed toward a very dark future. He must also discriminate, on the basis of *śāstric* descriptions, between different levels of devotees, which entails that he be aware of the lackings of less-than-consummate devotees.* As and when necessary, he must discreetly point out such failings, to correct the perpetrators and to warn others against emulating them.

Another common claim is that it is inappropriate for devotees to criticize others if (as in many cases) they themselves were recently engaged in illicit activities. This argument is blind to the dimension of compassionate belligerence, and presumes that all criticism is egoistic and meant to demean others. Moreover, it may be argued that devotees who have fresh memory of their previous vices are in the best position to apprise others of the iniquities thereof.

Those sworn to unqualified non-criticism not only fail to follow in the footsteps of the Vaiṣṇava *ācāryas* (who were highly critical), but by posing as more saintly and wise than they, are subtly offensive toward them. Actually, apart from the rare *uttama-adhikārī,* who is described as *nindādi-śūnya* (devoid of the propensity to criticize others),[1] the *madhyama-adhikārī* preacher is the only truly inoffensive person, for he avoids the offense of either directly or indirectly ratifying the nondevotees' offensiveness toward Kṛṣṇa. Moreover, to insinuate offensiveness in reference to such actually inoffensive devotees is itself an offense:

> Śrīla Jīva Gosvāmī has pointed out that when a first-class devotee or even a second-class devotee rejects the atheistic class of men, he is expressing the mission of the Supreme Personality of Godhead. A first-class or second-class Vaiṣṇava never actually becomes envious

* See SB 3.29.7–12, SB 11.2.44–47, and *Upadeśāmṛta* 5.

1 *Upadeśāmṛta* 5.

> of another living entity, but out of intense love for the Supreme Lord he becomes angry when the Lord is offended. Also, understanding the Lord's mission, he discriminates according to the position of a particular living entity. To consider such a Vaiṣṇava preacher an ordinary, envious person, or to consider him sectarian because of his proclamation of pure devotional service as the most exalted of all methods of spiritual advancement, reflects a materialistic vision called *vaiṣṇave jāti-buddhiḥ* or *guruṣu nara-matiḥ*. Such an offense drags the offender down to a hellish condition of life by the laws of nature.[1]

Still another fault of persons who deplore seeing faults is their hypocrisy in criticizing others for being critical. Those who condemn condemnation of nondevotees are infected by a kind of impersonalism, a monolithic view of reality that obstructs the *rasa* that arises from disliking dislike of Kṛṣṇa.

> A *kaniṣṭha-adhikārī* is disturbed if a second-class devotee criticizes the nondevotees of the Lord. In the name of compassion or kindness, a *kaniṣṭha-adhikārī* approves of the nondevotional activities of such materialistic men. He becomes angry when second-class devotees criticize the nondevotees.[2]

Overall, the plea to "see no evil, hear no evil, speak no evil," far from being saintly, is but irresponsible utopianism—an excuse to circumvent difficult issues and having to make moral judgments, a means to float in a dream of being spiritual without actually being deeply committed, a form of impotency masquerading as patience and wisdom, a dangerous subtle covering for deviation. There is a difference between humility and stupidity, and it is nonsense to laud the kind of passivity that remains undisturbed even amid arrant deviation.

1 SB 11.2.46.

2 SB 11.2.47, purport.

EIGHTEEN
LOVE AND COMPASSION

Materialistic people spend their whole life wallowing like hogs in the gutter of sense gratification. For them, "love and compassion" means to facilitate others' hoggish enjoyment—for instance, by being lenient and nonjudgmental and dealing with others so that they feel good. But such niceness is a trap, a foolish, ignorant semblance of actual love and compassion, for without proper guidance and correction, people will tend to devolve to the lowest level. Thus real love, real friendship, does not mean to indulge others in doing what they like, but to lead them to the proper path, even against their own will:

> Many are the sinful men in this world who speak agreeably, but rare is one who speaks that which is disagreeable but beneficial.[1]

> In this world there are multitudes of men who are given to hearing and uttering pleasant words. But few are the men who hear and utter words that are most salutary yet jarring to the ear.[2]

Śrīla Prabhupāda explicated this phenomenon by telling the story of a young man who had been raised liberally by his aunt. Gradually, by bad association, the boy became a thief. Out of affection, the aunt did not chastise him; rather, she encouraged him: "You

1 Vidura (in *Mahābhārata*).

2 *Rāma-carita-mānasa* (by Tulsīdāsa), 6.9.4–5.

are bringing so many things without any labor!" Eventually, he committed a murder and was sentenced to death. On the gallows, when granted a last request to speak into the ear of his aunt, he leaned toward her and bit off her ear, declaring, "If you had not spoiled me, I would not be here today!"[1]

Śrīla Prabhupāda explained the distinction between genuine and false love:

> The actual fact is that there is no love in this material world. That is false propaganda. What they call love here is lust only, or desire for personal sense gratification. Outside of loving God there is no possibility of loving. Rather, there is lusty desire only. So-called love here means that "you gratify my senses, I'll gratify your senses," and as soon as that gratification stops, immediately there is divorce, separation, quarrel, and hatred. Actual love means love of God, Kṛṣṇa. [Actual] love is not material, so it should not be judged on the false, sentimental platform of ordinary, mundane dealings. To say [that devotees] are not loving may be true from the materialists' point of view. They have given up affection for family, friends, wife, country, race, and so on, which is all based upon the bodily concept of life, or flickering sense gratification.[2]

Śrīla Prabhupāda compared material compassion to the attempt to relieve the pain of a boil by blowing on it:

> [Tamāla Kṛṣṇa Goswami:] In Rishikesh, Prabhupāda was every evening giving a class. The famous Maharishi Mahesh Yogi was also in Rishikesh at the time, and many of his teachers were coming to attend Prabhupāda's lectures. So at that point, Maharishi sent a note to Prabhupāda saying, "Swamiji, I have heard that you are quite ill. Perhaps you should not exert yourself so much. Better not to lecture in the evenings," because he felt worried that so many of his teachers were listening to Prabhupāda. One European lady was there, a very sweet lady, and she asked Prabhupāda, "It's very nice what you are

1 Lecture, 27 Oct 1974.

2 *The Science of Self-realization*, ch. 7 (d).

preaching, but what are you doing for the suffering of the people of the world?" And you would think that Prabhupāda would be very sensitive to her being an elderly European lady. Well, Prabhupāda just exploded. He said, "What do you know about mercy? What do you understand about compassion? It is simply sentiment." He said, "Your idea of giving some sort of relief to people's suffering is like blowing air on a boil that's full of pus. The kind act you can do for such a person is to cut it. So mercy means to cut through the ignorance that the persons are under, and our preaching is based on this understanding—that ignorance causes suffering and that to enlighten people is the way to free them from ignorance."[1]

A doctor who lances a child's boil despite the child's agonized screams may seem to be heartless, but no one else will object to his performing that noble, albeit messy, duty. Similarly, Vaiṣṇava compassion may seem like cruelty, and Māyāvāda and worldly compassion may seem gentle and caring—but the latter is violence, for it keeps *jīvas* in the illusion that compels them to suffer unendingly. A devotee's compassion for the rebellious *jīvas*, manifested as forceful attacks upon their foolishness and rascaldom, is not appreciated by persons on the platform of superficial love and misplaced compassion. Genuine love and compassion for all living beings distinguished Śrīla Prabhupāda both from his godbrothers (none of whom sacrificed their life to anywhere near the extent that Śrīla Prabhupāda did, simply to benefit others) and from materialistic do-gooders who divert attention away from peoples' actual need by advertising their own altruistic initiatives, such as feeding the underprivileged, offering education aimed at worldly advancement, and affording bodily medical treatment. Śrīla Prabhupāda's spirit of compassion reflected that of Prahlāda Mahārāja, who prayed to Nṛsiṁha-deva:

नैवोद्विजे पर दुरत्ययवैतरण्या-
स्त्वद्वीर्यगायनमहामृतमग्नचित्तः ।

---

1 *Following Srila Prabhupada*, DVD 11.

शोचे ततो विमुखचेतस इन्द्रियार्थ-
मायासुखाय भरमुद्वहतो विमूढान् ॥

naivodvije para duratyaya-vaitaraṇyās
tvad-vīrya-gāyana-mahāmṛta-magna-cittaḥ
śoce tato vimukha-cetasa indriyārtha-
māyā-sukhāya bharam udvahato vimūḍhān

O best of the great personalities, I am not at all afraid of material existence, for wherever I stay I am fully absorbed in thoughts of Your glories and activities. My concern is only for the fools and rascals who are making elaborate plans for material happiness and maintaining their families, societies, and countries. I am simply concerned with love for them.[1]

Prahlāda's referring to fools and rascals is not dismissive condemnation. Rather, his keen perception of the reality of suffering in material existence, coupled with his compassionate urge to deliver the unfortunate fools and rascals from that suffering, are prime symptoms of a truly advanced Vaiṣṇava. Similarly, Śrīla Prabhupāda's compassion manifested as a virtual war against all misleaders and cheaters and especially against Māyāvādīs and atheistic scientists. Devotees who follow the ideal of Prahlāda Mahārāja and Śrīla Prabhupāda in truly caring for Kṛṣṇa care also to rescue His estranged servants from their determined career into hell. Unless nondevotees are understood to be rascals in need of rectification, there can be no question of extending compassion toward them. Rather, to think of rascals as gentlemen is the antithesis of compassion, as it forestalls even the idea of trying to rescue them.

Confronted with a civilization that is being intentionally misled into hell, devotees are impelled to speak frankly. Out of devotional attachment to Lord Kṛṣṇa, and feeling poignant sympathy for

---

1 SB 7.9.43.

persons determined to forget Him, devotees cannot tolerate the pompous drivel spoken by rogues. They must boldly speak out to save the foolish rascals—and to save the world.

> Our leaders are simply misleading people, and the people in general are innocently following them to their ruin. So it is very much our duty to come to their aid and point out exactly how this sinful living—namely, slaughtering animals, intoxication, illicit sex life, and gambling—how these sinful activities are so much degrading to the humankind and how they are only producing hippies, wars, and endless suffering as a result. So we want to give the citizens the positive value of the Kṛṣṇa consciousness way of life, so for that activity we must always be preaching very strongly in the public.[1]

---

1 Letter, 28 May 1972.

NINETEEN
HUMILITY, AGGRESSION, AND ANGER

Does blunt speaking contradict the Vaiṣṇava principle of humility? Not according to Śrīla Prabhupāda:

> Kṛṣṇa is especially addressing [Arjuna] as "chastiser of the enemy." Where there is no excuse, you must be a chastiser. Not that, "Because I have become Kṛṣṇa conscious, I'll be very humble." You must be humble, but if there is a need, you shall be like a thunderbolt. That, Kṛṣṇa is instructing.[1]

And according to the teachings of Śrīla Bhaktisiddhānta Sarasvatī:

> The theist is by no means enjoined by the scriptures to be a nonviolent passive spectator of the violent acts of aggressive nontheists against Viṣṇu and His devotees. This is not the meaning of the teaching of the Supreme Lord Śrī Kṛṣṇa Caitanya by which the devotee is required to be humbler than a blade of grass and more tolerant than the tree. These qualities are to be exercised in upholding, and not for deserting, the cause of the Truth.[2]
>
> Such conduct on the part of the servant of the guru appears unpleasant to the *jīva* in the bound stage, but there is no other alternative. Conduct that is agreeable to the body and mind of the bound *jīvas* serves only to prolong his state of bondage. In such circumstances there would appear to be no other method of destroying

1 Lecture, 25 Nov 68.

2 *Harmonist* 29.113–14 (Oct 1931); SBV, vol. 1, pp. 144–45.

> the evil mental tendencies of the bound *jīva* than the performance of unalloyed *kīrtana* in the form of preaching the messages of the scriptures and of the pure devotees (viz., the Six Gosvāmīs), fully practicing them oneself. There is no other weapon available to the servant of the guru for cutting the tangled knot except for the words of the scriptures and of the guru. Accordingly, God Himself, the establisher of all religion, thus advised His beloved devotee Uddhava regarding the remedy, "The devotees will dissipate the evil mental tendencies of the bound *jīva* by their words."[1] The servant of the guru has no other means except following in the footsteps of Śrīman Mahāprabhu and Prabhu Nityānanda under the guidance of Śrī Guru. He is unable to act in accordance with the tastes and nature of the bound *jīva* thereby disobeying the injunctions of the guru and of the scriptures. This constitutes his proper function of honoring others. In such conduct there is no deficiency of the quality of humility that is greater than that of a blade of grass. This is the humble submission of the servant of the servants of the guru.[2]

Although such an attitude might seem not at all humble, the Vaiṣṇava understanding of humility does not entail mere quietude, cringing, or introvertedness, but a sense of total dependence on Kṛṣṇa in presenting His message. Śrīla Bhaktisiddhānta Sarasvatī definitively solved the apparent paradox of Vaiṣṇava humility vis-à-vis the need to speak strongly:

> A chanter of Hari-*kīrtana* is necessarily the uncompromising enemy of worldliness and hypocrisy. It is his constant function to dispel all misconceptions by preaching the truth in its most unambiguous form, without any consideration of person, place, or time. The form to be adopted is that which is least likely to be misunderstood. It is his bounden duty to clearly and frankly oppose any person who tries to deceive and harm himself and others by misrepresenting the truth, whether due to malice or genuine misunderstanding. This will be possible if the chanter of *kīrtana* is always prepared to submit to being

1 SB 11.26.26.

2 Harmonist 25.160–61 (Dec 1927); SBV, vol. 2, p. 227.

trodden upon by thoughtless people, if such discomfort will enable him to benefit his persecutors by chanting of the truth in the most unambiguous manner. If he is unwilling or afraid of considerations of self-respect or personal discomfort to chant *kīrtana* under all circumstances, he is unfit to be a preacher of the absolute truth. Humility implies perfect submission to the truth and no sympathy for untruth. Those who entertain any partiality for untruth are unfit to chant Hari-*kīrtana*. Any clinging to untruth is opposed to the principle of humility born of absolute submission to the truth.

Those who perpetually serve the truth with all their faculties, and who have no hankering for the trivialities of this world, are necessarily always free from malice born of competing worldliness. Thus they are fit to admonish those who are actively engaged in harming themselves and others by opposing or misrepresenting the truth for attaining rewards in the shape of a perpetuation of the state of misery and ignorance. The method employed by the servant of the good preceptor for preventing such misrepresentation of the truth is a part and parcel of the truth itself. It may not always be pleasing to the diseased susceptibilities of deluded minds, and may even be denounced by them as a malicious act with which they are only too familiar. But truthful words from the lips of a loyal and humble servant of Hari possess such beneficent power, that all effort to suppress or obstruct those words serves merely to vindicate to impartial minds the necessity of complete submission to the absolute truth as the only cure of the disease of worldliness. Humility employed in unambiguous service to the absolute truth is necessarily and qualitatively different from its perverted prototype, practiced by cunning people for worldly gain. The professors of pseudo-humility have reason to fear the preaching of Hari's servant, one of whose duties is to expose the enormous possibility of mischief inherent in various forms of so-called spiritual conduct when they are prostituted for serving the untruth.[1]

---

1 *Harmonist* 26.249–50 (Apr 1929);
SBV, vol. 1, pp. 145–46.

Śrīla Prabhupāda succinctly explained:

> Humility means that you are convinced beyond doubt that there is absolutely nothing in this world—not your money, not your family, not your fame, not your gun, not your education—nothing that will save you, except the mercy of Kṛṣṇa. When you are thus convinced, then you are humble.[1]

Śrīla Prabhupāda also wrote: "Humility means that one should not be anxious to have the satisfaction of being honored by others"—which does not preclude speaking strongly.[2] Persons raised with the fallacious belief that all opinions are equally valid might consider the combative preacher to be audacious, opinionated, and judgmental. Yet the preacher's confidence springs not from pride or dogmatism but from the certitude that Kṛṣṇa consciousness is the highest truth and must be preached by all means. Certainly, by representing the absolute truth he is actually right, whereas all others are disastrously wrong:

> The devotee is always right. The nondevotee in the shape of the empirical pedant is always and necessarily wrong. In the one case there is always present the Substantive Truth and nothing but the Substantive Truth. In the other case, there is present the apparent or misleading hypothesis and nothing but untruth.[3]

> Be intelligent and try to give them brain. And if you remain dull-brained like that, then you'll say, "Yes, yes, you are right." You are not right. At every step we shall say, "You are not right. You are wrong. You have no brain. You are all rascals."[4]

A genuine preacher's forcefulness is quite different from that of egoistic materialists, which is born of the desire to humiliate and dominate. A book distributor once asked Śrīla Prabhupāda how she could maintain humility while her engagement required being

---

1 *Following Srila Prabhupada*, DVD 6.

2 Definition of humility—See Bg 13.8–12, purport.

3 *Harmonist* 29.169 (Dec 1931); SBV, vol. 3, p. 143.

4 Conversation (2), 18 Feb 1977.

demandingly assertive. "Be aggressive for Kṛṣṇa," Śrīla Prabhupāda told her.[1] And later he clarified, "Aggression for the cause of Lord Caitanya Mahāprabhu is pure."[2] Although unpleasant for the recipient, a Vaiṣṇava's aggression is pure because it is actuated not by malice but by concern. Aggression seeks to force a response, whereas the polite presentation of even a strong message affords an opportunity to diplomatically ignore it.

"Aggressive pronouncement of the truth" is considered distasteful by persons opposed to truth, who, although themselves aggressive in pursuit of materialistic goals, and having sentenced sadhus to tepid insignificance, deplore any aggression on the part of sadhus. Certainly the sharp words of a sadhu are a kind of violence—they hurt. Yet such violence is kindness, comparable to the benign cutting of a surgeon.

A devotee's aggression and anger are not actuated by misanthropy, but by opposition to commonly expounded theories that are misleading and harmful. In decrying godlessness, a devotee does not have to abandon humility. It is his duty to speak out against illusion, blindness, and deceit—not to demean others but to uplift them. A Vaiṣṇava "hates the sin, not the sinner."

> We don't hate anyone; otherwise there will be no preaching. And Lord Jesus Christ said that you hate the disease, not the man who is suffering from disease. That is very nice. So we shall hate this influence of *māyā* but not the man who is now under the influence. Then how we can preach? That is our business.[3]

Therefore aggressive pronouncement of the truth is not the hostility of an enemy but the benevolent aggression of a true well-wisher. Those who know only the self-serving, artificial goodness of materialists can hardly understand that the aggressive preaching

1 Conversation, 13 Jul 1975.

2 Letter, 30 Jul 1975.

3 Lecture, 4 Apr 1972.

of a Vaiṣṇava is a real act of compassion, whereas mundane compassion is misplaced and thus liable to be harmful, as in the following anecdote related by Śrīla Prabhupāda:

> In front of our residence, our neighbor's daughter-in-law was beating her child. So I inquired through my servant, "Why is this young woman beating her child?" The servant brought me the news that this boy gave *parāṭha* to his elder brother, who is suffering from typhoid. In typhoid fever, solid food is strictly forbidden, but the boy did not know. He asked his younger brother, "If you steal one *parāṭha* and if you give me. I am very hungry." So he became very sympathetic to his brother, and he gave the *parāṭha*. And the boy was ill; he aggravated the illness. So as soon as the mother heard that he gave a *parāṭha* to him, she began to beat: "Why did you give?" It was charity—it was affection and sympathetic—but the result was beating with shoes.[1]

Only by shallow judgment can the aggressive benevolence of a Vaiṣṇava be considered unnecessarily harsh. The fact is that the world is harsh, repeated birth and death is harsh, and thus to assert this reality will always appear harsh to persons intent on avoiding reality. Actually, harshness is to not inform others of the harshness they will be forced to suffer for not accepting the direness of their predicament and not seeking to rectify it by the process of Kṛṣṇa consciousness. As demonstrated in the *parāṭha* anecdote, in fulfilling others' desires—doing what they think is good for them—one may unwittingly commit the worst violence toward them. Hence, the real duty of one who genuinely loves others is to act for their welfare even over their protests, and also to vehemently oppose persons who, even if seemingly well-intentioned, try to stymie acts of true benefit.

Satsvarūpa Dāsa Goswami analyzed the internal mood of a steadfast preacher:

---

1 Lecture, 27 Oct 1974.

> There are enemies to our movement. Scholars may disregard ISKCON as sentimental. Anti-cult groups may pursue us with charges of brainwashing or coercion. There are others. A devotee sees things philosophically. He sees the enemies as agents of karma and not really as enemies in their own right. After all, they are spirit souls whose eternal nature is as servants of Kṛṣṇa. This is the *mahā-bhāgavata* vision. Devotees cultivate this vision internally, but externally, they have to meet the demands of preaching and act on the platform of distinguishing between friends and enemies and protecting Kṛṣṇa from all attacks. Devotees are like knights at a jousting match. The scholar says, "Actually there is no person Kṛṣṇa. Kṛṣṇa has been mythologized from a conglomeration of tribal chieftains." Like *kṣatriyas*, we strike back: "Nothing personal, professor, but actually, your intelligence has been stolen by illusion." The professor might respond with an accusation of sentimentality. The devotee may call him a rascal or a dog. The argument can become heated, but the devotee maintains his internal vision that the scholar is a spirit soul in ignorance.[1]

Detractors cannot even begin to comprehend the profound humility of a devotee who, while aggressive and bold in preaching, feels himself to be minuscule, unqualified, and totally dependent on the mercy of guru and Kṛṣṇa. His use of strong language is not the egoism of presuming himself superior. A Vaiṣṇava considers himself most fallen and the unworthy recipient of the extraordinary mercy of Kṛṣṇa and His devotees, whereby he has been allowed to engage in devotional service. Wanting to share his good fortune, he exhorts others to not be foolish as he had formerly been but to accept the precious gift of Kṛṣṇa consciousness. Thus, as Śrīla Prabhupāda explained and exemplified, a Vaiṣṇava is humble and meek on his own account, but for Kṛṣṇa he can be angry like fire.[2]

> If you are fixed up as a servant of the Lord, even if you become angry for the Lord's service, that is not bad.[3]

---

1 *Nīti-śāstras* (by Satsvarūpa Dāsa Goswami), p. 25.

2 Cc 1.7.50, purport.

3 Conversation, 11 Jul 1973.

Although the *Bhagavad-gītā* (16.21) lists anger as one of the three gates to hell, properly directed anger is godly, as demonstrated in the central theme of the *Bhagavad-gītā*—Kṛṣṇa's exhorting Arjuna to fight. Girirāja Swami recalls Śrīla Prabhupāda's commenting on this:

> In Madras we were seated in Śrīla Prabhupāda's room, and His Divine Grace had just made an inspiring plea for Kṛṣṇa consciousness. Then a clean-cut European in his twenties exclaimed, "Yes, and then we can become more loving and less angry." His Divine Grace replied, "What is wrong with getting angry?" The boy was startled and stammered, "Well, uh, if we are angry, it is hard to have peace of mind." Prabhupāda interrupted and said, "Anyway, that is some speculation. Even Kṛṣṇa Himself gets angry. We are part and parcel of Kṛṣṇa, and the fact is that Kṛṣṇa spoke the *Bhagavad-gītā* to make Arjuna angry. Arjuna was not angry when he should have been. The whole *Gītā* was spoken just to make Arjuna angry so he would fight."[1]

The notion that a sadhu should always be calm is based on the rascal Māyāvādī idea that "nothing is real; therefore nothing is sacred; therefore nothing is worth getting upset about." But a Vaiṣṇava intensely feels for Kṛṣṇa and cannot tolerate belittlement of Kṛṣṇa by those who ignore or directly blaspheme Him. Being emotionally involved in Kṛṣṇa's mission to bring His lost children back to His shelter, a Vaiṣṇava cannot meekly disregard the demonic theories that beguile conditioned souls into remaining far from Him.

Therefore it is balderdash to contend that Vaiṣṇavas should not become angry. Rather, one who does not become angry about the pervading cheating that constitutes materialistic life (including most of what parades as religion) can only be a Vaiṣṇava of his own imagination, and never a follower of Arjuna or Hanumān or Śrīla Prabhupāda. A real devotee has a fire of desire burning within him

---

1 From a letter featured in *Śrīla Prabhupāda Nectar* (by Satsvarūpa Dāsa Goswami).

to establish everywhere that Kṛṣṇa is the Supreme Personality of Godhead. It is a preacher's glory, not a deficiency, if sometimes his devotional fire bursts forth as a volcano to annihilate all rascal theories that oppose Kṛṣṇa's overlordship of everything that be.

That a Vaiṣṇava should be meek and humble does not mean that he is a wimp. A Vaiṣṇava should be "like a lamb at home and a lion in the chase,"[1] as elaborated on by Śrīla Bhaktisiddhānta Sarasvatī, who in the following citation not only establishes the need for devotees to become angry but also warns against merely directing anger outward without first seeing to one's own purification:

> We should display anger toward those who are envious of devotees. This is a particular limb of devotional service. A lack of anger against blasphemers is unjustified. But we need to understand who is actually envious of devotees. Those who do not serve the Supreme Lord, the Supersoul and most blissful friend of all living entities, do not benefit themselves but instead invite trouble by their envy of Kṛṣṇa and the Vaiṣṇavas. Such people are branded as envious, and we should not show them mercy. These people become intoxicated by worshiping materialists. We should both ignore them and display our anger toward them.
>
> But before that, we have to see whether we ourselves are envious of devotees, whether we ourselves are actually serving Kṛṣṇa. Or are we serving something else on the pretext of serving Kṛṣṇa? How much are we attached to Kṛṣṇa? Are we trying to enjoy the objects meant for Kṛṣṇa's enjoyment?
>
> I think my enjoyment-prone material body is fiercely envious of Kṛṣṇa and His devotees, because instead of thinking constantly of Kṛṣṇa's lotus feet and happiness, I am busy worrying about my own happiness, blaspheming others, and looking for faults. I do not look at myself at all. I am such an offender at the feet of devotees that I should first learn to display anger toward myself. I am so envious of devotees that I should beat myself with shoes simply to purify

---

1 SB 1.12.22, purport.

> myself. Then I can set an example for others and sincerely engage in the service of Hari, guru, and the Vaiṣṇavas. I must remember that everyone is worshiping Hari but me. I am unable to do so. I should also remember that I may die at any moment.
>
> So first we should show anger toward our own sinful propensities, such as our desire for profit, adoration, and distinction and our propensity to cheat others. We must correct ourselves first. Otherwise, we cannot correct others. Then we have to correct those who are related to us, who are envious of the spiritual master and Kṛṣṇa and who are pulling us toward material enjoyment by tempting us. This is the secret of success.[1] *

Overall, although devotees may and in some circumstances should become angry, they should not be of angry temperament. Anger, when properly directed at suitable recipients and in a manner that is beneficial for them and others, becomes a further decoration to adorn the beautiful character of a Vaiṣṇava.†

* See also "Compassionate Belligerence and Genuine Humility," in *Śrī Bhaktisiddhānta Vaibhava* (vol. 2, p. 220), and also the comments regarding the restraining of anger on p. 156 of *Speaking Strongly.*

† For a discussion of the necessity to sometimes restrain anger, see p. 165.

1 From *Amṛta Vāṇī.*

TWENTY
SENTIMENTALISM AND PSEUDO-SAINTLINESS

Among the main detractors of strong speaking are the overly sentimental—those who presume that *bhakti* should fit their vague notions of what they consider "good" and "nice"—and the pseudo saintly, who resemble the sentimental but are even less sincere. Neither class seriously tries to understand the truth as presented by *śāstra* and the *ācāryas*. Unwilling to accept the trials and to muster the resolve that are necessary for actual surrender to Kṛṣṇa, they remain satisfied with a watered-down version of *bhakti* or merely a facade of being spiritual.

It is easier to attract people by sentimentalism than by stridency. The popular stereotype of a sadhu is a gentle, harmless religious figure with a dreamy far-away look. He holds a flower and smiles, speaks softly and sometimes giggles, and often utters words like *beautiful* and *wonderful*—or maybe speaks in riddles that no one can understand. He is sickeningly "nice," or maybe sickeningly jovial. He has no distinct or demanding message and avoids unpleasant exchanges. A sadhu can even become an icon if he is adept at getting people to "feel spiritual" amid their sense gratification. Such supposedly saintly persons enjoy the profile of being a holy man and feel disquieted by undeviating preachers whose jarring words challenge their own lack of conviction.*

Śrīla Prabhupāda warned devotees against such a hypocritical mentality:

> One may desire mundane reputation by making compromises with nondevotees ... these are pitfalls of personal sense gratification. Just to cheat some innocent people, one makes a show of advanced spiritual life and becomes known as a *sādhu, mahātmā,* or religious person. All this means that the so-called devotee has become victimized by all these unwanted creepers and that the real creeper of *bhakti-latā-bīja* has been stunted.[1]

An imitator who is cheaply advertised as a great preacher possessed of true saintly qualities swaps praises with his followers and imbues them with an artificial sense of being spiritual. Enamored by him, they collect more pseudo-spiritualists to be his disciples. They consider their shallow emotionalism to be superior to "lower matters," such as combating atheism or distributing Śrīla Prabhupāda's books.

Devotees themselves risk veering toward impersonalism should they imitate Māyāvādī cheaters who utter pious-sounding platitudes about love, peace, and compassion without clearly defining such qualities in relation to Kṛṣṇa. But, *santa evāsya chindanti mano-vyāsaṅgam uktibhiḥ:* true sadhus are meant to speak in a manner specifically meant to cut material attachments.[2] The principal characteristic of a genuine devotee is his full surrender to Kṛṣṇa.

---

* From *Śrīla Prabhupāda-līlāmṛta* (ch. 14, "Struggling Alone"): "Dr. Mishra was a dramatic, showy personality, given to flashing glances and making expressive gestures with his hands. He regularly used words like 'lovely' and 'beautiful.' Presenting an artfully polished image of what a guru should be, he was what some New Yorkers referred to as 'an uptown swami.'"

1 Cc 2.19.160, purport.

2 SB 11.26.26.

Kṛṣṇa wants His devotees to preach—and preaching means fighting. Devotees out in the hubbub of the world, fighting for Kṛṣṇa, confronting all hostile elements, not caring for comfort or reputation, are surely dearer to Him than ease-lovers. Even for those who do go out to preach, it is less troublesome and often apparently more successful to adopt a soft line, avoiding conflict by not pricking anyone's false ego. But Śrīla Bhaktisiddhānta Sarasvatī noted:

> When one contradicts those conceptions opposed to *bhakti*—namely karma, *jñāna*, and *anyābhilāṣa*—and establishes *bhakti-siddhānta*, it becomes necessary to buck the current thoughts of the world concerned with the body and mind. As the saying goes, "A dumb person has no enemies." If one simply sits in one's house silently, thinking of one's own welfare, there will certainly be nothing of import to tell the world.[1]

Those who maintain attachment to sentimental attitudes will ever remain neophytes. Although they may beguile themselves and others by posing as highly advanced, they have little idea of or inclination for actual surrender to Kṛṣṇa. In their meager understanding of Kṛṣṇa consciousness, they feel uncomfortable and threatened by forceful speaking because it hacks at and exposes their material attachments. Being on the mundane platform, they have no actual understanding of Kṛṣṇa consciousness—however pure, advanced, or saintly they may appear to their fellow sentimentalists.

Often those who are annoyed by incisive statements are uncommitted, and their spiritual life is mediocre. As *kaniṣṭha-adhikārīs* (materialistic devotees), they practice *bhakti* (but "not too much") and cultivate worldly desires along with their insipid devotional activities. These Vaiṣṇava-*prāya* ("almost devotees") can never understand that one who speaks penetratingly for the

---

1 SBV, vol. 1, pp. 149–150.

benefit of others is a greater saint than he who smiles to sanction the foolishness and hypocrisy of the bonded *jīvas.*[1]

In response to those who contend "Why not just talk about Kṛṣṇa?" Śrīla Prabhupāda answers:

> A common man cannot understand the Lord. He must first know the real position of his life under the influence of the illusory energy. In illusion one thinks that he can be happy only by fruitive activities, but what actually happens is that one becomes more and more entangled in the network of action and reaction and does not find any solution to the problem of life.[2]

To like only the "nice" features of Kṛṣṇa consciousness is redolent of the *prākṛta-sahajiyās,* who pick and choose topics of *bhakti* according to their own taste, and who consider that devotees who, unlike themselves, are not exclusively preoccupied with the "sweet" aspects of *bhakti* are on a lower level. Undoubtedly, *bhakti* is deliciously sweet, but to come to the level of genuine appreciation of that sweetness, all the garbage within the heart—material desires, attachments, and misconceptions—must be purged. And to effect such a cleansing, the *Bhāgavatam* prescribes that one hear the violently cathartic words of sadhus.[3] Those who want the nectar of *bhakti* without the "nastiness" of confrontational preaching are akin to those who like to hear only "sweet" *līlās*—about whom Śrīla Prabhupāda said:

> You can talk of Kṛṣṇa's pastimes with the *gopīs;* you can talk of Kṛṣṇa's pastimes of killing Pūtanā, Aghāsura, Bakāsura. Both are the same. Some of the rascals decide that to talk of Kṛṣṇa's embracing the *gopīs* is very good, and talk of Kṛṣṇa killing Pūtanā or other demons is not good. That is rascaldom.[4]

> The *sahajiyās* simply go to the pastimes of Lord Kṛṣṇa with the *gopīs.* Other things: "Oh no, that is not Kṛṣṇa's pastimes." They

---

1 Vaiṣṇava-*prāya*—See Cc 3.6.198.

2 SB 3.5.2, purport.

3 SB 11.26.26.

4 Lecture, 6 May 1973.

> differentiate between the absolute activities of the Absolute. That is called *sahajiyā*. The *sahajiyās* will never read *Bhagavad-gītā* because [sarcastic:] they have been elevated to the mellows of conjugal love. Therefore they have no interest in *Bhagavad-gītā*. Or when you discuss *Śrīmad-Bhāgavatam* on the philosophical point *janmādy asya*, they also do not attend.[1]

Just as *Śrīmad-Bhāgavatam* records more *līlas* of Kṛṣṇa's killing demons than of dancing with the *gopīs*, Śrīla Prabhupāda more combatted various materialistic, atheistic, and demonic theories than directly describing the beauty of Kṛṣṇa's form and pastimes. Devotees who are serious about fulfilling the mission of Śrīla Prabhupāda should, as he did, challenge the whole current of worldly thought, and not ape the putative sadhus, welfare workers, mundane gurus, or others who offer adjustments to or palliatives for the material condition. Such misguiders directly or indirectly perpetuate the notion that temporal existence is basically congenial to human happiness, and accordingly they offer various antidotes to its anomalies other than the only and ultimate solution: total subordination to Kṛṣṇa, the Supreme Personality of Godhead.

A sincere devotee models himself on the ideal of the authentic Vaiṣṇava *ācāryas*, not on the phony piety of effete persons with an agenda to be revered as saints and well-wishers of human society. One who is more attached to maintaining the profile of a sadhu than to understanding and selflessly serving the Absolute Truth is an actor, not a genuine sadhu.

---

1 Lecture, 14 Feb 1971.

TWENTY-ONE

IDEAL BEHAVIOR, SWEET AND UNSWEET SPEECH, ARTIFICIAL POLITENESS

Many devotees base their preaching on Śrīla Prabhupāda's advice that "we must all become ideal in our character and then people will be very impressed with such purity."[1] Commendably, such devotees strive to develop peacefulness, detachment, and other such attributes considered typical of saintly persons. Indeed, the public expects sadhus to behave commensurately with the divine ideals and higher knowledge they profess. As Śrīla Prabhupāda said, "A devotee is a perfect gentleman, because he has developed all good qualities,"[2] and "A preacher must behave very nicely."[3]

Thus, devotees who are pledged to presenting Kṛṣṇa consciousness straightforwardly should know that the essence of strong speaking is strong arguments, not mere name-calling. As required, a devotee may employ slurs like *animals, fools,* and *rascals,* in accord with Śrīla Prabhupāda's statement "Sometimes strong words are needed to arouse a sleeping man."[4] But it is not enough to simply dub people as fools and rascals; devotees should make it evident to

---

1 Letter, 1 Feb 1975.

2 Lecture, 7 Apr 1976.

3 Lecture, 24 Jan 1977.

4 Jayādvaita Swami, *Following Srila Prabhupada*, DVD 1.

them why they are fools and rascals, and how they can stop being fools and rascals.*

> This Kṛṣṇa consciousness movement is to give the greatest benefit to the human society, to clear their rascal brain. We declare that they are all rascals. Let any scientist, philosopher come here, I shall prove that he is nothing but a rascal. I shall prove that. I challenge them. What are they doing? Nonsense.[1]

Yet Śrīla Prabhupāda also said, "A devotee is never rude to anyone."[2] Thus, strong speaking does not necessarily entail becoming excited or irritated nor even raising the voice. A devotee is not arrogant, brash, insulting, or nasty, nor ambitious to defeat others for the sake of self-aggrandizement, nor does he wantonly provoke quarrels. And as a general rule, devotee-preachers should eschew physical violence. Fighting is meant to defeat all errant ideas, but it is not an end in itself. Rather, it is intended to facilitate the real aim, which is to convince others of the message of Kṛṣṇa consciousness: "Our mission is not to fight; our mission is to convince."[3] Therefore Śrīla Prabhupāda warned against unnecessary and unproductive anger:

> There is some gentlemanly behavior: even if you are angry with some person, you do not show your anger. You talk with him. Actually these people are demons, but because we are preaching, if we simply become angry and cannot convince him, that means imperfect preacher. Basically you are angry, that's all. But because we are preachers, if I simply become angry then my preaching work will be stopped. Just like politicians—they are angry upon the enemy, but sometimes, by diplomatic means, they take their work from the enemies. Not that they show anger always. Similarly, when you go to preach, first of all

* This parallels a frequent comment by Śrīla Prabhupāda—for instance, in a letter of 23 Aug 1968: "Simply to know that God is great is not perfection, but to know how He is great is perfect knowledge."

1 Lecture, 8 Jun 1974.

2 Lecture, 7 Apr 1976.

3 Lecture, 23 Jan 1967.

> try to convince him that "How have you become God? What is your definition of God?" You simply ask, "What do you mean by God that you are claiming to be God?"[1]

> Regarding your tendency to become angry in public, that is alright provided there is positive reaction. Otherwise we do not wish to create any unnecessary enemies, and you should curb your anger by your advanced intelligence in Kṛṣṇa consciousness. We have to better correct the faulty habits of the conditioned souls by persuasive authoritative preaching and personal example without stop.[2]

Politeness, speaking sweetly, and dealing with sensitivity and empathy for others are social skills that every gentleman should cultivate. But being "good" and "nice" is not in itself sufficient to convey Kṛṣṇa consciousness or to convince others to adopt it. There are millions of "good" and "nice" people in the world who have no interest in becoming Kṛṣṇa conscious. Therefore courteousness is not an end in itself—as demonstrated by Śrīla Prabhupāda, who, although an ideal gentleman, sometimes upset people who expected saintly persons to be more passive. Tamāla Kṛṣṇa Goswami perceived that "Prabhupāda does not care an iota for anyone's position. He simply preaches absolutely and condemns totally all illusions, irrespective of anyone's sentiments."[3]

Undoubtedly, inconsiderate crudeness is uncouth; but conversely, being a stickler for manners can be more a fault than a virtue. Persons who develop an affectation beyond the needs of civility consider that "what you say is not so important as how you say it"—which preempts the possibility of any meaningful discussion.

Devotees can learn from the example of Vidura, a *mahā-bhāgavata* whose expertise in political and social affairs (as recorded in *Vidura-nīti,* a series of instructions from the *Mahābhārata*) is still revered today. Although a consummate diplomat, Vidura could

1 Lecture, 21 Mar 1969.

2 Letter, 4 Jan 1971.

3 *TKG's Diary*, 19 May.

occasionally be shockingly outspoken, not caring that someone might be offended by his "lack of empathy and compassion." At least twice, Vidura directly told Dhṛtarāṣṭra that to save the Kuru dynasty, Duryodhana should be killed. How do you sweetly tell a father, "Your son should be killed"?

Gentlemanliness, sweetness, and empathy are undoubtedly laudable, but the prime consideration should always be to expound the truth at all cost, no matter how bitter that truth may seem. Actually, the truth of the *jīvas'* dependence on Kṛṣṇa is delectably sweet, but for persons jaundiced by a false sense of independence from Him it can seem repulsive. Nonetheless, frank speaking is better than speaking sweetly to pacify persons who are unlikely to take serious interest in Kṛṣṇa consciousness, for there cannot be an ultimately better method for preaching the truth than to directly present the truth—nor can any other method substitute, for anything short of the truth contains at least a modicum of falsity. Sweet speech may be employed for ornamenting the truth, but it should not be used to waylay the truth and thus become a decoration on a dead body.

Some devotees profess that although Śrīla Prabhupāda spoke disparagingly about politicians, questionable religionists, and "so-called scientists and scholars," when meeting with such persons he would often speak in a respectful, diplomatic manner, encouraging them to consider adopting Kṛṣṇa consciousness. In this vein, Girirāja Swami related that in Los Angeles in 1973 he asked Śrīla Prabhupāda, "When you speak about the scientists, you use phrases like *fools, rascals,* and *kick them in the face with boots.* When we speak to them, should we use the same terms?" and Śrīla Prabhupāda replied, "No, you should speak like a gentleman." Certainly, when drilling his disciples Śrīla Prabhupāda was generally more forthcoming in using unflattering terms than when he was personally addressing those very same kinds of people that he had described by such invectives. Yet there are also many examples of Śrīla Prabhupāda being devastatingly blunt in such circumstances.* He cited the precedent set by Lord Caitanya for doing so:

> Chand Kazi, a Muslim magistrate, challenged Caitanya Mahāprabhu. Caitanya Mahāprabhu said, "What is your religion? You are eating your father and mother"—directly. Not that because He was talking with a magistrate, He should be a little respectful. No. In spiritual matters, everything spoken frankly—no compromise. Just like we say, "If you are not a Kṛṣṇa conscious person, then you are a rascal. You may be the president, that doesn't matter. But because you are not Kṛṣṇa conscious, you are rascal." There is no compromise—"Oh, here is a big man. How he is speaking?" So many scientists come. I say, "You are rascal. You are demon." *[Laughter]* I say it. And they tolerate. I prove that he is a rascal. I prove that he is a rascal, he is a demon. Then he tolerates, "Yes." We have got sufficient strength to prove to any materialistic man that he is a rascal.[1]

Following Śrīla Prabhupāda's example, a preacher can take risks. But he is not reckless. He neither shies from controversy nor is controversial simply for the sake of being so. His aim is not merely to be perceived as a gentleman, nor specifically to be outspoken or aggressive, but to serve Kṛṣṇa, the Absolute Truth, by doing whatever is required to help *jīvas* forgetful of Kṛṣṇa to come as soon as possible to the proper position of surrender to Him. Yet a devotee knows that so-called gentlemanliness, if placed above service to the Absolute Truth, obliterates the very purpose of living. Hence, while behaving in a manner that upholds the exalted philosophy and culture of Kṛṣṇa consciousness, and while maintaining ordinary courtesy in everyday dealings, a mature preacher does not partake in the pretentious civility of hypocrites, knowing that the artificial politeness and charm of supposedly cultured materialists is merely a charade of mutual deception, a veneer that covers selfishness, greed, and exploitation.

---

* Many such examples are given in this book, especially in chs. 1 and 2.

1 Lecture, 31 Dec 1973.

Deceitful persons avoid speaking plainly because they want something from others (albeit perhaps only subtle advantages, such as endorsement or approval), or because they simply care too little to act for others' real benefit. In the society of cheaters and the cheated, good manners is a social mechanism for overlooking that which should not be overlooked, thus allowing everyone to pursue sense gratification without fear of castigation:

> "I praise you and you praise me. I say you are very big; you say I am very big." And compromise: "I don't criticize you; you don't criticize me."[1]

By mutual flattery everyone might feel good about each other, but the purpose of life is not served. A committed preacher does not cultivate such fraudulent politeness or pseudo saintliness, but rather seeks to demolish such affectation.

> "You are OK, I am OK"—our proposal is not that. Our proposal is "You are not OK. I am OK."[2] *

> When [nondevotees] say they are as good as we are, we must say that only we are good and that they are not good. This is not our obstinacy; it is the injunction of the *śāstras*. We must not deviate from the injunctions of the *śāstras*.[3]

These stark statements counter all that is considered civil and reasonable in the world. But such civility and reasonableness are derived from humanistic concepts devoid of knowledge of dharma and the purpose of life, and are practiced within a "civilization" that upholds all kinds of abominable activities, not least a daily holocaust of tens of millions of animals. Hence devotees should not be overly concerned about being considered civil and reasonable

* *I'm OK—You're OK* (by Thomas A. Harris, M.D.; first published in 1969) became a bestseller and its title a popular saying.

1 Conversation, 21 Oct 1975.

2 Lecture, 22 Jun 1975.

3 Cc 1.17.24, purport.

by hypocrites who cannot brook any kind of preaching that impinges on their abominable status quo, for whom observance of social niceties is a convenient policy for living pleasantly in sin.

It is not that gentlemanliness is to be eschewed—but a devotee must not tolerate nonsense:

> I am very much encouraged to learn that you are bold enough to challenge any nondevotee as you did with that impersonalist yoga student. That should be the temperament of all our preachers. We should not be aggressive, but we should not tolerate any sort of nonsense.[1]

And for that intolerance the preacher is likely to be perceived as outspoken and aggressive. Of course, it is natural for a devotee to become animated when, for instance, he describes how certain persons posing as spiritual leaders are misleading people into hell. But however excited he may become, he should maintain internal balance and not lose self-control. Nor need a devotee become disturbed by inevitable counterchallenges. He may rather welcome them as a platform to dispel misconceptions and to clarify the Vaiṣṇava position.

As Śrīla Prabhupāda perfectly demonstrated, being a gentleman and being an uncompromising preacher are not mutually exclusive. Devotees had better look to Śrīla Prabhupāda's example of ideal behavior than that of persons concerned with mundane conventions and unconcerned with discovering absolute reality. Śrīla Prabhupāda was exceptionally personable. He was always strong but never nasty, and most people who met him were struck by his genuine saintliness, even if they understood little of his message. Yet Śrīla Prabhupāda exemplified the principle that ideal behavior should give rise to bold preaching: "Become first-class man. Everyone will hear you. And you can face any so-called first-

---

1 Letter, 28 Jan 1969.

class man and talk with him straightforward, that 'You are fourth class.'"[1]

No one can validly fault a devotee whose behavior is unimpeachable, who clearly is not personally motivated. Undeniable truths spoken by such persons resonate powerfully, for the force of their veracity is bolstered by the purity and conviction of the speaker. Hence, to be effective, those who speak cuttingly must properly practice devotional service—for instance, by rising early, ingesting only Kṛṣṇa-*prasāda,* remaining constantly and meaningfully engaged in devotional service without ulterior motive, spurning sense gratification, and being genuinely anxious for the welfare of all living beings:

> Our method is very simple. The preacher should be ideal, sincere, serious, and strictly adhering to our principles, chanting sixteen rounds and following the restrictive rules.[2]

Those who espouse righteousness but do not themselves follow the basic tenets of devotional service, or even basic moral principles, rightly become despised, and their preaching will be ineffectual:

> To make a show of devotional service will not help one. One must be a pure devotee following the devotional process; then one can convert others to devotional service. Śrī Caitanya Mahāprabhu practiced devotional service and preached (*āpani ācari' bhakti karila pracāra*). If a preacher behaves properly in devotional service, he will be able to convert others. Otherwise, his preaching will have no effect.[3]

1 Conversation, 15 May 1975.

2 Letter, 20 Nov 1971.

3 Cc 2.24.98, purport.

TWENTY-TWO

RESTRAINT, CAUTION, AND INDIRECT PREACHING

There are many dedicated preachers who deliberately eschew confrontational methods, considering them more likely to alienate than to enlighten. They deliberately adopt a restrained manner, whereby they aim to impress people that Kṛṣṇa consciousness is "nice," and to induce them to gradually accept it. Particularly for the many persons who are at least somewhat open to spiritual messages, a cautious approach is meant to accommodate and foster their pious inclinations rather than push them too hard too soon, at the risk of crushing them.

Proponents of this indirect style argue that it is necessary for reaching a wider audience. The very nature of conditional existence is that people are inclined to accept only that which appeals to their perverse outlook. The message of Kṛṣṇa consciousness, of forswearing sense gratification and surrendering to Kṛṣṇa, is decidedly unappealing to their perverse outlook, and thus very few people are sufficiently sincere or fortunate to immediately accept much of the *Bhāgavata* teachings. Therefore preachers of mildness advocate the administering of truth in small palatable doses, in the hope that open-minded and intelligent individuals will gradually accept Kṛṣṇa consciousness to some extent, whereas (it is postulated that) too much of the absolute truth given all at once to nondevotees would more likely drive them away forever.

Some preachers deem it wise, as a prelude to attempting to introduce direct Kṛṣṇa consciousness, to try to win people's confidence by sharing casual talk with them, offering them *prasāda*, and generally attempting to put them at ease. Carefully averting discord by not disturbing false egos, and speaking what people like to hear rather than what they need to hear, such preachers shun confrontation and controversy. They might also try to capture the attention of shallow persons by, for instance, making jokes or telling stories.

This type of friendly approach certainly has its utility—for instance, in greeting first-time visitors to an ISKCON center, who are more likely to be curious than to be truth-seekers. By affability and genuine concern, this style seeks to make it easy for people to make the often difficult transition from their present manner of thinking and acting so that they may incrementally adopt the understanding and behavior of pure devotees. Generally, even preachers who are committed to straightforwardness also first try to strike some rapport with people rather than lashing into them from the outset. And it is practically observed that by careful cultivation many people have been brought to Kṛṣṇa consciousness who probably would not have come via an instant zapping.

An extension of the sociable method is wholly indirect preaching, which is designed to bring people into contact with devotees, gradually befriend them, and then introduce them step by step to Kṛṣṇa consciousness. Thus some devotees offer courses in subjects, such as yoga exercises and time management, that have nothing to do with devotional service—and for that very reason, to appeal to a greater number of people than would an undisguised presentation of Kṛṣṇa consciousness. Proponents of indirect preaching generally cite Śrīla Prabhupāda's statement, "An *ācārya* should devise a means by which people may somehow or other come to Kṛṣṇa consciousness. First they should become Kṛṣṇa conscious, and all the prescribed rules and regulations may later gradually be introduced."[1] Such tactics, although in many circumstances unnecessary, can be legitimate if, as Śrīla Prabhupāda cautions in the above-quoted purport, "the ultimate goal is never neglected."

1 Cc 1.7.37, purport.

Indirect preaching can be effective if undertaken with a clear understanding of the principle of total surrender to Kṛṣṇa, and also with a clear plan for bringing people to that platform. Without such understanding and commitment, indirect preaching, even if helpful in bringing many persons to Kṛṣṇa consciousness, cannot bring them to pure, unmixed Kṛṣṇa consciousness. By popularizing Kṛṣṇa consciousness mixed with extraneous processes, indirect preaching tends to foster *bhakti* mixed with misconceptions and material desires, and to thus obscure the actual process and become a deviation.

Indeed, the very stratagem of tweaking the presentation as a concession to the diseased conditioned mentality is itself a kind of compromise. The preacher himself becomes compromised if, in making others feel comfortable, he becomes enamored by their favorable responses and thus, as a policy, never tells them what they really need to hear. Such a policy is condemned in *Śrīmad-Bhāgavatam:*

स्वयं निःश्रेयसं विद्वान् न वक्त्यज्ञाय कर्म हि ।
न राति रोगिणोऽपथ्यं वाञ्छतोऽपि भिषक्तमः ॥

svayaṁ niḥśreyasaṁ vidvān
na vakty ajñāya karma hi
na rāti rogiṇo 'pathyaṁ
vāñchato 'pi bhiṣaktamaḥ

A pure devotee who is fully accomplished in the science of devotional service will never instruct a foolish person to engage in fruitive activities for material enjoyment, not to speak of helping him in such activities. Such a devotee is like an experienced physician, who never encourages a patient to eat food injurious to his health, even if the patient desires it.[1]

To not discuss philosophy, to not state the difference between truth and falsity, between right and wrong, means to subscribe

---

1 SB 6.9.50.

to the common impersonalistic norm of "accepting people as they are" no matter what their outlook is—thus implying that philosophy is unimportant and that Kṛṣṇa consciousness is not a compelling necessity but just one path among many. Therefore Śrīla Bhaktisiddhānta Sarasvatī considered it a defect if a preacher is overly anxious to accommodate others:

> Everyone is eager for adoration by others, not for the absolute truth. Those who make a show of being preachers do not disturb mankind, but rather maintain everyone's present mentality while busily protecting their own existence. Therefore there is no propagation of the truth, since one's popularity is not served by speaking or hearing the truth.[1]

And, as quoted previously, Śrīla Bhaktisiddhānta Sarasvatī defined the "constant function" of a chanter of Hari-*kīrtana* as being "to dispel all misconceptions by preaching the truth in its most unambiguous form, without any consideration of person, place, or time."[2]

Śrīla Prabhupāda lived according to that policy. His aim was not to share intellectual pleasantries, but to convince others of the veracity of his message:

> Whenever anyone would come to see him, Prabhupāda wouldn't waste time—he talked philosophy, with reason and argument. He constantly argued against atheism and impersonalism. He spoke strongly to prove the existence of God, and the universality of Kṛṣṇa consciousness. He talked often and vigorously, day and night, meeting all kinds of questions and philosophies.[3]

Even during Śrīla Prabhupāda's manifest presence, a sub-group of his disciples (headed by Siddha-svarūpānanda Swami) regularly criticized orthodox ISKCON devotees for their strong preaching tactics. Siddha-svarūpānanda's people had their own approach,

---

1 SBV, vol. 1, p. 137.

2 *Harmonist* 26.249–50 (Apr 1929); SBV, vol. 1, p. 145.

3 SPl ch. 18, "Breaking Ground."

which was designed to avoid generating controversy with the public. When Guru-kṛpā Swami opined that they were not following what Śrīla Prabhupāda was doing, but had created their own way to spread Kṛṣṇa consciousness, Śrīla Prabhupāda agreed: "Yes, that idea is there." Although he always encouraged them to chant and maintain the regulative principles, Śrīla Prabhupāda frankly analyzed that Siddha-svarūpānanda and his followers were "thinking of their own way. That is bad." Expressing faith in Śrīla Prabhupāda's direction, Guru-kṛpā Swami said, "You know how to spread Kṛṣṇa consciousness. Therefore I follow. I don't even know what Kṛṣṇa is. I'm just trying to follow. Therefore that will be successful." "That is my preaching," Śrīla Prabhupāda said. "What Kṛṣṇa said, you say as it is. Don't change. How you can give interpretation? And if he thinks that he can give another interpretation, what is this nonsense? Then he's not following guru or Kṛṣṇa, both. One has to receive the mercy of guru and Kṛṣṇa. Through guru, Kṛṣṇa's mercy."[1]

Notwithstanding, presenting Kṛṣṇa consciousness in a manner calculated to appeal to a defective mentality can be effective for bringing apathetic or seriously deluded people (who constitute the vast majority of the world's population) into contact with Kṛṣṇa consciousness. This approach is acceptable, according to Śrīla Prabhupāda's direction that we either defeat challengers or turn them into friends.[2] Nārada Muni's upliftment of Dhruva offers an example of how, by indirect preaching, a expert preacher can deliver even a person who is far from pure devotional service, and that it is not necessary to begin all exchanges forcefully if persons are eventually brought to the right point.[3]

Devotees who are more inclined to restraint than to brazenness can certainly perform important services for spreading the holy name and creating a favorable situation for the propagation of Kṛṣṇa consciousness. However, they should not resent those who

1 Adapted from *A Transcendental Diary*, vol. 2, p. 16.

2 Letter, 5 Feb 1977.

3 See SB 4.8–9.

speak strongly, but should recognize the essential role that such outspoken devotees play.

And those who advocate the initial dispensation of mild dosages must not fail to elevate their spiritual wards to the point of accepting the full dose. Small doses of truth should prepare persons for the full, absolute truth, not for avoiding it or being content with partial truths. To give sugar-coated pills without substance is cheating. The bulk of the pill must be pure medicine. This principle is as valid in spiritual treatment as it is in medical care. As a godbrother wrote me in 2011:

> A prominent doctor was recently arrested here in San Diego. He was given a severe sentence and is condemned by all. What was his shocking and debased crime? He was secretly watering down expensive cancer medicines to the point that they had no effect. If we do the same to the life-saving message of our *ācāryas*, aren't we also criminal?

It may seem axiomatic that to make friends is better than to make enemies, but the real crux of preaching is the attempt to convince others of the reality and effectiveness of Kṛṣṇa consciousness. If we become overly concerned with what the *karmīs* think, becoming involved in the likes and dislikes of others, then we cannot possibly present the simple truth.[1] Notwithstanding that various devotees have differing styles, every preacher's task is to impart to the uninformed the understanding that Kṛṣṇa consciousness affords a compellingly distinctive and meaningful perspective that at the very least warrants their thoughtful consideration. Furthermore, according to the example of our *ācāryas*, it is distinctly better to be known as an enemy of envious persons (like Māyāvādīs) than to make friends with them, which is positively dangerous.

A further danger of the low-key approach is that by descending to the platform of those he is meant to uplift, the devotee becomes

1 See Cc 2.2.86.

affected by their consciousness and thereby compromised into acting, talking, and ultimately thinking like them. By connecting with others at their level of triviality, he trivializes the incalculably profound message of Kṛṣṇa consciousness. If he speaks in the humdrum manner that others are accustomed to, they will reply in their usual, stereotyped way and will treat the devotee as another mundane person—with no benefit to either party. Hence, bolder preachers who deliberately violate the unspoken social rule of keeping conversation light (and thus unthreatening to peoples' insipid, insubstantial existence), thereby protect themselves while attempting to uplift others. The outspoken preacher considers that unless the clear message is consistently spoken, people are unlikely to get it, and that the tactic of starting weakly with the plan to later switch to strong is more likely to confuse people than convince them.

At the very least, speaking the plain truth should not be inordinately delayed, because in and of itself "friendly talking cannot decide any serious question; it does not come to any conclusion."[1] While waiting for others to be "ready" for the real message, we or they could die, or they might lose interest in associating with devotees. Also, speaking the plain truth can be a litmus test for revealing the underlying offensiveness or the insincerity of persons who initially seem friendly toward devotees, but are actually not inclined to make any serious attempt to improve themself in Kṛṣṇa consciousness.

Even if devotees choose not to directly call the nondevotees rogues or rascals, they should at least know that nondevotees definitely *are* rogues and rascals:

> All these leaders, all these rascals—they are all rascals. At least you must know. You may behave gentlemanly, that is your duty. But you should know that he is a rascal number one.[2]

---

1 Lectures, 15 Aug 1973 & 25 Feb 1975.

2 Lecture, 4 Apr 1972.

> If we also become enamored by the so-called scientists, politicians, and philosophers, then we cannot preach. We must definitely be convinced that they're all rascals. As a gentleman, I can give him some respect—that is another thing. But he's a rascal. You must know that "I am talking with a rascal number one." He cannot deviate me from my position, but I can talk in a nice way, gentlemanly. That is another thing; that is courtesy. But I know that these rascals, number one fools, they have no idea.[1]

> You must know that they are all rascal, unbelievers. You have to convert them to be sane men. That is preaching.[2]

Although it might seem safer to not risk provoking others, it is questionable how much others can be benefited by a preacher's withholding from them the facts that they need to know. Certainly it is spiritually safer for himself, and unquestionably auspicious for others, if a devotee maintains the principle of always presenting Kṛṣṇa consciousness straightforwardly.

Ideally, devotees should be conservative in their own practice of devotional service and in understanding of *siddhānta,* and also liberal in making Kṛṣṇa consciousness available to persons who are far removed from it. Devotees should not be so conservative as to insist that things always be done in the same way in all circumstances, regardless of the outcome. Real preachers have to be sensitive to people and circumstances, and sufficiently flexible to make adjustments as required for bringing people to Kṛṣṇa consciousness. They should aspire for the expertise of Śrīla Prabhupāda and Śrīla Bhaktisiddhānta Sarasvatī in maintaining the core principles of Kṛṣṇa consciousness while promulgating it with an innovative spirit based on the maxim *phalena paricīyate:* "Judge by the result."

1 Conversation, 13 Apr 1977.

2 Conversation, 11 Dec 1973.

TWENTY-THREE
SOFT AND HARD

Devotees who consider the radical approach to be incongruous with the sweetness of Kṛṣṇa consciousness should consider that Lord Caitanya was not only as soft as a flower but could also be as hard as a thunderbolt.[1] It may be difficult to comprehend how the all-merciful Lord can be both hard and soft, since softness of heart is the inherent nature of the soul and thus the prime characteristic of a devotee, and is naturally expected to be overwhelmingly manifest in the Lord's most magnanimous descent as Śrī Caitanya Mahāprabhu. However, "these opposing qualities can easily be understood in terms of the Lord's transcendental nature and purpose."[2] A devotee's softness can manifest as hardness toward all that is not Kṛṣṇa conscious, and as the hardness necessary for preaching Kṛṣṇa consciousness in a hard world.

Followers of Lord Caitanya need not always preach like a thunderbolt, but neither should they always be like a flower. To opine that devotees should only be soft like a flower and never hard like a thunderbolt indicates a superficial, imbalanced understanding of Kṛṣṇa consciousness. Śrīla Prabhupāda, the ideal follower of Śrī Caitanya Mahāprabhu, was decorated with innumerable flowerlike transcendental qualities and was

1 Cc 2.7.72.

2 SB 11.11.32, purport.

undoubtedly the greatest saintly person, yet like a thunderbolt he untiringly lambasted the demons—and relished doing so:

> [Prabhupāda:] These animals are passing on as big scientists, philosophers, theologicians, and so on. We have to stop them. *Na māṁ duṣkṛtino mūḍhāḥ prapadyante narādhamāḥ*. This is the qualification of a person who does not accept God. *Duṣkṛtina, narādhama, mūḍha, māyayāpahṛta-jñāna*—although highly educated, no knowledge. *Āsuraṁ bhāvam āśritāḥ*—simply atheist. So as Kṛṣṇa conscious leaders, we have to punish them, chastise these rascals. They are demons.
>
> [Girirāja:] It's actually relishable to chastise them.
>
> [Prabhupāda:] Yes, *(laughs)* it is a pleasure sport.[1]

> That is my business: to punish all these rascals. I become very angry if anyone says before me, "I am God, he is God, everyone ..." I cannot control myself. *[Laughter]* Yes. I am so obstinate enemy of these rascals. I want to kick them on their face, but it is incivility. But I want to kick them. It will be my pleasure. Never mind I go to hell.[2]

However, just as a devotee should not simply be soft, neither should he be exclusively hard. A devotee may be hard externally but should be soft internally. One who is only hard is hardly a devotee, for implacable hardness typifies demons. Yet it is doubtful whether those who are so soft as to not like to fight for Kṛṣṇa even when He is misrepresented and blasphemed, actually have any feeling for Him. Devotees should not emulate those pseudo-sadhus who present themselves as being mild and humble just to enjoy being respected, and to avoid the censure that is inevitably directed at true sadhus who, being deeply concerned for the suffering *jīvas*, speak in a manner intended to shatter the misconceptions at the root of their suffering.

---

1 Conversation, 19 Apr 1977.

2 Lecture, 26 Apr 1972.

Devotees who by nature are soft can also become bold—if they are sincere:

> You mentioned that you are not yet a very bold preacher, but you will become bold, if you have got sincerity. In the beginning also I could not speak. But Kṛṣṇa is within you, and when you are serving Him sincerely He will give you courage, boldness, everything. We are not going to bluff anyone or cheat others, and we are delivering the message on behalf of the Supreme Lord, so we haven't got anything to fear and we should be always mindful of our topmost position of occupation of life.[1]

1 Letter, 16 Jun 1972.

TWENTY-FOUR
POSITIVE AND NEGATIVE

A positive approach in preaching may be defined as one in which hearers are presented with aspects of Kṛṣṇa consciousness that are likely to appeal to them, that promise to enhance their life without adding difficulties; a negative approach may be defined as one that stresses that everything and everyone without Kṛṣṇa consciousness is useless, foolish, and wicked.

Surely, it may seem, it is better to present a positive outlook. "Why not emphasize the joy and sweetness of *bhakti*? What need is there for pointing out others' faults and dwelling on the miseries of material existence? Why be habitually negative?"

Śrīla Bhaktisiddhānta Sarasvatī had a different understanding:

> The truth (*satya*) is propagated in a twofold way, viz., positively, by the method of direct support, and negatively, by the method of opposition. The truth cannot be made sufficiently known by the positive method alone. Propaganda by the method of opposition, more than the presentation of the positive aspect, brings about more brilliantly in this world the appearance and glorification of the truth.[1]
>
> The positive method by itself is not the most effective method of propaganda in a controversial age like the present. The negative

1 *Harmonist* 25.5–6 (Jun 1927); SBV, vol. 3, p. 37.

> method which seeks to differentiate the truth from nontruth in all its forms, is even better calculated to convey the directly inconceivable significance of the Absolute. It is a necessity which cannot be conscientiously avoided by the dedicated preacher of the truth if he wants to be a loyal servant of Godhead. The method is sure to create an atmosphere of controversy in which it is quite easy to lose one's balance of judgment. But the ways of the deluding energy are so intricate that unless their mischievous nature is fully exposed, it is not possible for the soul in the conditioned state to avoid the snares spread by the enchantress [*māyā*] for encompassing the ruin of her only-too-willing victims. It is a duty which shall be sacred to all who have been enabled to attain even a distant glimpse of the Absolute.[1]

Once a woman wrote to Śrīla Prabhupāda complaining that she had met two of his young disciples who had "a very negative outlook." In reply, Śrīla Prabhupāda explained:

> In order to withstand the attack of *māyā* and remain strong under all conditions of temptation, young or inexperienced devotees in the neophyte stage of devotional service will sometimes adopt an attitude against those things or persons which may possibly be harmful or threatening to their tender devotional creepers. They may even overindulge in such feelings just to protect themselves, and thus they will appear to some nondevotees, who are perhaps themselves still very much enamored by the material energy of *māyā*, to be negative or pessimistic.
>
> But the actual fact is that this material world is a miserable, negative place, full of danger at every step; it is *duḥkhālayam aśāśvatam*, a temporary abode of death, birth, disease, and old age, a home of suffering and pain only. To come to the platform of understanding these things as they are is not very common, and therefore persons who attain to it are described as "great souls."
>
> *mām upetya punar janma duḥkhālayam aśāśvatam*
> *nāpnuvanti mahātmānaḥ saṁsiddhiṁ paramāṁ gatāḥ*

---

1 *Harmonist* 29.72–73 (Sep 1931);
SBV, vol. 1, p. 142.

> This means that those who have understood that the material worlds are places of misery and temporality (*duḥkhālayam aśāśvatam*) never return here again, and because they are *mahātmānaḥ*, the great souls, Kṛṣṇa keeps them with Him because they have qualified themselves to escape this nasty place by becoming His pure devotees. This verse is spoken by Kṛṣṇa, or God Himself, in the *Bhagavad-gītā* (8.15). Who can be a more final authority? The point is that to make advancement in spiritual life, one must view everything material with a pessimistic eye unless it is utilized to serve and please Kṛṣṇa. We are not very much hopeful for any lasting pleasure or satisfaction for our deepest cravings within this realm of gross matter.[1]

When questioned if his outlook was negative, Śrīla Prabhupāda replied:

> Why negative? It is the fact. That is the positive understanding. Why do you take it as negative? If you are suffering and if you say, if I say, "Don't suffer," is that negative or that is positive?
>
> [Bali-mardana:] In other words, if you are suffering and I tell you "Don't suffer," it may sound negative but actually it's positive.
>
> [Śrīla Prabhupāda:] Yes, positive. But they are rascals, they are taking it as negative.[2]

Certainly, Kṛṣṇa consciousness is the only true positivity; yet it cannot be entered without negating the negative. Śrīla Prabhupāda repeatedly pointed out that all that is materially desirable—such as wealth, beauty, friends, and education—are all zeros. Yet he often tempered this seeming negativity by further stating that by placing a one—*the* one: Kṛṣṇa—in front of all those zeros, they become transformed into millions. While requesting people to "just add Kṛṣṇa" to their lives, Śrīla Prabhupāda averred, "We never say to stop everything material," yet qualified this by continuing, "but we have to stop anything which is against Kṛṣṇa consciousness (such

---

1 *The Science of Self-realization*, ch. 7 (d).

2 Conversation, 16 Jul 1976.

as meat-eating)."[1] It thus appears that even when presenting Kṛṣṇa consciousness in what could be termed a "positive manner," Śrīla Prabhupāda did not try to hide certain essential aspects of Kṛṣṇa consciousness that are unlikely to appeal to many people. Adding Kṛṣṇa is a beginning, but to really advance in Kṛṣṇa consciousness requires an eventual wholesale change of outlook and conduct.

That Śrīla Prabhupāda did not approve of habitual one-sided negativity that neglects to present the positive is indicated in the following anecdote. One morning, Tamāla Kṛṣṇa Goswami related that the lecturer in the temple had, along with speaking on other topics, criticized false gurus. Śrīla Prabhupāda became displeased and said that we must be positive and speak about real gurus. "This criticizing tendency will not attract. We must ourselves be ideal."[2] (This was less than a day after Śrīla Prabhupāda had himself scaldingly attacked politicians in the presence of a politician.)

1 E.g., see: Lecture, 1 May 1973.

2 *TKG's Diary*, 20 May.

TWENTY-FIVE
UNPALATABLE TRUTH

अनुद्वेगकरं वाक्यं सत्यं प्रियहितं च यत् ।
स्वाध्यायाभ्यसनं चैव वाङ्मयं तप उच्यते ॥

anudvega-karaṁ vākyaṁ satyaṁ priya-hitaṁ ca yat
svādhyāyābhyasanaṁ caiva vāṅ-mayaṁ tapa ucyate

Austerity of speech consists in speaking words that are truthful, pleasing, beneficial, and not agitating to others, and also in regularly reciting Vedic literature.

This austerity of speech is symptomatic of *sattva-guṇa,* the mode of goodness. In his purport to this verse (Bg 17.15), Śrīla Prabhupāda states: "One should not speak in such a way as to agitate the minds of others. Of course, when a teacher speaks, he can speak the truth for the instruction of his students, but such a teacher should not speak to those who are not his students if he will agitate their minds." Similarly, a well-known Vedic guideline prioritizes pleasantness over truth—*satyaṁ brūyāt priyaṁ brūyāt mā brūyāt satyam apriyam:* "Speak truthfully, speak palatably, do not speak unpalatable truths."[1]

These are general recommendations for social dealings among cultured people. Ideally, all that is spoken should be very sweet to

1 *Manu-saṁhitā.*

hear, full of meaning, appropriately presented, and perfectly true.[1] However, such an ideal is only realizable among persons who are ready to accept the truth, for the message of ultimate truth tends to upset rather than to please.* Often one must choose whether to speak the truth or to speak pleasingly, or to not speak at all to persons who are likely to become agitated by hearing the truth. Particularly on the platform of service to God, the principle of speaking the truth overrides that of speaking palatably:

> When you speak of higher truths, you don't care whether it is palatable to others or not.[2]

> *Satyam,* truthfulness, means that facts should be presented as they are, for the benefit of others. Facts should not be misrepresented. According to social conventions, it is said that one can speak the truth only when it is palatable to others. But that is not truthfulness. The truth should be spoken in a straightforward way, so that others will understand actually what the facts are. If a man is a thief and if people are warned that he is a thief, that is truth. Although sometimes the truth is unpalatable, one should not refrain from speaking it. Truthfulness demands that the facts be presented as they are for the benefit of others.† That is the definition of truth.[3]

> People may not like it. It may be very unpalatable, but the fact is like that. *Satyaṁ brūyāt priyaṁ brūyāt mā brūyāt satyam apriyam.* It is social convention that if you want to speak truth, you speak truth very palatable, flattering, don't speak unpalatable truth. But we are

* I challenge any devotee who disbelieves this to put it to a test: For a week, or at least a day, tell as many nondevotees as you can (in as pleasing a manner as possible) that this world is miserable due to the unavoidable miseries of birth, death, old age, and disease, and that human life is meant not for sense enjoyment but for making a solution to these problems.

† The importance of this point is evident from Śrīla Prabhupāda's stating it twice within this paragraph.

1 Adapted from SB 1.19.22.

2 Lecture, 10 Jul 1968.

3 Bg 10.4–5, purport.

> not meant for that purpose—social convention. We are preacher. We are servant of God. We must speak the real truth. You may like it or may not like it.[1]

Śrīla Prabhupāda intricately discussed this principle in correspondence with Sumati Morarji (a follower of Vallabhācārya), who had taken umbrage at a *Back to Godhead* article describing Lord Caitanya's comparing Vallabhācārya to an unfaithful wife.[2] Śrīla Prabhupāda apologized: "It is certainly unpleasant, but the officers who publish the magazine do not know *satyaṁ brūyāt priyaṁ brūyāt.*" He went on to state that the cause of Lord Caitanya's agitation was much the same as Mrs. Morarji's: "As you are irritated by the criticism of Śrī Vallabhācārya, similarly Śrī Caitanya Mahāprabhu was also agitated when Vallabhācārya criticized Śrīdhara Svāmī." Śrīla Prabhupāda explained that Lord Caitanya and Vallabhācārya were friends, and that their arguing may be compared to the wrangling of two lawyers in a courtroom; after the parley they again relate as friends. Śrīla Prabhupāda's concluding remarks serve as a guide to Vaiṣṇava etiquette when dealing with delicate controversial topics:

> Devotees always humbly offer respect to everyone, but when there is a discussion on a point of *śāstra*, they do not observe the usual etiquette, *satyaṁ brūyāt priyaṁ brūyāt*. They speak only the *satyam* [truth], although it may not necessarily be *priyam* [pleasing].[3]

Elsewhere, *śāstra* states:

प्रियमुक्तं हि तं नैतदिति मत्वा न तद्वदेत् ।
श्रेयस्तद्रहितं वाच्यं यद्यप्यत्यन्तविप्रियम् ॥

priyam uktaṁ hi taṁ naitad iti matvā na tad vadet
śreyas tad-rahitaṁ vācyaṁ yadyapy atyanta-vipriyam

---

1 Lecture, 20 Oct 1968.

2 BTG 10-08 (Aug 1975). For the incident re Lord Caitanya and Śrī Vallabhācārya, see Cc 3.7.109–18.

3 Letter, 9 Aug 1976.

> A statement that seems pleasant, but that is not actually beneficial, should not be uttered. But even if extremely unpleasant, the ultimate good should be spoken.[1]

In the above-quoted correspondence, Śrīla Prabhupāda expertly asserted the truth (*satyam*) without compromise, without backing down from his position, yet did it pleasingly (*priyam*). This should be the standard for devotees who are highly concerned with being pleasing (even though that was not Śrīla Prabhupāda's prime concern).

The *satyaṁ brūyāt* verse may also be understood as a direction to speak the truth in a manner meant to benefit others. To speak the truth but with the intention to exploit others or for self-promotion—to flaunt one's own qualities or achievements, or to pose as a great preacher—does not serve the cause of the *ācāryas* or please Kṛṣṇa. Similarly, to speak the truths of *śāstra* in a harsh and mean-spirited manner meant to harm the persons spoken to, or others being spoken about, is influenced by the mode of ignorance and is as bad or worse than untruth; it cannot bring people toward Kṛṣṇa, and is more likely to drive them away.

---

1 *Viṣṇu Purāṇa*, 3.12.44; *Hari-bhakti-vilāsa*, 11.713.

TWENTY-SIX
DISCRETION AND TACT

Along with the need to present Kṛṣṇa consciousness clearly and spiritedly, another important principle is "Discretion is the better part of valor" (which Śrīla Prabhupāda sometimes quoted).[1] An important feature of a *madhyama-adhikārī*, which distinguishes him from a neophyte, is that he is careful not to fall into the pit of false arguments;[2] he chooses his battles and does not get entangled in useless squabbles (for instance, over trivialities, or with fanatical Christians). A seasoned preacher also tends to concentrate his efforts on persons who are most likely to accept the Kṛṣṇa conscious message, knowing that many people are highly impervious to it: "While rendering first aid service in the battlefield the Red Cross men, although equally disposed to all the wounded soldiers, give first preference to the hopeful ones. The hopeless ones are sometimes neglected."[3]

Śrīla Prabhupāda also cited the Bengali maxim "Enter like a needle and come out like a plow."[4] Certain circumstances particularly call for prudence and diplomacy, such as in countries whose oppressive governments disfavor devotees, or to avoid unnecessarily alienating influential persons. And although all devotees are mandated to preach Kṛṣṇa consciousness strongly and distinctly,

1 E.g.: SB 1.15.24.

2 Cc 2.25.279.

3 Letter, 7 Jul 1958.

4 Conversation, 9 Oct 77.

those who spend much of their lives in secular situations generally cannot speak as freely as can full-time, dedicated preachers. For instance, in many cases it would not be advisable for devotees who are employed in an office or a factory, attending college, or transacting business to preach forthrightly and thus risk, respectively, being fired, being expelled, or losing financial deals. Similarly, interacting with nondevotee relatives may also warrant restraint.

During his years as a married man doing business, Śrīla Prabhupāda mostly preached by assisting various of his godbrothers who were full-time preachers and via his strident *Back To Godhead* magazine. This fact, however, does not negate the overall thesis of this book, for even during his household life Śrīla Prabhupāda was high-spirited. For example, sometimes he would urge a certain sannyasi godbrother to accompany him in charging Gandhi and Nehru as to why they were not following the principles of the *Bhagavad-gītā*![1]

Thus the need for tact is by no means a call to compromise; rather, it entails a sense of knowing the right moment and method for presenting delicate points in a manner conducive for their acceptance. In the following letter, Śrīla Prabhupāda outlined a method of carefully outlining philosophical arguments and thereby preparing listeners to hear unwelcome facts:

> If we speak the naked truth to the people, sometimes they may get angry because unpalatable truth is not tolerated. If we call a black man black he will be angry because it is unpalatable. So we have to present our case very carefully. The best way of presentation will be like this: 1) Yoga system is recommended in the *Bhagavad-gītā*; 2) It is an approved system; 3) But it is not suitable for ordinary man, especially in this age of Kali; 4) The so-called yoga system practiced by the people of this age is not bona fide. They cannot follow all the

---

1 SPl ch. 5, "The War."

> rules and regulations of yoga practice; 5) Therefore it is conclusive that so-called yoga followers are simply cheated and they are wasting their time. I have already explained these points in the *sāṅkhya*-yoga chapter of the *Bhagavad-gītā As It Is*, so you read them carefully and present it, point by point, in suitable occasions.[1]

In another letter, Śrīla Prabhupāda promoted boldness yet also endorsed specifically palatable presentations if they were faithful to the spiritual authorities and actually effective in convincing others:

> Our presentation of Kṛṣṇa consciousness must be always very bold—if we are king, we must act like king.... Still, it was my method to make Kṛṣṇa consciousness palatable to you Western boys and girls, how else could I attract you to give up your habits of sense gratification? Kṛṣṇa philosophy can be approached from every angle because it is the Complete Whole, *pūrṇam*. So if your scientific explanation, beginning from the point that sound vibration is the root cause of everything, and leading to the understanding that Kṛṣṇa is the cause of the sound vibration is having good effect, why not continue in this way? Only thing is to remain true to the authorities—Kṛṣṇa, the great saints and *ācāryas*—and everything you say will come out nicely. People are of different natures so we have to use our talents how to convince people in different circumstances.[2]

Best is if devotees can impart the genuine message of Kṛṣṇa consciousness to people without disturbing them:*

> The highest development of Kṛṣṇa conscious understanding will be when you are able to give anyone the truth but in such a manner that they will respond in a positive way.... The idea is not what you are saying, so much as how you say it. If you understand this properly,

* That to do so is not always possible has been stated at various places in this book—for example, on p. 110.

1 Letter, 19 Mar 1969.

2 Letter, 15 Nov 1971.

> then you may be able to say the truth at all times in the most palatable way, according to the situation and the type of hearer.[1]

Similarly, Śrīla Prabhupāda wrote: "We have to speak the truth but very palatably."[2] In the following exchange, Śrīla Prabhupāda resolved the apparent dichotomy between straightforwardness and tact:

> [Paramahaṁsa:] Our position in preaching should be to encourage people in all respects to associate with us.
>
> [Prabhupāda:] Yes.
>
> [Paramahaṁsa:] That means sometimes we might have to compromise in certain ways.
>
> [Prabhupāda:] Why compromise? Don't compromise. If you compromise, you associate with him. Then gradually you'll also go down. When we see some person, we do not associate with him, but we give him chance to associate with me. Why you should make compromise? What is the reason? If you know something positively, why should you compromise? When people come to talk with me, I don't make any compromise. Do I make any compromise?
>
> [Devotees:] No.
>
> [Prabhupāda:] Then why shall we make compromise? That gentleman ... said, "It has taken eighteen years to write these books." I said, "Still, there are so many mistakes." Immediately I said. And he could not say anything. Immediately I said, "Yes, you have labored eighteen years. Still, there are so many mistakes."
>
> [Nitāi:] Anyone else would have said, "Oh! Very nice."
>
> [Prabhupāda:] *(Laughs)* I did not say.
>
> [Puṣṭa Kṛṣṇa:] He said that morning, "What can we do, Prabhupāda?" He said, "What can we do? If we do not compromise, we will make enemies."

1 Letter, 31 Dec 1972.

2 Letter, 31 Aug 1975.

[Prabhupāda:] No, you'll not compromise; at the same time, you'll not make enemies. That is tactics. If you make enemies, then what is your tactics? You must speak the truth; at the same time he'll not be displeased. That is tactics. If you can defeat him by your argument, then he'll not be displeased. After all, everyone is human being. If you can find out his defect, why he shall be enemy? Therefore it is said, "You better make a reasonable man an enemy, but don't make a friend [of a] fool." Don't make friendship with a fool, but if a man is intelligent, better make him an enemy. Because, because he's intelligent, although he's an enemy he'll not do any harm, because [he is] intelligent. But a fool may pose himself as friend, and he can do anything which is very harmful.

[Paramahaṁsa:] So we should be able to see the quality of man we are preaching to.

[Prabhupāda:] Yes, you have to make him intelligent. Everyone is fool, *mūḍha*. Everyone within this material world is supposed to be a fool.[1]

Śrīla Prabhupāda further explained how not to compromise and yet be tactful:

[Young man:] Śrīla Prabhupāda, how does one surrendering to Kṛṣṇa discriminate between being tactful in his speech, on one hand, and on the other hand compromising?

[Prabhupāda:] To surrender to Kṛṣṇa is the best tactfulness, and if you surrender He will give you instruction. Then all tactfulness will be there.

तेषां सततयुक्तानां भजतां प्रीतिपूर्वकम् ।
दद‍ामि बुद्धियोगं तं येन मामुपयान्ति ते ॥

teṣāṁ satata-yuktānāṁ bhajatāṁ prīti-pūrvakam
dadāmi buddhi-yogaṁ taṁ yena mām upayānti te

If you become a completely surrendered devotee of Kṛṣṇa—He is within your heart—He will give you the right instruction so that in

1 Conversation, 11 Jun 1974.

every sphere of life you'll be perfect.[1]

We should not compromise in any way just to accommodate the public idea, but we can so tastefully present the real thing that we will change the people to accommodate us.[2]

Śrīla Prabhupāda himself was expert at communicating unpalatable truths in a manner that others could accept. When once passing by the mansion of one of the world's richest oil tycoons, he told his disciples that if ever they were able to meet that man, they should tell him that he was a big thief who would be punished for usurping so much oil that belongs to God. Dayānanda Dāsa, who was present on that walk past the mansion, also witnessed (some years later) how in the course of a friendly conversation Śrīla Prabhupāda cornered a businessman into admitting being a thief.[3] Hari Śauri Dāsa described that exchange:

Prabhupāda welcomed [a certain Life Member] and asked what his business was.

The man told him he owned a glass manufacturing factory. When Prabhupāda asked what the glass was made from, he replied, "From silicon, Swamiji, from sand."

"And who owns the sand?" Prabhupāda asked.

"Bhagavān, God, owns the sand."

"Oh, you are stealing from Bhagavān?" Prabhupāda challenged.

The man laughed. He was slightly embarrassed but obviously appreciated Śrīla Prabhupāda's swift expose and lesson in proprietorship. He thought for a minute, and then, as if to offset the implied criticism, ventured that he gave a lot in charity.

Prabhupāda got him a second time. "Oh, then you are just a little thief," he said teasingly.

1 Lecture, 22 Apr 1976. The verse cited is Bg 10.10.

2 Letter, 16 Feb 1972.

3 *Śrīla Prabhupāda Nectar.*

> Everyone laughed and the man was happy to be further enlightened as to his real position as subordinate to God.[1]

Śrīla Prabhupāda once demonstrated a simple but powerful technique for preparing potential doubters and antagonists to hear unpalatable facts. When a reporter asked him about the "moon expedition," Śrīla Prabhupāda responded, "Should I flatter you or shall I tell the truth?"[2]

Inseparable from tact is patience. In Hamburg in 1969, Śrīla Prabhupāda discussed with an Indologist over the course of several days before the man understood the unpleasant point that Śrīla Prabhupāda wished to convey. Kṛṣṇa Dāsa recalled:

> A couple of days after Prabhupāda arrived in Hamburg, Dr. Bernhardt came.... Prabhupāda talked with him, and the entire conversation was in Sanskrit. As a matter of fact, every now and then Prabhupāda would put in a couple of words of English for our benefit. For three or four days there were continual meetings between Prabhupāda and Dr. Bernhardt. They culminated in a statement by Dr. Bernhardt. He lapsed into English and said, "What you are saying is that all my knowledge is useless without devotional service." Prabhupāda said, "Yes, now you've understood." Then Dr. Bernhardt said, "What you're saying is that all my studies and entire library are just like an ass laden down with so many books that are ultimately pushing him to his grave." Again Prabhupāda said, "Yes, that is right."[3]

Notwithstanding his being the recipient of such an unflattering appraisal, Dr. Bernhardt remained favorable to devotees.*

In Manila in 1972, Śrīla Prabhupāda demonstrated tact in dealing with a philosophical opponent:

* For instance, in 1971 he helped Kṛṣṇa Dāsa to contact Indologists in Russia (SPl ch. 34, "Jet-age Parivrājakācārya").

1 *A Transcendental Diary*, vol. 1, p. 285.

2 Recounted in a lecture of 30 Sep 1972.

3 *Prabhupāda-līlā*, 7-7: "Preaching in Germany, 1969."

After his lecture, Prabhupāda called for questions. An Indian man stood up and said in a loud voice, "Isn't it true that the all-inclusive conception of the Absolute ..." He rambled on. After about three minutes, the audience began fidgeting.

Prabhupāda leaned toward the microphone and asked, "Are you finished?" "No," the man retorted, and he continued for another two minutes. Again Prabhupāda asked, "Are you finished yet?" "No, let me speak." His monologue of disjointed, spiritual-sounding phrases continued. After another three minutes, the audience began to wax angry. Prabhupāda again gently spoke into the microphone, "Are you finished yet?"

"Yes, now I am finished."

Prabhupāda thundered into the microphone, "Then sit down!" The hall filled with laughter and cheering.

Had Prabhupāda interrupted the man before he was able to "ask" his self-serving "question," the audience would have favored the man. Prabhupāda waited and allowed the man to parade his foolishness. When the audience had sufficient time to realize the man's motives, Prabhupāda, with the full backing of the audience, demanded that the man sit down. Prabhupāda was expert.[1]

In the following anecdote, Śrīla Prabhupāda first calmed the emotions of an upset visitor, then reiterated the very point that had disturbed him:

When he first met Śrīla Prabhupāda, an elderly gentleman who was connected with a yoga society respectfully stated, "Swamiji, I like your movement very much, but one thing is that one of your disciples said that Swami [name withheld] is a rascal.Yet it always seemed to me that he was a very holy man, so I don't understand why your disciple would say that you said he's a rascal."

Prabhupāda asked, "Who has said this?"

---

1 *My Glorious Master*, pp. 167–68.

The man replied, "You didn't say?"

Prabhupāda answered, "If they say that I have said and I have not said, then they are rascal."

The man became pacified.

After a little conversation, Śrīla Prabhupāda took an edition of the *Bhagavad-gītā* from his bookshelf and handed it to the man, saying, "You know this book?"

The man looked at it and responded, "Oh, Swami [name withheld], Dr. [name withheld]. Oh, Vedanta Society. Oh, yes!"—seeming quite pleased at seeing something familiar to him.

Śrīla Prabhupāda opened the book and told the man to read the translation of a certain verse. The man read, "Always think of Me, devote yourself to Me, worship Me, offer your homage to Me."

Śrīla Prabhupāda said, "Yes, he has done it nicely. He is a very good scholar. Then the commentary, what does he say?"

So the man began reading, "It is not to Kṛṣṇa that we have to surrender but to the unborn impersonal ..."

Śrīla Prabhupāda interjected: "Just see! Therefore I say they are all rascals!" And then he explained why such persons are rascals. He quoted *na māṁ duṣkṛtino mūḍhāḥ prapadyante narādhamāḥ/ māyayāpahṛta-jñānā āsuraṁ bhāvam āśritāḥ*—that they are either miscreants, the lowest of mankind, those whose knowledge is stolen by illusion, or who are demonic. "Because just see: Kṛṣṇa is saying "Me" and they are saying "not Kṛṣṇa." Therefore I say."[1]

When in Melbourne in 1976 a discussion with a Māyāvādī professor degenerated to the point of both the scholar and Śrīla Prabhupāda

---

1 Jayādvaita Swami, *Following Srila Prabhupada*, DVD 1.

accusing each other of being a fanatic, Śrīla Prabhupāda deftly turned the subject away from philosophy. The conversation soon became light-hearted, and the professor calmed down, dropped his defensiveness, and developed a friendlier demeanor. After the meeting, the professor took *prasāda* with the devotees. Finally, fully relaxed, he apologized for any misunderstandings and left.[1]

In San Francisco, in 1967:

> Almost every night someone would come to argue with Prabhupāda. One man came regularly with prepared arguments from a philosophy book, from which he would read aloud. Prabhupāda would defeat him, and the man would go home, prepare another argument, and come back again with his book. One night, after the man had presented his challenge, Prabhupāda simply looked at him without bothering to reply. Prabhupāda's neglect was another defeat for the man, who got up and left.[2]

In dealing with people who are not inclined to hear our message, Śrīla Prabhupāda often recommended the tactic of first briefly flattering them and then, having gained their favor, speaking the hard and straight truth:

> If you say, "Oh, you are a *karmī*, you are a *mūḍha* ..." Actually he's a *mūḍha*, but in the beginning if you say like that, then there will be no opportunity to speak. He is a *mūḍha*, there is no doubt—working like hogs and dogs day and night for sense gratification. Certainly he is a *mūḍha*, a *karmī*. We have to preach, but if we say directly "You are all *mūḍhas*, *māyayāpahṛta-jñānā*, and *duṣkṛtina*," they will be angry. Because *satyaṁ brūyāt priyaṁ brūyāt:* you have to speak the truth very cautiously. Otherwise they will be angry. *Murkhāyopadeśo hi prakopāya na śāntaye:* "If you give good instruction to a rascal, he'll be angry."
>
> Therefore Prabodhānanda Sarasvatī is teaching us how we should present our case. *Dante nidhāya tṛṇakam:* "Sir, I have come to you,

1 *The Great Transcendental Adventure* (by Kūrma Dāsa), pp. 597–598.

2 SPl ch. 22, "Swami Invites the Hippies."

taking this grass in my teeth." In India, this is a symbolic representation of becoming very humble. They take a grass. *Dante nidhāya padayor nipatya*: "And I am falling down on your feet." *Kāku-śataṁ kṛtvā*: "And I am flattering you. You are very grand. You are very nice. You are very learned. You are so on, so on." If you flatter, people become puffed up. So, *dante nidhāya tṛṇakaṁ padayor nipatya kāku-śataṁ kṛtvā cāham*: "I have one submission."

"What is that?" "*He sādhavaḥ*: You are a great learned sadhu. My one request is that whatever nonsense you have learned, please forget it. This is my submission." "I have learned so many things, and I have to forget? Then what do I have to do?" "*He sādhavaḥ sakalam eva vihāya dūrāt caitanya-candra-caraṇe kurutānurāgam*: You just submit yourself to Caitanya-candra. Then everything will be perfect."

This should be the preaching method, because you cannot enforce. The atheistic party, the godless civilization, is so strong. So you are not weak. You are protected by the Supreme. But our mission is not to fight; our mission is to convince. So this is the method to be accepted by devotees, those who are in Kṛṣṇa consciousness, to preach the philosophy in the world.[1]

Śrī Caitanya Mahāprabhu turned the minds of the Māyāvādī *sannyāsīs*. They were melted by the sweet words of Śrī Caitanya Mahāprabhu and thus became friendly and spoke to Him also in sweet words. Similarly, all preachers will have to meet opponents, but they should not make them more inimical. They are already enemies, and if we talk with them harshly or impolitely their enmity will merely increase. We should therefore follow in the footsteps of Lord Caitanya Mahāprabhu as far as possible and try to convince the opposition by quoting from the *śāstras* and presenting the conclusion of the *ācāryas*. It is in this way that we should try to defeat all the enemies of the Lord.[2]

Ācāryas in the disciplic succession of Lord Caitanya teach us that we shall try to place the message of Lord Caitanya very humbly to the people in general and that will make us successful in our service to the Lord.[3]

1 Lectures, 17 Nov 1976 & 23 Jan 1967.

2 Cc 1.7.99, purport.

3 Letter, 26 Apr 1968.

An excellent way to get points across without making offense is by humor, a technique often expertly employed by Śrīla Prabhupāda—getting others to laugh at their own folly. To a challenging mini-skirted reporter who asked, "Why do you people have bald heads?" Śrīla Prabhupāda retorted, "Why do you have bare legs?" She was speechless. Śrīla Prabhupāda then offered, "Better to have warm legs and a cool head." Everyone, including the reporter, laughed with delight. Śrīla Prabhupāda added, "You must have a cool head to understand this Kṛṣṇa consciousness philosophy."[1] However the use of humor also risks insulting people even more deeply than if they had been addressed straightforwardly.

Another aspect of tact is to introduce topics of Kṛṣṇa consciousness according to and in the language of various areas of interest, such as ecology or vegetarianism. In this vein, Śrīla Prabhupāda founded the Bhaktivedanta Institute as a parallel organization to ISKCON, specifically for presenting the philosophy of Kṛṣṇa consciousness in a manner suitable for scientists and other intellectuals. However, in approaching various interest groups, devotees must be careful not to simply find common ground, but to remain focused on promoting Kṛṣṇa consciousness.

> We will present our program at Bhaktivedanta Manor exactly in the line of Lord Caitanya, by *kīrtana*, *prasāda* distribution, and speaking from *Bhagavad-gītā*. We cannot deviate even an inch in order to attract the followers of the ecology philosophy or any other materialistic utopian movement.[2]

Although Śrīla Prabhupāda's instructions regarding tact and fighting may appear equivocal, the conclusion is not difficult to understand: although tact is sometimes advisable, and public chanting and similar outreach programs must go on, the general tenor of the preaching movement should be to combat and overcome the demonic civilization:

---

1 *Śrīla Prabhupāda Nectar.*

2 Letter, 3 Mar 1974.

> You should not be simply chanting and dancing. Along with that, you must know philosophy. There are so many Māyāvādīs. You have to defeat them. It is not that we are cowards. We are Kṛṣṇa's soldiers. So as soon as there is Māyāvādī attack, you must immediately defeat them. That is wanted.[1]

Neither of these directives—to preach unpretentiously and to preach with tact—can be given up. Preaching is not solely logic and argument, but neither is it all sweetness and effusion. The art of administering medicine must be learned from an expert doctor. The doctor whom we have accepted is Śrīla Prabhupāda, who sometimes charmed and sometimes blasted. As a practical, experienced preacher, Śrīla Prabhupāda was acutely familiar with the realities of attempting to communicate the message of *śāstra* to persons disinclined to hear it. Adept in presenting controversial topics to tough audiences, Śrīla Prabhupāda nonetheless was never unclear—and could be bluntly straightforward:

> We have to follow in the footsteps of Lord Caitanya Mahāprabhu, executing our mission peacefully, or, if necessary, kicking the heads of such protesters.[2]

In other words, however peaceful devotees may want to be, they may sometimes have to use "the chopping technique":

> Compromise and flattery have no effect where strong words are required.[3]

Thus, Śrīla Prabhupāda advocated both strong preaching and preaching with discretion. The art is to present Kṛṣṇa consciousness directly, but with tact and circumspection as necessary. The experienced preacher, remaining robust both in his principles and presentation, is expert in communicating Kṛṣṇa consciousness to the various persons he meets, according to their individual

1 Lecture, 16 Jun 1972.

2 Cc 1.17.218, purport.

3 *Perfection of Yoga*, ch. 4.

personality and disposition, and knows how and when to apply tact without compromising his position. Devotees should aim at being uncompromising—depending on the circumstances, sometimes presenting the message starkly and sometimes employing tact and diplomacy:

> Deal tactfully in your preaching. Do not compromise the truth, but speak palatably so he does not reject it but accepts it. That is preaching.[1]

> Straightly preach. Of course, you may say all these things in soft language just so as not to make any agitation.[2]

Although Śrīla Prabhupāda sometimes cautioned his followers to be tactful, he himself typified aggressiveness in preaching and particularly appreciated the same in his disciples. Hence, notwithstanding the case for careful preaching, the spirit of combating rogues and rascals should never be abandoned:

> We say these are all rascals. Generally I say this very strong word, but that is the only word to be used for them: rascals. Simply rascals. We have no business with them that we have to flatter. We say you are rascals—that's all. Straight, blunt.[3]

Although discretion is an important principle, it remains ever subordinate to serving the truth. To consider otherwise converts us into mundaners who "live and let live," and thus live and die in ignorance. Therefore, if on the plea of tact the message is tailored principally to titillate mundane sensibilities, then the preacher ceases to be a sadhu, and joins the ranks of the cheaters.

---

1 Letter, 1 Sep 1975.

2 Lecture, 5 Oct 1974.

3 Conversation, 13 Jun 1976.

TWENTY-SEVEN
TO NAME OR NOT TO NAME

When at the ashram of Mahatma Gandhi in Wardha, central India, Bāsu Ghoṣa Dāsa ventured, "Śrīla Prabhupāda, Mahatma Gandhi ..." Śrīla Prabhupāda cut him off: "Don't criticize Gandhi here. This is his place. They won't understand." On another occasion, Śrīla Prabhupāda quoted the saying "In private one may say that the queen is a prostitute, but one cannot say it publicly."[1] * In the same vein, Śrīla Prabhupāda advised:

> I have heard with delight of your preaching attempts. That is one of our businesses: to expose these rascals who are cheating and who have no spiritual asset. We don't say publicly that they are rascal; otherwise they will condemn also. But by practical action they will see and compare. Simply chant and dance, distribute *prasāda*, and, where possible, some books. Nobody will be grudged.[2]

A similar point regarding tact was mentioned (p. 189) in the exchange with Sumati Morarji, about which Śrīla Prabhupāda had previously cautioned:

> We cannot attack anyone directly in writing. There is a proverb in Sanskrit that you can speak something one thousand times but don't

* The advent of the internet has blurred the distinction between public and private. Even if spoken in a small group, usually any controversial statement of a prominent person becomes public.

1 *ISKCON in the 1970s*, vol. 1, p. 28.

2 Letter, 4 Jun 1976.

> give it in writing. Similarly, we may use some strong words against all this nonsense, but if we write it in black and white, that will not be good. So instead of naming these rascals directly, you change the word to "mental speculators."[1]

Śrīla Prabhupāda further elaborated on this topic in his reply to a disciple who had proposed composing a book to discuss the failures of various famous persons:

> *Satyaṁ vada mā likha:* you can criticize them with your mouth, but don't put into writing. That will create a section of enemy. Then we'll have to fight with the enemy one after another. That will be wasting of time and energy. What is the use of criticizing them? They are failure. Let us prove by action that all others are failures. To criticize them means to give them some importance, that "the rival to Hare Kṛṣṇa." We don't care for them. We go on positively, and automatically they are failure. There is a proverb in Bengali, *chuco mere hāte gandha:* if you want to kill a *chuco* [a type of small rodent], then your hand will [get a] bad flavor. Keep your position respectable. Don't create many enemies.[2]

In his books, Śrīla Prabhupāda several times obliquely criticized the Ramakrishna Mission, but without naming it.* He explained why not to Jayapatākā Swami, who was preaching in Bengal, where the Ramakrishna Mission was based and was most prominent: "We should not criticize the Ramakrishna Mission by name, or directly, for they have become somehow or other popular and people are against us for it. So carefully avoid this type of preaching."[3]

Once Patita-pāvana Dāsa was climbing the stairs to Śrīla Prabhupāda's apartment in Juhu, Mumbai, when a man came bounding down, flushed with anger. When Patita-pāvana reached the top, he saw through the slightly open door to the apartment

* Examples: Bg 10.42, purport; SB 4.27.11, purport.

1 Letter, 30 Aug 1969.

2 Conversation, 5 Jul 1977.

3 Letter, 22 Sep 1976.

that Śrīla Prabhupāda was sitting inside, shaking his head and saying to himself, "I just can't do it. I just can't do it. I just can't criticize Ramakrishna like that any more."[1] *

In one exchange, devotees noted to Śrīla Prabhupāda his technique of undermining the importance of known persons and smashing their philosophy without personally attacking them: "Every time I've seen a reporter say, 'Swamiji, what do you think about so and so?' you [Śrīla Prabhupāda] said, 'I do not know about such persons.' Immediately that person becomes very unimportant. You don't even know about him! And then you'd begin to preach."[2] Another way that Śrīla Prabhupāda often responded when asked his opinion about various supposedly important persons was to inquire, "What is his philosophy?" Śrīla Prabhupāda advised, "Let others present the philosophy of [So-and-so], and then you smash it, crush it by kicking."[3]

However, Śrīla Prabhupāda did not always himself adhere to this principle:

> We sometimes criticize big men. On what strength? That strength is because we have taken shelter of Kṛṣṇa consciousness, Caitanya Mahāprabhu. Otherwise, any ordinary man can criticize. Just like the consulate general in San Francisco—he was speaking to me that "Swamiji, you have called Maharishi a rascal?" "Yes. I may have called. What is that?"[4]

When reporters in Hong Kong in 1974 pushed him to comment about one "Guru Maharaj Ji," mentioning that he claimed to be Kṛṣṇa, Śrīla Prabhupāda at first evaded the question, but when

* See also the anecdote on p. 3, which also describes a man leaving in anger after Śrīla Prabhupāda had named and spoken unfavorably of a so-called avatar (presumably Ramakrishna).

1 Told by Patita-pāvana Dāsa to Bhakti Vikāsa Swami.

2 Conversation, 5 Jul 1977.

3 Ibid.

4 Lecture, 24 May 1969.

the reporters further prodded him, Śrīla Prabhupāda suddenly responded, "This Guru Maharaj Ji is a cheat! Yes, he is a cheat. But Kṛṣṇa is God. He can be a bigger cheat! Guru Maharaj Ji is a cheat, but he will get cheated by Kṛṣṇa."[1] Śrīla Prabhupāda's comments received international news coverage, which very much pleased Śrīla Prabhupāda and very much displeased that cheater's followers. Śrīla Prabhupāda commented, "I did not want to speak against him, but they insisted. I could not help myself."[2]

Some months later, when discussing with a few of his own disciples about that same rascal, Śrīla Prabhupāda ordered them:

> Preach against him. What is the proof that he is God? If we remain silent, then that means we accept whatever he says. I can kick on the face of this ... I can urine on the face of ... What can he do? If he's God, then let him kill me by his power. When I go to kick on his face, let him stop me; then I shall accept that he's God. So why don't you do that? He's saying [he is] God. You just kick on his face. In this way, make some counterpropaganda. If we allow him to go on, then so many people are falsely being misled. We must make some counterpropaganda. At least we should not allow the people to be in darkness and accept him as God. We have got our meeting. We shall say that he is a rascal. Call him by all ill names. He should be insulted everywhere. A cheater. He does not believe in the authoritative scriptures. And he has become God? What he has done? How you have become so foolish? God has created the universe—what he has created?[3]

When a devotee told Śrīla Prabhupāda that at one of Guru Maharaj Ji's meetings, someone had thrown a pie in his face, Śrīla Prabhupāda recommended that "our men" do the same.[4]

To a reporter who asked Śrīla Prabhupāda if he had ever met people like Sai Baba or Bala Yogeshvar (another name for Guru Maharaj Ji), Śrīla Prabhupāda responded:

---

1 *My Glorious Master*, p. 198.

2 *Life with the Perfect Master*, ch. 3.

3 Conversation, 13 Aug 1973.

4 Ibid.

> Why shall I meet these nonsense? Fools and rascals may meet them. Why shall I meet? What can I get from them? What is their special value? Tell me, why shall I meet? What is the business I have got to meet him?[1]

When some disciples asked Śrīla Prabhupāda how to answer the contention of Dr. Radhakrishnan that one should not worship Kṛṣṇa, Śrīla Prabhupāda retorted:

> Who cares for Radhakrishnan? In India who cares for Radhakrishnan? They worship Kṛṣṇa. So therefore they have urinated on the face of Radhakrishnan. Say like that *[laughter]*, that "Indian people have passed urine on his head, and they are worshiping Kṛṣṇa. This is Radhakrishnan." Tell him like that.[2] *

Śrīla Prabhupāda himself (in 1958, in articles in two editions of *Back to Godhead*) named Dr. Radhakrishnan, first offering him due respect as a scholar, then proceeding to lacerate his ideas.

Thus, Śrīla Prabhupāda instructed both to avoid naming philosophical adverseries and charlatans, and also to openly name and attack certain cheaters. Which of these approaches to follow poses a dilemma. On the one hand, not naming them helps to keep the discussion more philosophically focused, which is actually the point, since devotees have no personal contention with anyone but wish to expose everything that is misleading. By keeping a philosophical focus, devotees' rebuffs become templates that can be applied in the future, regardless of who the forthcoming propounders of similar errors may be. On the other hand, by naming persons whose position we wish to assail, the immediate issue comes unmistakably into focus (persons and issues being inextricably connected) and tends to generate significantly

* Another fiery response of Śrīla Prabhupāda's to this contention of Dr. Radhakrishnan's is described on p. 7.

1 Conversation, 25 Mar 1976.

2 Conversation, 11 Jan 1977.

greater interest than the more discreet approach. However, naming of persons is usually taken as a personal attack, which in contemporary culture is considered reprehensible; and hence, the actual issue commonly declines into emotional altercations on the platform of "friends and enemies," rather than consisting of constructive philosophical exchanges.

Still, followers of Śrīla Prabhupāda should be known to oppose all kinds of bogus persons and ideas—which inevitably means that we sometimes directly engage or name them. Many uninformed people consider devotees of Kṛṣṇa to be similar to "other Indian groups;" but it is deplorable that Vaiṣṇavas be lumped in with impersonalists and other sundry charlatans. So devotees should make the difference known by loudly broadcasting it. However, it is best not to publicly name persons who are widely respected if doing so is likely to create popular outrage against devotees to the extent that almost everyone becomes unwilling to hear our message. It also is generally inadvisable to overtly name powerful persons who could create serious difficulties for devotees.

On the whole, devotees should be cautious about openly criticizing prominent persons, but if they do so, they should not simply slang others but should present cogent arguments to demonstrate that those personalities deserve to be attacked.

TWENTY-EIGHT
MILDER TECHNIQUES

Some devotees contend that since most people in the modern age are too dull-headed to understand philosophy, we should follow Lord Caitanya's example of preaching to the masses primarily by *saṅkīrtana* and *prasāda* distribution.[1] But actually, along with propagating *saṅkīrtana* among the general public, Lord Caitanya also taught basic philosophical truths—for example, that human life is temporary and should not be uselessly whiled away but utilized for worshiping Kṛṣṇa.[2] Lord Caitanya Himself ordered His followers to instruct others (*yāre dekha…*),[3] and Śrīla Prabhupāda vigorously continued the *paramparā* principle of preaching such elementary points to one and all. For indeed, without being awakened to awareness of such fundamental topics, no one can properly take to Kṛṣṇa consciousness.

However, it is a fact that preaching entails much more than speaking out forthrightly. Most people are more likely to respond favorably to the joy and attractiveness of Kṛṣṇa consciousness if their first contact is, for instance, via *harināma-saṅkīrtana* or *prasāda* distribution, or at a festival, rather than by hearing only a delineation of philosophy. Following the Gauḍīya tradition, Śrīla Prabhupāda introduced a variety of essential programs aimed at "cultural conquest," meant for introducing the conditioned souls to Kṛṣṇa consciousness, for awakening their dull covered

1 See Cc 2.8.56, purport.

2 See Śrīla Bhaktivinoda Ṭhākura's song that begins *Udilo aruṇa….*

3 Cc 2.7.128. For the full verse, see p. 71.

consciousness, and preparing them to hear and accept the Kṛṣṇa conscious message.

Among all such programs, Śrīla Prabhupāda declared *harināma* to be the main weapon in the war against *māyā*:

> Lord Caitanya's movement is also fighting, but it is a fight in a different way, declaration of war by this chanting process—Hare Kṛṣṇa, Hare Kṛṣṇa, Kṛṣṇa Kṛṣṇa, Hare Hare. The transcendental vibration will clarify the whole atmosphere, and as soon as these Kṛṣṇa conscious soldiers come out victorious, the whole world will be peaceful.[1]

> By the mercy of Lord Caitanya even materially absorbed persons can be extricated from their entanglement in *māyā* by contact with offenseless chanting of the Lord's holy names, Hare Kṛṣṇa mantra. If you vibrate these transcendental sounds everywhere continually, it will pierce their ears and enter their hearts, and then their natural attraction for Kṛṣṇa will be revived.[2]

Śrīla Prabhupāda confirmed that for the general public, *saṅkīrtana* is the most effective method to awaken Kṛṣṇa consciousness,[3] and warned his disciples not to get too much into the mood of challenging and defeating:

> Although Lord Śrī Caitanya Mahāprabhu and His devotees in disciplic succession can defeat all kinds of learned scholars, scientists, and philosophers in arguments, thus establishing the supremacy of the Personality of Godhead, their main business as preachers is to introduce *saṅkīrtana* everywhere. Simply to defeat scholars and philosophers is not the occupation of a preacher. Preachers must simultaneously introduce the *saṅkīrtana* movement, for that is the mission of the Caitanya cult.[4]

Śrīla Prabhupāda also stressed the importance of *prasāda* distribution:

---

1 Lecture, 30 Mar 1971.

2 Letter, 16 Nov 1970.

3 Cc 2.8.56, purport.

4 Cc 1.16.8, purport.

> Ours is not a dry philosophy—simply talk and go away. No. We distribute *prasāda*, very sumptuous *prasāda*. In every temple, we offer *prasāda* to anyone who comes. If you eat *bhagavat-prasāda*, then gradually you become spiritualized; it has this potency.[1]

Repeated exposure to blissful *harināma-saṅkīrtana* and delicious *prasāda* should eventually soften the hearts of the agnostic, antagonistic, and apathetic, and prepare them for accepting the message of Kṛṣṇa consciousness:

> Our method should be to convert fools gradually by asking them to come and take *prasāda* and chant and dance with us.[2]

Prasāda restaurants allow devotees to "be themselves" and simultaneously introduce nondevotees to a feature of Kṛṣṇa consciousness that many of them find irresistibly attractive. Vegetarian cooking courses are a further method of making friends and gradually familiarizing people with broader aspects of Kṛṣṇa consciousness. But even in the first of a series of cooking classes, the importance of offering food to Kṛṣṇa should be stated.

Dioramas can be a novel and intriguing way of demonstrating Vedic truths to newcomers. Particularly the "Changing Bodies" model has graphically revealed to thousands of Westerners the reality of reincarnation. Dioramas are excellent preaching tools in that they can convey a poignant message without the need of many words. Śrīla Prabhupāda wanted dioramas ("doll exhibitions") in every center of ISKCON,[3] and portable dioramas have also proved a great success in traveling festival programs.

Śrīla Prabhupāda also instructed: "Dramas about Kṛṣṇa, Kṛṣṇa's pastimes, and also Lord Caitanya's pastimes, are very much desirable for presenting to the public widely. So if you can organize your traveling party to present such dramas all over your country and other places that will be very much appreciated."[4]

---

1 *Journey of Self-Discovery*, 4.2.

2 Cc 1.9.53, purport.

3 Letter, 9 May 1973.

4 Letter, 18 Sep 1972.

Hare Kṛṣṇa festivals can combine all or most of the elements mentioned above in a smorgasbord of color, fun, and exotica that is practically guaranteed to give even casual participants a good impression of Kṛṣṇa consciousness, and for some can be a life-changing experience. And indeed, Śrīla Prabhupāda sometimes even said to not speak philosophy to newcomers but to instead present only those aspects of Kṛṣṇa consciousness that are naturally pleasing:

> We are requesting everyone: "Chant Hare Kṛṣṇa and take *prasāda* and go home." That's all. Philosophy later on. Because unless one has got a clear brain, unless has actually purified senses, one cannot take the lesson of the Kṛṣṇa consciousness movement. One cannot understand the lessons which are given in the *Śrīmad-Bhāgavatam*, *Bhagavad-gītā*. Therefore in the beginning we do not ask any outsider to read *Bhagavad-gītā*. No. "Please come, chant with us Hare Kṛṣṇa." That is required. Chant Hare Kṛṣṇa and you will feel. Because this method will cleanse your heart. The more you chant the Hare Kṛṣṇa *mahā-mantra*, the more you become fit to understand the philosophy of Kṛṣṇa consciousness.[1]

However, unless Kṛṣṇa conscious teachings are conveyed, the actual purpose of preaching is not served. Thus other programs should augment, or at least prepare people for hearing, the clear Kṛṣṇa conscious message, not substitute for it—as Śrīla Prabhupāda exemplified by vigorously promoting Hare Kṛṣṇa festivals yet always (whenever personally attending such festivals) delivering a speech in his typical unequivocal style. People should know that we are not simply minstrels or gourmets, but have a message worth hearing:

> They should not think that these Kṛṣṇa devotees are sentimentalists, simply chanting and dancing. That is, of course, the ultimate goal. But they do not understand. They think that we are simply sentimental. Yet we are the greatest scientists, we are the greatest philosophers, we are the greatest humanitarians. They should know that.[2]

1 Lecture, 21 Jan 1974.

2 Lecture, 3 May 1973.

Therefore, along with plenty of harināma-saṅkīrtana and profuse prasāda distribution, a strong and clear presentation is required. Śrīla Prabhupāda underlined this principle by stating that distribution of prasāda without distribution of spiritual knowledge is insufficient:

> The best humanitarian work is to give knowledge to humanity. If I give some food, that is good work, but that is not sufficient. I may give food, that's alright. You give. We also give *prasāda* free. But that does not mean simply by giving *prasāda* we are silent. We give knowledge also. This is Kṛṣṇa consciousness movement. Food, automatically you have to give; there is no prohibition. But at the same time, knowledge. Without knowledge-giving, if he remains ignorant ... Just like the same example: if you have got some children, if you don't give them education and simply feed them, that is not your proper duty. You must give knowledge.[1]

As in the aforementioned case of the Paris city officials, the easily appreciable pleasure of *harināma* and *prasāda* can help buffer the jarring message of Kṛṣṇa consciousness, which nondevotees need to hear. Indeed, a mix of pleasing and "painful" approaches is likely to intrigue people into inquiring into the apparent paradox of why devotees are so blissful yet their message so devastating.

As every follower of Śrīla Prabhupāda must be aware, he repeatedly stressed distribution of Kṛṣṇa conscious literature as most effective for spreading Kṛṣṇa consciousness:

> My first concern is that my books shall be published and distributed profusely all over the world. Practically, books are the basis of our movement. Without our books, our preaching will have no effect.[2]

> Preaching means book distribution.[3]

> Distribution of literature is our real preaching; the success of your preaching will be substantiated by how many books are sold.[4]

---

1 Lecture, 9 Sep 1975.

2 Letter, 20 Jan 1972.

3 Conversation, 31 Dec 1976.

4 Letter, 30 Sep 1972.

Considering that Śrīla Prabhupāda said "Real preaching [is] selling books. Who can speak better than the books?"[1] it could be questioned, "What is the need for this treatise on strong speaking?" Clearly, the mass distribution of Śrīla Prabhupāda's books, and also of supplementary titles, is a better strategy for widely spreading Kṛṣṇa consciousness than trying to personally convince individuals, one by one. Yet this does not undermine the importance of verbally presenting the message within those books, for several reasons, including:

- Creating interest in others to purchase and read them.*
- Devotees who distribute the books must be intimately attuned to the philosophy and know how to present it to all kinds of people and to respond on the spot to all manner of challenges.
- For persons who have tried reading the books but find the meaning difficult to grasp, hearing the philosophy spoken can really help to bring it alive.
- Oral explanation often serves to awaken understanding in persons who have read Śrīla Prabhupāda's books yet, due to previous conditioning, have not registered certain crucial points therein (for instance, that all paths are not the same, or that demigod worshipers possess paltry intelligence).
- The *paramparā* cannot be passed on exclusively through books, for it is impossible to explain everything in them sufficiently for each recipient's understanding.

---

* Nowadays, most of the book distribution that I am directly involved in is via public lectures. My consistent experience is that the stronger I speak, the better the sales tend to be. (NB "The success of your preaching will be substantiated by how many books are sold."—Letter, 30 Sep 1972)

1 Letter, 30 Sep 1972. (These four are just a sampling of the many statements by Śrīla Prabhupāda that establish the paramount importance of book distribution to his mission.)

• If devotees do not verbally articulate what is in the books, then among both devotees and nondevotees it may come to seem that the message in the books is not our actual message and that perhaps there is something wrong with what is stated in the books.*

• Thoughtful outsiders who have read Śrīla Prabhupāda's books will notice and be unimpressed if devotees' teachings and commitment do not match the vital, demanding message therein, which devotees are supposed to represent.

• Devotees must be prepared to defend inevitable attacks on what is written in the books.

• Devotees for whom Śrīla Prabhupāda's books are their life and soul will have to resist attempts to revise the message in those books.

• Verbal presentation is required for illiterates, as illiteracy is not a disqualification for devotional service.

• Śrīla Prabhupāda himself gave more importance to hearing and explaining than to reading: "To hear and explain them [the revealed scriptures] is more important than reading them. One can assimilate the knowledge of the revealed scriptures only by hearing and explaining."[1] †

---

* Another danger is that of devotees speaking from the books but misrepresenting the message—for instance, by explaining it in terms of modern psychology, or by unduly emphasizing one aspect of a teaching over others, such as one-sidedly repeating advice to not criticize while largely overlooking the huge body of instructions to speak strongly.

† More on the need for regular preaching of the message within the books is given in ch. 31, "Preach Strongly or Perish."

1 *Harmonist* 29.169 (Dec 1931); SBV, vol. 3, p. 143.

TWENTY-NINE
PREACHING VIA WRITING

A major medium for presenting Kṛṣṇa consciousness is the written word. The basic principles governing straightforward presentation apply to both speaking and writing, yet the effect of written communication is different than that of addressing a physically present audience. The guidelines in *The Back to Godhead Handbook* should be consulted by all devotees who are serious about preaching via the written word.[1] A sample of the valuable advice given therein is to get one's facts straight, and to articulately express and defend one's ideas.

Traditionally, devotional writing about Kṛṣṇa, the Vaiṣṇavas, and *bhakti* was composed in a manner that primarily establishes and upholds their divinity. However, some Vaiṣṇava *ācāryas* made concessions to win the attention and confidence of persons unready to immediately accept Vaiṣṇava conclusions. For instance, in *Śrī Caitanya Mahāprabhu—His Life and Precepts,* Śrīla Bhaktivinoda Ṭhākura stated that he would be satisfied if readers not prepared to recognize Nimāi Paṇḍita as the Supreme Lord would at least accept Him as a noble and holy teacher. However, the pronounced majority of Śrīla Bhaktivinoda Ṭhākura's writings were of the traditional, unmitigatedly Vaiṣṇava genre, and even when making

1 This handbook is out of print. It is included in *The Bhaktivedanta Vedabase.*

concessions, he never attempted to cloak his own purely Vaiṣṇava position.

After Śrīla Bhaktivinoda Ṭhākura, the two great *ācāryas* Śrīla Bhaktisiddhānta Sarasvatī and Śrīla A.C. Bhaktivedanta Swami Prabhupāda both wrote in a direct, aggressive style. Notwithstanding Śrīla Bhaktisiddhānta Sarasvatī's having specifically warned of the dangers of misunderstanding Śrīla Bhaktivinoda Ṭhākura's apparent accommodating of non-Vaiṣṇava elements,* some recent Vaiṣṇava writers, claiming to follow the lead of Śrīla Bhaktivinoda Ṭhākura, almost habitually make qualified statements. As a theoretical example, such writers would prefer the cautious "Śrī Caitanya Mahāprabhu, who Gauḍīya Vaiṣṇavas consider to be a 'full incarnation' of Kṛṣṇa, whom they accept as the supreme deity" to the assertive "Śrī Caitanya Mahāprabhu, who is nondifferent from Kṛṣṇa, the Supreme Personality of Godhead." The first phraseology makes no claim for the divinity of Lord Caitanya or Kṛṣṇa—the author presents himself as a mere relayer of information, as uncommitted as his target audience—whereas the second affirms the faith of the author and of all Gauḍīya Vaiṣṇavas and squarely challenges agnosticism.

An area of Vaiṣṇava writing that requires special expertise is that meant to gain the attention and respect of academicians. Undoubtedly, devotees who attempt to be heard within orthodox academia, sworn as it is to reason and logic (as defined by the academia itself), face tremendous challenges in composing writings that are true to Vaiṣṇava *siddhānta* yet also are perceived by contemporary intellectuals as sound, readable, thorough, well-argued, balanced, and dispassionate—because the outlook and spirit of Vaiṣṇava *siddhānta* are in so many respects contradictory

* See "Perspectives on Śrīla Bhaktivinoda Ṭhākura," in *Śrī Bhaktisiddhānta Vaibhava*, vol. 2, p. 201.

to those of the academic establishment. Mundane academicians consider as serious scholarship only writings of the above-mentioned "indefinite style." The academia requires clinical analysis, which cannot possibly inspire anyone toward devotion.

A terrible danger in presenting Vaiṣṇavism in terms agreeable to the scholarly class is that of introducing and normalizing relativism within Gauḍīya society. Better to follow the example of Śrīla Bhaktisiddhānta Sarasvatī and his followers, who engaged with academic types, not by catering to their multiple misconceptions but by unalleviated attack on their endemic errors—yet in a style so brilliantly scholarly that the mundane scholars, even begrudgingly, were obliged to take note. This approach reinforces, rather than risks diminishing, the precious faith of Vaiṣṇava readers, and at every step challenges the supercilious agnosticism of academia, which must be demolished as a precondition for solidly establishing true theism in the world. Śrīla Prabhupāda also ordered his disciples to "write very strongly, vehemently. Even if it is a little offensive, still these rascals should be taught a good lesson."[1] *

In contrast, the pandering style expresses acquiescence with the pseudo neutrality of academia. For instance, even though to present *Rāmāyaṇa* as a folk story and Bhagavān Śrī Rāma as a legendary hero might reach a wider audience, such a presentation does not inspire *bhakti,* and is in fact offensive. The plethora of such academically neutral writing in post-1977 Vaiṣṇava society has almost certainly been a major, if not subtle, factor in the ethos of diminished faith that has enveloped and enervated it, imperceptibly polluting it at every level.

---

* This was spoken in the context of countering spurious scientific propaganda.

---

1 Conversation, 19 Apr 1973.

Early in 1977, some leading disciples complained to Śrīla Prabhupāda that the team producing *Back to Godhead* had deliberately changed its tenor. For several months, *Back to Godhead* had pitched at making Kṛṣṇa consciousness accessible to all types of people, even houswives, and at giving nondevotees a favorable opinion of our movement; but in doing so, they had presented Kṛṣṇa consciousness in an almost commonplace manner. For instance, nondevotional books rather than *śāstra* were cited, and recipes were given without instructions to offer the prepared food to Kṛṣṇa. Photos of people in regular American dress were featured along with their mundane testimonies on the benefits of chanting Hare Kṛṣṇa: "Chanting makes me calmer," "Chanting makes me more perceptive," "Chanting makes me more open-minded." Throughout the whole magazine, there were no pictures of Lord Caitanya or Kṛṣṇa. Śrīla Prabhupāda's response was to change the editor. The first issue under the new editor (Satsvarūpa Dāsa Goswami) included articles like "Beyond Animal Technology," "Kṛṣṇa—The Personal Form of God" (accompanied by a full-page photo of Rādhā-Kṛṣṇa Deities), "Man on the Moon—A Case of Mass Brainwashing," and "Calling the Blind Scientists' Bluff."[1] Later that year came the article, "The Demons Among Us," with the classic observation:

> A demon need not be a huge monster with ten heads and a thousand arms, nor a little red fiend with a pitchfork. Of course, there may very well be demons with grotesque features and supernatural powers, but the demons who live among us generally appear quite ordinary. Your mailman might be a demon. So might your grocer, your congressman, or anyone else you know. For that matter, so might you.[2]

The article then proceeded to analyze the nature of demons according to modern contexts (subheadings: "The Divine and the Demonic," "The Killers of the Soul," "The Blind Leaders," "The Godless Scientists") and descriptions from *śāstra*, especially

1 BTG 12-05 (1977).

2 BTG 12-07 (1977).

chapter sixteen of the *Bhagavad-gītā*. This represents the standard of preaching to the public that Śrīla Prabhupāda approved, not the spineless, fuzzy style, which he rejected for *Back to Godhead*, his flagship literary medium for presenting broader society with Kṛṣṇa conscious perspectives on topical issues.

Today many more devotees are writing than during Śrīla Prabhupāda's presence, and most of their writing appears on the internet. The internet is ironic: while affording practically unlimited dissemination of information and ideas, it seems to ratchet down mass stupidity to ever lower depths. It provides wide opportunities for preaching Kṛṣṇa consciousness, yet it also exposes devotees to multiple influences that they would be better off without.

Much of devotees' internet writings focus on internal matters, including news, views, and also controversial issues such as the roles of gurus, women, and homosexuals within Vaiṣṇava society. Unfortunately, polemic exchanges are rarely well moderated and thus tend to be dominated by innuendo and intimidation. Furthermore, such dialogues seldom come to a satisfactory conclusion, but tend to peter out in unresolved disharmony. A better overall approach for addressing such topics might be for differing parties to post papers that comprehensively present their respective positions, thereby leaving it to others to draw their own conclusions. Position papers should forestall having to repeatedly restate the same arguments, and may be cited or referred to when issues that have already been deliberated ad nauseum are raised yet again.

The internet is also host to profuse propaganda of the kind composed by Vaiṣṇavas or quasi-Vaiṣṇavas who believe it their calling to widely broadcast the downsides and failings—real, imagined, or exaggerated—of ISKCON and its leaders. Arguably, a good antidote to such propaganda is for concerned insiders to promptly rebutt postings that are untrue, misconceived, and malicious, and to openly, realistically, and constructively analyze the actual downsides and failings of ISKCON. Traditionally, respectable people kept internal problems to themselves, but the advent of the internet has made that almost impossible. The reality is that via the internet, mistaken ideas will continue to be widely propagated about Vaiṣṇavas and Vaiṣṇavism, which require to be countered; otherwise, wrong notions will gain currency and unnecessarily spread distrust and disharmony among Vaiṣṇavas.

THIRTY
TRUTH WILL PREVAIL

Outspokenness and struggle are unlikely to make Kṛṣṇa consciousness immediately popular, but in the long run, such preaching will prove effective—because when people become disappointed by the cheaters whom the devotees constantly berate, they will ultimately come to recognize the veracity of the devotees' message.

> By agitation, our position will be improved. Prahlāda Mahārāja was suppressed in so many means. What was the loss on his part? He improved more and more, more and more. If Christ were not crucified, then his cult would not have spread so much all over the world. Because he was persecuted, his cult became so spread.[1]

> If we sincerely try to present our philosophy at every opportunity, eventually it will be heard and appreciated.[2]

> Our unique asset is our purity. No one anywhere can match it. That will be noticed eventually and appreciated, as long as we do not diminish or neglect the highest standard of purity in performing our routine work. Our pure standard is enough. Let us stand on that basis.[3]

> People are appreciating the purity of our teachings. Gradually they will appreciate such teachings more and more, simply if we stick to our principles.[4]

---

1 Conversation (3), 19 Feb 1977.

2 Letter, 15 Nov 1971.

3 Letter, 28 Dec 1971.

4 Letter, 11 Jun 1971.

> This Kṛṣṇa consciousness is authorized, practical, and simple, and those who have enough intelligence will recognize this fact and will join with us. Our program is to simply chant Hare Kṛṣṇa, follow the regulative principles, and preach this philosophy without any adulteration. If we stick to this policy, then by our good example, people will see the potency of this great movement.[1]

> Our movement is the greatest gift to the human race. They may not immediately appreciate it, but time will come and history will give evidence that this movement saved the human society from being fallen into barbarianism.[2]

The fact is that our movement is unique, professes the highest truth, and is based on the highest principles. We are on very firm ground.

> Our so-called religion is unique in the world, simply because we stand solidly on philosophy, and because we are strong in that way, no one can refute or defeat us. So we are wiping out sentimental religion wherever we penetrate and it appears the people everywhere are accepting us more and more.[3]

There is no need to hide ourselves or our philosophy. Clear, insistent, and persistent promoting of Kṛṣṇa consciousness will surely create all-auspiciousness.

> We stand on our Kṛṣṇa philosophy, and because it has the full potency of Kṛṣṇa Himself, there is no limit to the effect it will have upon the world if we remain sincere and convinced for spreading this philosophy purely.[4]

> If we simply repeat this philosophy exactly as it is, without any misrepresentation or adulteration, then this movement will never be checked, and we will conquer the world.[5]

---

1 Letter, 25 Mar 1972.

2 Letter, 13 Nov 69.

3 Letter, 5 Feb 1972.

4 Letter, 30 Nov 1971.

5 Letter, 27 Mar 1972.

Such words of our *ācārya* should not be taken lightly. Preachers who are on the cutting edge can experience how Kṛṣṇa responds to devotees who persevere in all circumstances without ever dreaming of compromising. Kṛṣṇa makes the impossible possible. Doors open, magic happens, mercy rains, demons join the *kīrtana*, the world changes.

THIRTY-ONE
PREACH STRONGLY OR PERISH

In untiringly explaining the substantial philosophy of the absolute truth as delineated in *śāstra*, Śrīla Prabhupāda necessarily spoke against all flawed and nonsensical perspectives held by nondevotees. But in today's ISKCON, it is unusual—and in some circles almost taboo—to raise a voice of challenge against cheating so-called religionists, scientists, welfare workers, educationists, et al.

Annadā Devī Dāsī reminisced that during a *Śrīmad-Bhāgavatam* class in 1975 in Delhi, Śrīla Prabhupāda was talking about hogs, dogs, camels, and asses. Her parents were present, and her father's response was, "What kind of lecture was that? He was just talking about hogs, dogs, camels, and asses." She commented:

> Śrīla Prabhupāda gave us just what we needed to hear, but we're not always willing to accept. But it was very interesting. He was talking about *gṛhamedhī* life and hogs, dogs, camels, and asses. No "Rādhe, Rādhe" or intimate pastimes, anything like that. When you look back now, it's so much clearer how his preaching was medicinal on the level that we needed to hear these things, and we still need to hear these things. He is giving the right medicine, the right dose, at the right time—not like a quack who will give you something that you like to take but it doesn't actually do the job.[1]

---

1 Annadā Devī Dāsī, *Following Srila Prabhupada*, DVD 8.

Śrīla Prabhupāda's direct, lucid, and powerful delineation of the philosophy of Kṛṣṇa consciousness convinced thousands of nondevotees to dedicate their life to Kṛṣṇa, and furthermore, helped devotees to remain fixed on their goal and ever striving for new heights in devotional service. Today also, according to the spiritual science that Śrīla Prabhupāda represented and taught, regular undisguised and undiluted exposition of the *Bhāgavata* teaching is required to bring nondevotees to Kṛṣṇa consciousness and to help devotees remain fixed in their determination to assiduously practice and propagate devotional service.

As Kṛṣṇa is all-attractive, His instructions in *Bhagavad-gītā* and His literary manifestation as *Śrīmad-Bhāgavatam* are also all-attractive. Failure to present to devotees the full message of these essential works in the manner that Śrīla Prabhupāda presented it is to fail to give Kṛṣṇa as He intended Himself to be given via Śrīla Prabhupāda. To consider some portions unpalatable means to deny those aspects of Kṛṣṇa's attractiveness, and demonstrates a misunderstanding of Kṛṣṇa and Kṛṣṇa consciousness.

Therefore candid speaking is particularly required in temple classes and in all preaching directed specifically toward devotees. Although persons may be brought to Kṛṣṇa consciousness by sweet words and enjoyable programs, and nourished by the soul's natural attraction to *harināma*, if they are not subjected to the full, unedited, *anartha*-shattering message of *śāstra*, they will never properly imbibe the seriousness of Kṛṣṇa consciousness or be able to distinguish it from the many prevalent forms of pseudo-spiritual sense gratification; they will never gain the strength to remain fixed on the path in the face of inevitable tests.

To combat misconceptions (among both devotees and nondevotees) does not directly foster *bhakti*, but is necessary to protect *bhakti*—for as long as erroneous notions remain, *bhakti* can never be properly understood or practiced. *Prema-pracāraṇa* (preaching about divine love) without *pāṣaṇḍa-dalana* (quelling of deviations) will allow fallacies to fester within devotional society—perennially weakening it and diverting it from the goal—and to sometimes erupt as full-fledged heresies.* Particularly in the modern world, materialistic propaganda is so ubiquitous and pernicious that devotees cannot but be affected by it, unless they continually distinguish reality from illusion by mutual discussion of the absolute truth as described in *śāstra.* Indeed, unless various misconceptions are regularly raised and refuted, and thus purged, devotees are likely to harbor deep, subtle attachments to such delusions. To not unmitigatedly oppose various aberrations means to accord them tacit approval, for silence indicates consent—"*Maunaṁ sammati-lakṣaṇam:* if there is some argument and you remain quiet, that means indirectly you accept."[1] Thus, an atmosphere is nurtured wherein no one can be clear as to what Śrīla Prabhupāda taught and wanted, wherein no one can properly advance in Kṛṣṇa consciousness.

Mild speaking and glossing over issues often means philosophical laziness, an unwillingness to try to deeply understand philosophical truths. Such dullness dooms any possibility of spiritual advancement. *Siddhānta-alasa jana anartha to' chāḍe nā:* "A person who is slack in accurately comprehending *siddhānta* does not give up *anarthas.*"[2] Therefore:

সিদ্ধান্ত বলিয়া চিত্তে না কর অলস ।
ইহা হইতে কৃষ্ণে লাগে সুদৃঢ় মানস ।।

siddhānta baliyā citte nā kara alasa
ihā haite kṛṣṇe lāge sudṛḍha mānasa

* *Prema-pracāraṇa, pāṣaṇḍa-dalana*—from Cc 3.3.149. For the full verse, see p. 2.

1 Conversation, 9 Jul 1975.

2 "Prākṛta-rasa-śata-dūṣiṇī," by Śrīla Bhaktisiddhānta Sarasvatī, 28.

> A sincere student should not neglect the discussion of such conclusions, considering them controversial, for such discussions strengthen the mind. Thus one's mind becomes attached to Śrī Kṛṣṇa.[1]

To not continually repeat the full and unadulterated message within Śrīla Prabhupāda's books is itself a minimization of that message. Consequently, those books will come to be seen as anachronistic and irrelevant, and thus the devotee community, no longer guided by Śrīla Prabhupāda's teachings, will be divested of his mercy and defined by teachings other than his. If anything but the undiluted truth is regularly discussed, half-truths or lies will come to be accepted as the actual truth.* Due to the deeply rooted perversions of conditioned souls, unless aspiring transcendentalists frequently hear exposés and condemnations of all that is opposed to Kṛṣṇa consciousness, they are unlikely to grasp even basic concepts. Retaining attachments to various misconceptions and concomitant *anarthas,* they will remain stuck in the very thought patterns they are supposed to rise above.

For instance, without regularly hearing that material existence is excruciatingly nasty, devotees are likely to maintain the depraved tendency to mistake this hostile world as an arena for their own enjoyment. Hence they will have little impetus to surrender to Kṛṣṇa—nor even know that they are meant to surrender, or what surrender entails. Similarly, if the prominent iniquities of modern society—impersonalism, atheism, mundane welfare work, cheating religiosity, cheating philanthropy, quasi-scientific bamboozling, and so on—are not regularly discussed, devotees

* In December 2010, after a lecture I had delivered, a devotee commented that it was good that I was speaking the truth—as if he was unaccustomed to hearing devotees speak the truth. But what else, I wonder, am I, or anyone else who purports to represent Śrīla Prabhupāda, supposed to speak?

1 Cc 1.2.117.

might consider that perhaps those *anarthas* are not so bad after all. Consequently the whole society of devotees will be open to poisonous contaminations. Particularly the resolve to preach, to save the misguided populace, will erode, and the very purpose of Śrīla Prabhupāda's mission will be lost: "Without preaching, our institution becomes all rubbish."[1]

Māyā is so tricky that unless we are firm in our position against the *mūḍhas*, there is every danger that we ourselves will again become *mūḍhas*. "If you compromise, then gradually you'll also go down."[2] Unless our preaching is solid, our conviction will diminish. Not to fight against bogus ideas means to compromise with them—at first maybe only subtly, but from the subtle comes the gross. For instance, devotees who become inordinately influenced by social niceties start to doubt the principle of absolute correctness and thus consider Prabhupāda-style condemnation to be excessive. They complain about the severe style of presentation, but their real objection is to the content. Such persons cannot be considered genuine followers of Mahāprabhu, being akin to the *apa-sampradāyas* who opposed Śrīla Bhaktisiddhānta Sarasvatī. Their becoming "reasonable" according to mundane standards—their preferring to be accepted and respected by fools and rascals rather than to faithfully maintain the Vaiṣṇava position—is their acknowledgement of capitulation to *māyā*.

Śrīla Prabhupāda warned that without strong preaching, our movement would become ruined:

> We have to become very strong preachers. Then this movement will stay. If you simply take the temple worship, it will not stay very long.[3]
>
> Don't compromise. This principle must be observed. Then you'll remain strong. As soon as you compromise, then it is finished.[4]

1 Letter, 11 Apr 1974.
2 Conversation, 11 Jun 1974.
3 Conversation, 9 Jul 1974.
4 Conversation, 2 Jul 1974.

> We have to fight against all this nonsense—nonsense scientists, nonsense religionists. It is not an easygoing, sleeping business. We have to fight with so many demons. Otherwise, *khāwā dāwā dukāna*, my guru-mahārāja used to say: "Beg some rice and bring it and cook it and eat and sleep."[1]

By no means should the Hare Kṛṣṇa movement come to be seen as merely sentimental:

> Just demonstrate sincerely that we have got solid ground beneath us, not that we have only some sentiment.... This is our substance—real philosophical information—not some weak sentiments.[2]

Śrīla Prabhupāda cautioned that "anything without substance will not last.... Many fanatic spiritual movements have come and gone.... Without the flawless philosophy of Kṛṣṇa, they cannot stand."[3]

Nothing is gained by becoming superficial to cater to superficial people. We can attract sincere people by giving the clear, consistent understanding that Śrīla Prabhupāda gave us. By giving anything else, we ourselves become superficial, and satisfied to attract superficial people. Anything less than direct delineation of the purely spiritual message of *śāstra* means descending to the bodily, mental, and intellectual platforms, on which speculations abound and confusion prevails. Devotees then become diverted to peripheral concerns such as money, relationships, and health, rather than the crucial consideration of fully surrendering to guru and Kṛṣṇa in the fire of the *saṅkīrtana* movement.

Hence, before we can save the world, we must first save ourselves and Śrīla Prabhupāda's movement. As Śrīla Prabhupāda warned, if preaching is compromised, everything else becomes compromised.[4] The path of *bhakti* is extreme and demanding—*mām ekaṁ śaraṇaṁ*

1 Conversation, 2 Jul 1976.

2 Letter, 27 Nov 1971.

3 Letter, 27 Nov 1971.

4 See Conversation, 12 Dec 1973.

vraja: "Surrender unto Me utterly"[1]—and can be traversed only by the fully dedicated. It is true that strong preaching risks alienating others, and that an ethos of strong speaking, unless carefully monitored, is likely to attract and foster some fanatics. Yet habitually mild preaching much more dangerously risks losing the sense of urgency and commitment to save others, and of altogether compromising the preaching spirit by reshaping our mission into an insipid, ignoble bid for social acceptance. Whereas those who preach strongly are obliged to follow strongly, those who advocate a relaxed, accommodating approach to Kṛṣṇa consciousness *ipso facto* lack dynamism and focus. By accommodating *māyā,* they make gradual adjustments to their practices and thus risk eventually becoming totally mundane.

Widespread lack of faith in the absolute correctness of Kṛṣṇa consciousness, evidenced by averseness to presenting Kṛṣṇa consciousness "as it is" (that is, as Śrīla Prabhupāda presented it) is undoubtedly a major factor in the decline of standards within ISKCON since Śrīla Prabhupāda's departure. When Śrīla Prabhupāda was here with us, he kept us in line. Nowadays among many putative devotees, "anything goes." Watching movies, eating unofferable food, wearing T-shirts with nondevotional themes—somehow everything has become unquestionably acceptable. Today many so-called devotees do not like to clearly differentiate between devotees and nondevotees, and disapprove the use of words like *karmī* or *demon,* which Śrīla Prabhupāda regularly used. And those who rightly identify nonsense masquerading as Kṛṣṇa consciousness are conveniently labeled "old school" or "fundamentalist," their protestations being neglected by persons who are very serious about not taking Kṛṣṇa consciousness seriously: "That's just his opinion"; "That's alright for him because he's a sannyasi. I'm not, so I don't have to follow so strictly." However, at least senior devotees cannot shun their duty to point

---

1 Bg 18.66.

out discrepancies that inevitably arise even within a Vaiṣṇava institution.

Still, frankness in dealing with devotees should be tempered by the special honor due Vaiṣṇavas. It is appropriate to first praise the qualities of (especially a respected) person before calling attention to his apparent faults. Śrīla Prabhupāda once quoted a Sanskrit verse related to criticizing, the gist of which is that one should say, "The beautiful tree with luxuriant foliage, delicious fruits, and aromatic flowers has lost its juice," rather than merely saying, "The tree is dry."[1] Although both statements convey the same meaning, the appreciative tone of the former is far less likely to offend than the blunt four words of the latter. This is appropriate etiquette and is in accord with the vital principle of avoiding offenses to devotees. However, such etiquette is wrongly invoked if speaking out about various deviations is from the outset assumed to be Vaiṣṇava-*aparādha* and is thus rejected out of hand.

Some devotees argue that members of ISKCON have no right to highlight others' faults because too many among us have failed to maintain proper devotional standards. However, the solution is not to placidly tolerate that which should not be, but to make ISKCON what it should be. If ISKCON is not the worldwide pacesetter in genuine spirituality, capable of and dedicated to "completely rejecting all religious activities which are materially motivated," if we flop into accepting internal depravity as being unavoidable, then ISKCON will not be the society that Śrīla Prabhupāda is the founder-*ācārya* of—but a sham, just another middling religious institution posing as spiritual for cheating the public.[2]

According to the principle of unity and diversity that Śrīla Prabhupāda often stressed,[3] the Kṛṣṇa consciousness movement

1 Told by Girirāja Swami to Bhakti Vikāsa Swami.

2 "Completely … motivated"—See SB 1.1.2.

3 E.g.: Letter, 18 Oct 1973.

can and should accommodate a variety of approaches toward the practice and propagation of devotional service. Yet in many cases the difference is not simply of approach, but a fundamental divergence in understanding what Kṛṣṇa consciousness entails and of the very purpose of the Kṛṣṇa consciousness movement. For instance, members of the Kṛṣṇa consciousness movement who consider strong speaking to be too dangerous are themselves dangerous, since knowingly or unknowingly they undermine the mission of the *ācāryas*. Yet an even greater threat are those who deliberately downplay the fact that Śrīla Prabhupāda spoke strongly and who thus obliquely try to redefine him as the kind of harmless sadhu they think he should have been.

At least the leaders of ISKCON should uphold the philosophical, behavioral, and preaching standards given by Śrīla Prabhupāda and the previous *ācāryas*. If the heterodox becomes predominant, then all is lost.*

* Arguably, this has already happened within ISKCON. Can the situation be retrieved? Hopefully, *Speaking Strongly* will engender thoughtful discussion of this vital topic, the scope of which, however, is beyond this volume. A call for reform is the underlying purpose of this book, the publication of which suggests a hope that transformation is possible. Yet presumably, effecting required changes will be a trying and prolonged task.

THIRTY-TWO
SUMMARY

Regardless of how they attempt to do so, glorious indeed are all devotees who resolutely strive to transform the contrary inclination of conditioned souls. Yet there will always be a divergence, for some devotees revel in an acute frankness that may sometimes disturb certain people, while others are commitedly non-confrontational. Both approaches are admissible, but which should be the prevalent one in ISKCON?

Ultimately it all boils down to the question, "Did Śrīla Prabhupāda want his followers to speak strongly or did he advocate a non-confrontational style?" This book has attempted to demonstrate that Śrīla Prabhupāda desired that his preachers speak strongly, subject to certain caveats. The general principles of strong speaking are:

- Preachers' statements (written or oral) should be solidly based on *śāstra* and the teachings of the *paramparā*; this includes being loyal to the spirit and style of *śāstra* and the *paramparā*, which entails being bold, clear, provocative, frank, realistic, uncompromising—all grounded in conviction in the veracity of *śāstra* and the teachings of the previous *ācāryas*.

- Preaching should be conducted in the spirit of creating a spiritual revolution; generally, opposition from mainstream society should be seen as indicative that we are on the right course.

• Subject to the caveats below, the truth, even when unpalatable, should be stated fully for the benefit of the recipient, having regard to his personality and disposition.

Caveats to strong speaking are:

• It should be undertaken in a spirit of selfless service to Kṛṣṇa and in a judicious manner, preferably by well trained, experienced devotee preachers who have firm *sādhana* and thorough śāstric knowledge.

• It is not called for in all cases; the mature preacher must determine how best and in which manner to present the message of the *ācāryas* under varying circumstances and to disparate individuals.

• It should not be employed out of malice but out of compassion for the conditioned *jīvas*.

• It should be presented scientifically and cogently to establish sound, persuasive conclusions.

• It should not consist of mere name-calling, threats, or similar misbehavior.

• Generally, miscreants should not be openly exposed by name; occasionally this may be done if is calculated that the overall reaction will help to spread the message of Kṛṣṇa consciousness rather than alienate the public.

• Prudence and diplomacy are especially called for when dealing with government officials, employers, business partners, and other important persons.

• A consummate, composite preacher is as aware of and skilled in employing tact and discretion as he is in speaking strongly; his aim is to always serve the truth, for which purpose he may sometimes employ tact and sometimes be deliberately confrontational.

Strong speaking significantly differs from "soft" speaking, which is characterized by a fear of disturbing others and resulting reluctance to straightforwardly speak the seemingly harsh truths stated in *śāstra*. This attitude is typically wedded to a low-key preaching style aimed more at creating a good impression of Kṛṣṇa consciousness than impressing it on others. The soft approach favors cultural performances, *prasāda* distribution, and other agreeable presentations, all of which are essential to the preaching strategy of the Kṛṣṇa consciousness movement—but which should complement and not become substitutes for direct delineation of its core message. Proponents of the soft approach should not oppose on principle the clear utterance of śāstric truths that was Śrīla Prabhupāda's trademark; nor should softness decline into or foster arrant compromise.

If (as is largely the case in ISKCON today) straightforward speaking of the style that Śrīla Prabhupāda inculcated is considered axiomatically unacceptable, then *ipso facto* ISKCON has significantly departed from Śrīla Prabhupāda's practice and precept. This new paradigm might help to increase ISKCON's numerical strength and level of public approval, but it is symptomatic of spiritual decline and can only augur further inauspiciousness. Only if ISKCON members again embrace Śrīla Prabhupāda's uncompromising mood, and cooperate to preach and to manifest Kṛṣṇa consciousness "as it is," can ISKCON fulfil Śrīla Prabhupāda's mandate to revolutionize the world.

With this conviction and sense of mission, devotees who have implicit faith in the message of *śāstra* as presented by Śrīla Prabhupāda and all bona fide *ācāryas*, who live by that message (not merely paying it lip service), who regularly, thoroughly, and prayerfully study Śrīla Prabhupāda's books, who are sufficiently experienced and expert to present the knowledge thereof in a confident, coherent manner and to answer all objections and overcome all opposition—and who have the pluck to do so—should continue to preach strongly. And indeed they will, because they know they must.

That devotees speak strongly should be the norm, not an oddity. Strong speaking is necessary for defeating challengers, counteracting common misconceptions, answering doubts, goading the complacent and the apathetic, and for keeping keen the understanding of already committed devotees.

Not all devotees will understand or accept this. Possibly in every generation there will be a majority who in the name of preaching attempt to denature the *paramparā* message, and a minority who maintain the *paramparā* principle by rigidly adhering to the *ācāryas*. Many cringe upon hearing the truth expressed explicitly, even though that is the idiom of *śāstra*, and do not like that devotees straightforwardly present the truth to others. They strongly preach against strong preaching and think that the worst possible thing a devotee can do is to upset someone. They become disturbed at the apparent arrogance of preachers who deride the position of nondevotees. Not being convinced of Kṛṣṇa's teachings, they propose various "reasons" for covering them up or understating them (for instance, by perversely misapplying Śrīla Prabhupāda's statements to propose that no one should speak as strongly as Śrīla Prabhupāda did because no one is as qualified as he). Some of those who protest against strong preaching seem to be opposed to the very enterprise of preaching, for they themselves hardly do anything that resembles actual preaching and often seem more concerned to obstruct actual preaching than to promote it. However, just as proponents of "being nice to all" may feel disturbed by clear-cut, incisive preaching, forceful preachers are disturbed by wishy-washiness.

The widespread misconception among both nondevotees and neophyte devotees that a saintly person should not speak strongly is one of the many misconceptions that the Kṛṣṇa consciousness movement must address. Unless the spirit of powerful speaking is kept prominently alive within ISKCON, it will become a bog of sentimentalism, lacking proper discrimination and philosophical understanding, and thus indistinguishable from the morass of pseudo-spiritual organizations. It will be incapable of fulfilling the mission of Śrīla Prabhupāda and the previous *ācāryas*: to give to the world the knowledge it needs. Better that ISKCON be felt as a threat to materialistic civilization than as nice but insignificant, like the Salvation Army or an old women's crochet club. Beware, devotees, lest we sell our souls and, by altering the tenor and character of his movement, betray Śrīla Prabhupāda.

Śrīla Prabhupāda preached with a hatchet and warned against mental speculation. He demonstrated how to be direct and strong, firm in *śāstra* and philosophy, uncompromising, unabashed, and unflinching, yet also sensitive and considerate. Many could not accept Śrīla Prabhupāda's message, but those who did became fixed in Kṛṣṇa consciousness. Śrīla Prabhupāda did not operate on the platform of mundane emotion. He aimed to convince people, elevate them to the transcendental platform, and give them an experience of the happiness of genuine spiritual life. We must model ourselves after Śrīla Prabhupāda—not by imitation but by faithful following. Śrīla Prabhupāda saved us from illusion, doubt, and confusion by relentlessly speaking the vital, transformational truth of Kṛṣṇa consciousness. To think that we can better spread Kṛṣṇa consciousness by presenting anything different is arrogant, foolish, and offensive and a disservice to Śrīla Prabhupāda and to the world. Much better than becoming overly cautious is to insistently propagate the undiluted teachings of *śāstra,* while simultaneously endeavoring to become ever more expert and realized. To do so requires a mature commitment to studying, absorbing, and intelligently preaching the philosophy that Śrīla Prabhupāda so elaborately presented in his books.

Let us not neglect the challenge to present Kṛṣṇa consciousness vigorously and frankly, as Śrīla Prabhupāda did—always praying to him for guidance so that our preaching may be authoritative, poignant, and effective in dispelling illusion.

THIRTY-THREE
AFTERWORD

I am very neophyte in spiritual life. My vision of Kṛṣṇa consciousness is very limited. I do not know anything beyond what I have learned from my spiritual master, nor do I know how to behave as a Vaiṣṇava. Therefore, I have simply studied the character and activities of my spiritual master and have, within my limited capacity, tried to follow him. Others may emphasize different traits in his multifaceted personality, but I cannot ignore the immovable, uncompromising preacher who is Śrīla Prabhupāda.

As a disciple of Śrīla Prabhupāda and a sannyasi, I am mandated to speak strongly, as he did. But some deem that I am not advanced enough to speak straightforwardly. If that is so, then why should it be supposed that I am capable of speaking so expertly that peoples' hearts melt and they automatically abandon their envy of Kṛṣṇa? Factually, I am not fit for preaching work of any capacity, nor even for chanting Hare Kṛṣṇa or wearing *tilaka*. But my spiritual master has ordered me, so I cannot give these up.

I cannot imagine changing my style of presenting Kṛṣṇa consciousness. It is beyond my power of self-control to simply keep quiet while anti-devotional twaddle is expounded. Not that I always speak sharply, but apparently often enough to have earned a reputation for it.

As I continue to preach strongly throughout this life and maybe also in many future lives, I offer apologies to those whom I have or will upset, and further apologize that I cannot compromise with all of your nonsense. But I feel more sorry for your remaining unattached to Kṛṣṇa than for my having disturbed your mundane sentiments. Hence, I might continue to upset you again and again until you finally stop upsetting Kṛṣṇa and surrender to His lotus feet.

You may accuse me of being arrogant or immature, that I do not know how to deal with people, am not a real sadhu, or so many things. While admitting my multifarious faults, I must counter that mostly people are not agitated by my forthright style. Indeed, many thank me for having enlightened them. Even if my words make them feel uncomfortable, they appreciate that I do not speak from hostility, and respect that my commitment to an ideal is more important than to mollify others for maintaining artificial bonhomie. So to those few people who do become annoyed at me, I request you to look into your own heart to see if perhaps there is a plethora of false ego there. I can only conclude that those who still consider myself and others of my ilk to be unreasonable and fanatical—notwithstanding the extensive quotes and arguments offered herein—are themselves unreasonable and fanatical.

I am a tiny soul, a small fish in a great ocean. Yet I aspire to follow in the footsteps of the previous *ācāryas* in whatever negligible way I can. Although I certainly cannot claim to be anywhere near the level of the mighty *ācāryas*, I must at least try to serve their mission by repeating their message forcefully and with conviction, even if it opposes the current of public opinion.

GLOSSARY

Words explained herein may also have other meanings. The definitions given apply specifically to usage within this book.

Absolute Truth—an English rendering of *brahman;* (1) the ultimate source of everything; (2) the supreme independent reality. *See also* Supreme Personality of Godhead.

Ācārya—a guru who has realized the import of *śāstra* (q.v.), and by practice and precept establishes Kṛṣṇa consciousness.

Ādi-Śaṅkara—(686–718?) the proponent of Māyāvāda who spread it all over India.

Anartha—"(that which is) useless or harmful"; an activity, attitude, or tendency that is an impediment to devotional advancement (e.g., gambling, lust).

Anyābhilāṣa—any desire other than for satisfying Kṛṣṇa.

Apa-sampradāya—a deviant sect. *See also* **Sampradāya.**

Arjuna—the devotee and intimate friend of Kṛṣṇa's to whom Kṛṣṇa spoke the *Bhagavad-gītā.*

Bhagavān—"possessor of all opulences in full"; Supreme Personality of Godhead.

Bhāgavata—"in relation to Bhagavān"; (1) *Śrīmad-Bhāgavatam;* (2) great devotee.

Bhakti—*See* Devotional Service.

Bhakti-siddhānta—the correct scriptural conclusion of the *jīva's* constitutional position as a loving servant of Kṛṣṇa.

Brāhmaṇa—a devotee who has been initiated as a spiritual leader of society.

Caitanya-caritāmṛta—the most famous and authoritative biography of Śrī Caitanya Mahāprabhu.

Caitanya Mahāprabhu—(1486–1534) recognized by Gauḍīya Vaiṣṇavas (which includes members of ISKCON) to be the Supreme Lord, Kṛṣṇa, manifested as His own devotee to impart love of Himself. In English He is often referred to as Lord Caitanya.

Conditioned—pertaining or subject to the conditions of material life.

Dāsa—"servant"; a surname given to a devotee at initiation, denoting him as a servant of Kṛṣṇa.

Demigod—a resident of the higher planets. Principal demigods are assigned roles by the Supreme Lord for overseeing universal affairs, and are worshiped for material boons by materialistic followers of Vedic culture.

Devotee—a person who identifies himself as a servant of Kṛṣṇa, recognizing Him to be the Supreme Personality of Godhead. *See also* **Vaiṣṇava.**

Devotional service—the process of worshiping the Supreme Personality of Godhead, Śrī Kṛṣṇa, by dedicating one's thoughts, words, and actions to Him in loving submission. *See also* **Kṛṣṇa consciousness.**

Gauḍīya—(1) pertaining to the Vaiṣṇava *sampradāya* derived from Lord Caitanya; (2) a disciplic descendant of Śrī Caitanya Mahāprabhu.

Gītā—the *Bhagavad-gītā.*

Goloka Vṛndāvana—the spiritual world.

Gopī—a spiritual cowherd damsel who serves Kṛṣṇa in His most intimate pastimes.

Hare Kṛṣṇa mahā-mantra—the great incantation for deliverance from material existence and which bestows love of Godhead: Hare Kṛṣṇa, Hare Kṛṣṇa, Kṛṣṇa Kṛṣṇa, Hare Hare/ Hare Rāma, Hare Rāma, Rāma Rāma, Hare Hare.

Hare Kṛṣṇa movement—the movement for spreading the chanting of the Hare Kṛṣṇa *mahā-mantra. See also* ISKCON.

Harināma—(1) the holy name(s) of the Supreme Lord; (2) *harināma-saṅkīrtana.*

Harināma-saṅkīrtana—*See* Saṅkīrtana.

Hiraṇyakaśipu—an ancient infamous despot.

Impersonalism—*See* Māyāvāda.

ISKCON—International Society for Krishna Consciousness. Founded in 1966 in New York by His Divine Grace A.C. Bhaktivedanta Swami Prabhupāda, it is the principal manifestation of what is popularly known as the Hare Kṛṣṇa movement.

Jīva—one of the innumerable living entities who are eternal individual souls, atomic particles of the Supreme Lord's energy.

Jñāna—(1) knowledge; (2) abstruse spiritual knowledge, based on Vedic texts, purported to lead to liberation; the quest for the absolute truth through philosophical speculation and with an impersonalist bent.

Jñānī—a seeker of the absolute truth through philosophical speculation, usually with an impersonalist bent.

Kali—the personification of vice.

Kaniṣṭha-adhikārī—a neophyte devotee, on the lowest level of devotional service, having little knowledge or understanding.

Karma—(1) action; (2) fruitive activity performed in accordance to *karma-kāṇḍa* injunctions; (3) the principle governing material action and reaction; (4) reactions to previously performed activities; destiny.

Karmī—a person engaged in materialistic work and having little or no spiritual inclination.

Kīrtana—chanting of the names and glories of the Supreme Lord. *See also* **Saṅkīrtana.**

Kṛṣṇa—the original, all-attractive form of the Supreme Personality of Godhead.

Kṛṣṇa consciousness—acting in knowledge of one's relationship with Kṛṣṇa, the Supreme Absolute Truth. *See also* Devotional service.

Kṣatriya—a member of the Vedic martial class.

Līlā—transcendental activities of Bhagavān or His liberated devotees.

Lord Caitanya—*See* Caitanya Mahāprabhu.

Madhyama-adhikāra—the intermediate level of devotional service.

Madhyama-adhikārī—a devotee on the intermediate level of devotional service.

Mahāprabhu—*See* Caitanya Mahāprabhu.

Mahārāja—"great king"; (1) a title and term of address for a king; (2) a term of address for a sannyasi or saint; (3) used in conjunction with *guru* to emphasize the majesty of the spiritual master.

Māyā—illusion; forgetfulness of one's eternal relationship as servant of Kṛṣṇa.

Māyāvāda—the philosphical thesis of absolute identity between *jīva* and Brahman, Brahman being considered formless and impersonal or void; monism.

Māyāvādī—an adherent of Māyāvāda.

(Lord) Nityānanda (Prabhu)—an avatar who appeared as the foremost associate of Śrī Caitanya Mahāprabhu.

Paramahaṁsa—a self-realized saint, completely beyond the influence of material nature.

Pastimes—*līlā* (q.v.).

Prabhu—a respectful appellation for devotees.

Prākṛta-sahajiyā—an aberrant performer of devotional activities who neglects prescribed regulations and whose philosophical understanding is deviant.

Prasāda—"mercy." Conventionally refers to food or other items received from the Supreme Lord or high-level devotees after having first been offered to them.

Prema—transcendental love.

Pure devotee—one who is free from all desires other than to please Kṛṣṇa through pure devotional service.

Pure devotional service—activity performed solely for the pleasure of Kṛṣṇa, uncontaminated by any other motive.

Rādhā—Lord Kṛṣṇa's internal potency and most intimate consort.

Sampradāya—a sect of spiritual practitioners maintained by the principle of preceptorial succession and distinguished by a unique philosophical position.

Saṅkīrtana—congregational chanting of the Supreme Lord's holy names.

Śāstra—(1) revealed scripture; (2) the four Vedas and literature in pursuance of the Vedic version.

Satya—truth.

Siddhānta—the ultimate conclusion of any philosophical proposal or system.

Spiritual master—guru.

Śrī—an honorific prefix to names of persons, books, places, or other objects.

Śrīla—an honorific prefix to names of exalted devotees.

Śrīla Bhaktisiddhānta Sarasvatī—(1874–1936) a powerful *ācārya* of Kṛṣṇa consciousness, and the guru of Śrīla A. C. Bhaktivedanta Swami Prabhupāda.

Śrīla Bhaktivinoda Ṭhākura—(1838–1915) the inaugurator of the modern-day *bhakti* movement and the father of Śrīla Bhaktisiddhānta Sarasvatī Ṭhākura.

Śrīla Prabhupāda—*(in this book, refers to)* His Divine Grace A.C. Bhaktivedanta Swami Prabhupāda (1896–1977), the founder-*ācārya* of ISKCON and the most prominent preacher of Kṛṣṇa consciousness in the modern era.

Śrīmad-Bhāgavatam—an ancient extensive treatise that presents confidential and definitive understanding of Lord Kṛṣṇa, His devotees, and pure devotional service to Him.

Supreme Personality of Godhead—Kṛṣṇa (God), the supreme creator, maintainer, and controller of all that be.

Surrender—*(in Vaiṣṇava parlance)* full submission (of oneself as a servant of guru and Bhagavān).

Tapasya—austerity undertaken for spiritual advancement.

Tapasvī—a person dedicated to *tapasya*.

Tilaka—auspicious clay-markings on the upper part of the body, principally the forehead, signifying one's membership within a *sampradāya*.

Uttama-adhikārī—a topmost, fully perfect devotee; a *paramahaṁsa* (q.v.).

Vaiṣṇava—(1) a devotee of Viṣṇu (Kṛṣṇa), especially a pure, fully perfect devotee; (2) of or pertaining to devotees of Viṣṇu.

Vaiṣṇava-aparādha—offense to devotees.

Viṣṇu—the Supreme Lord, especially His majestic four-armed forms in Vaikuṇṭha and His expansions for creating and maintaining the material universes.

ACKNOWLEDGEMENTS

My thanks to everyone who helped produce this book, prominent among whom were:

Bengali and Sanskrit script composition—Kiśora Dāsa

Cover design—Gokula-candra Dāsa, Mādhava Dāsa, Rasikaśekhara Dāsa

Editing—Guru-Kṛṣṇa Dāsa

Layout—Vṛndāvana-candra Dāsa

Printing supervision—Śrī Giridhārī Dāsa

Proofreading—Indirā-sakhī Devī Dāsī, Kiśora Dāsa and Ananta-sarovara Dāsī, Murāri Dāsa, Prāṇa-vallabhī Devī Dāsī, Śrī Giridhārī Dāsa

Review—Kṛṣṇa-kīrti Dāsa, Patrick Boch

ABOUT BHAKTI VIKĀSA SWAMI

The author was born in Britain in 1957, and joined ISKCON in London in 1975. Later that year he was formally accepted as a disciple of His Divine Grace A.C. Bhaktivedanta Swami Prabhupāda, the founder-*ācārya* of ISKCON, and renamed Ilāpati Dāsa.

From 1977 to 1979 Ilāpati Dāsa was based in India, mainly distributing Śrīla Prabhupāda's books throughout West Bengal. In the following ten years, he helped pioneer ISKCON activities in Bangladesh, Malaysia, Myanmar, and Thailand.

In 1989 the author accepted the order of *sannyāsa*, receiving the name Bhakti Vikāsa Swami, and again made his base in India. Since then he has been preaching Kṛṣṇa consciousness mostly throughout the subcontinent—lecturing in English, Hindi, and Bengali—and also for a few months each year in other parts of the world. His television lectures in Hindi have reached millions worldwide.

Bhakti Vikāsa Swami writes extensively on Kṛṣṇa conscious themes. His books have been translated into over twenty languages, with over a million in print.

Lightning Source UK Ltd.
Milton Keynes UK
UKOW042324260912

199667UK00001B/8/P

9 789382 109044